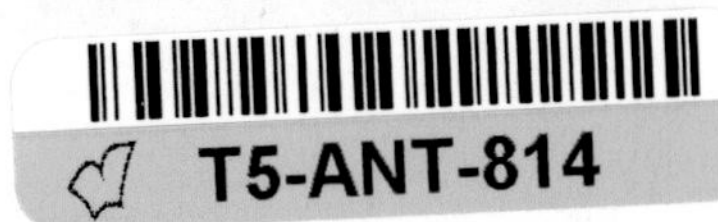

THE HEAVENS DECLARE THE GLORY OF GOD

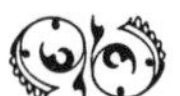

THE HEAVENS DECLARE THE GLORY OF GOD

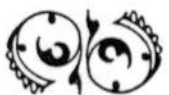

Daily Devotionals
in Defense of
Biblical Christianity

Dr. Henry M. Morris

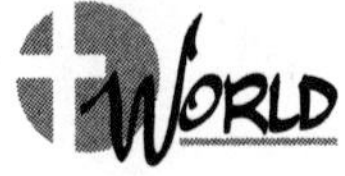

The Heavens Declare the Glory of God

Published by World Publishing, Inc.
Grand Rapids, MI 49418

Cover design by Paetzold Design, Batavia, IL.
Interior design by David C. Den Boer
Typesetting by The Composing Room of Michigan, Inc., Grand Rapids, MI.

ISBN 0-529-10829-1

Library of Congress Catalog Card Number 97-060498

Printed in the United States of America

2 3 4 5 6 7 02 01 00 99 98

Introduction

The popular devotional quarterly, *Days of Praise,* published by the Institute for Creation Research and edited by the writer, has received wide use by Christian readers for over eleven years now, ever since its first issue was distributed for the winter quarter beginning December 1985. Many and thrilling have been the unsolicited testimonies from people using it in their daily quiet times.

They have indicated their appreciation of the simple, yet substantive, Bible studies on many subjects related to our Christian life and witness. The devotionals do not include stories or poems or other extraneous material that might distract from seriously feeding on the milk and meat of the Word of God. Many have also expressed appreciation that we still use the time-tested King James Bible, with its singular beauty, clarity and power.

A number of these devotional studies have stressed the inerrant authority of the Bible and the many evidences of its divine inspiration, including the truth of recent literal creation of all things by the Lord Jesus Christ, God's eternal Son. These particular devotionals are the ones selected for inclusion in this volume, slightly modified and updated when preferable, and arranged whenever appropriate to correlate with special dates (Christmas, July 4, etc.).

They are not intended to take the place of one's daily Bible study, of course, but rather to supplement and to encourage it. The devotionals have also been selected to comprise a sort of companion volume to go with my *Defender's Study Bible,* which also seeks to honor the written Word of God and to strengthen the Christian faith and understanding of all who use it. My desire and prayer is that this devotional volume, as well as the *Defender's Bible,* will be used to lead people to strong conviction of the full truth of God's Word and to great faith in the Lord Jesus Christ as omniscient Creator, personal Savior and soon-coming King.

I believe *The Heavens Declare the Glory of God* can be adapted for use in any year, and it should always be up to date, until the Lord returns. This is because, at least to the best of my understanding, every devotional Bible study in the volume is founded solely on the unchanging Word of God, eternally settled in heaven (Psalm 119:89).

Henry M. Morris
October 1996

Acknowledgments

My secretary-at-a-distance, and beloved daughter, Mrs. Mary Ruth Smith, typed and edited the manuscript, and my equally beloved son, Dr. John D. Morris, new president of the Institute for Creation Research, reviewed all the devotionals for content and expression. My sincere thanks to both!

I also appreciate the gracious and efficient publishing ministries of Mrs. Doris Rikkers and Mrs. Carol Ochs, of World Publishing Co., who have coordinated the publication of the book.

Creation and the New Year

❦

In the beginning God created the heaven and the earth (Genesis 1:1).

It is appropriate for Christians to begin the New Year by referring back to the beginning of the very *first* year. The first verse of God's Word is also its most important verse, since it is the foundation on which everything else is built. Even God's great work of salvation is irrelevant and futile without His prior work of creation, for only the *Creator* of all things could become *Savior* of all things.

If a person really believes Genesis 1:1, he or she should have no difficulty believing anything else in the Bible. The very first object of *saving* faith (Hebrews 10:39) is the fact of special creation by the Word of God (Hebrews 11:3).

The verse is comprehensive and scientific, viewing space ("the heavens") and matter ("the earth") as functioning in a framework of time ("in the beginning"). This space/matter/time "continuum" (as scientists call it) has not existed eternally, nor is it still being created, both of which heresies are standard beliefs of all forms of evolutionary pantheism (including most of the world's religions and philosophies, ancient or modern). It was *created*—an event *completed* in the past.

This foundation of all foundations is, clearly, the only sure foundation upon which one should build a life, or an organization, or anything. A firm renewal of one's commitment to special creation, as literally recorded by divine revelation in the inerrant Word of God, is thus the proper way to begin a New Year, or a new home, or a new career, or a new family, or any phase of a Christian life. This is the time to confess and forsake all doubts, and trust God's Word!

In the beginning of the *first* year, God created all things. At the beginning of *this* year, we should resolve to believe and obey all things in His Word.

JANUARY 2

The New World

And I saw a new heaven and a new earth: for the first heaven and the first earth were passed away; and there was no more sea (Revelation 21:1).

As a new year begins, men and women customarily turn over a "new leaf" and make "new resolutions" for improving their behavior. For the Christian, however, the new year—indeed a whole new life—begins when he or she accepts Christ. "Therefore if any man be in Christ, he is a new creature: old things are passed away; behold, all things are become new" (II Corinthians 5:17).

He receives from Christ a "new commandment . . . that ye love one another" (John 13:34). He has come to "Jesus the mediator of the new covenant" (Hebrews 12:24), and, in a sense, he lives in a whole new world.

The ultimate new year is yet to come, however, when Christ returns—perhaps this year, perhaps today! He will surely keep His promise, and "we, according to His promise, look for new heavens and a new earth, wherein dwelleth righteousness" (II Peter 3:13). Peter *looked for* this world to come, and so do we, but John—translated in time by the Holy Spirit—actually *saw* the new heaven and new earth, and so shall we someday! In fact, as Isaiah prophesied, when God finally does "create new heavens and a new earth . . . the former shall not be remembered, nor come into mind," so glorious will be that new world (Isaiah 65:17).

Then we shall have "a new name written" by Christ Himself, sing "a new song" with new voices, and live in that "holy city, New Jerusalem" (Revelation 2:17; 5:9; 21:2). We shall have new bodies, new homes, new ministries, new lives, forever. In fact, the Lord Jesus assured John: "Behold, I make all things new, . . . these words are true and faithful" (Revelation 21:5). *All* things will be eternally new in that great new year soon approaching.

All Things New

And He that sat upon the throne said, Behold, I make all things new. And He said unto me, Write: for these words are true and faithful (Revelation 21:5).

The coming of a new year is a good time to consider that glorious time to come when Christ will make everything new again. In the present age, all things "shall wax old as doth a garment" (Hebrews 1:11) under the bondage of the universal law of decay and death; indeed "the whole creation groaneth and travaileth in pain together until now" (Romans 8:22).

"Nevertheless we, according to His promise, look for new heavens and a new Earth, wherein dwelleth righteousness" (II Peter 3:13). There, in the "New Jerusalem," we shall each have "a new name" and sing "a new song" (Revelation 21:2; 2:17; 5:9). We shall have new bodies, "fashioned like unto His glorious body" (Philippians 3:21), and a new dwelling-place, prepared by Christ Himself among the "many mansions" in His "Father's house" (John 14:2).

And all the old and dying things will be completely and forever gone. "There shall be no more death, neither sorrow, nor crying, neither shall there be any more pain: for the former things are passed away" (Revelation 21:4). "And the ransomed of the LORD shall return, and come to Zion with songs and everlasting joy upon their heads: they shall obtain joy and gladness, and sorrow and sighing shall flee away" (Isaiah 35:10).

What a "Happy New Year" that will be! In the meantime, we have His "new covenant" and have each been made "a new creature" in Christ (Hebrews 12:24; Galatians 6:15). Since all His words "are true and faithful," we know His promises are sure. Therefore, already, "old things are passed away; behold, all things are become new" through faith in Christ (II Corinthians 5:17).

JANUARY 4

The Generations to Come

That the generation to come might know them, even the children which should be born; who should arise and declare them to their children (Psalm 78:6).

Each generation of people tends to regard its own times as the most significant of all, toward which all past history has been merely a preparation. The fact is, however, that God has "been our dwelling place in *all* generations" (Psalm 90:1), and He is equally concerned about any generations yet to come.

This is why He stresses repeatedly that the great truths concerning God's creation, His character, His great work of salvation and His long-range plans for the ages to come be transmitted faithfully from one generation to another. "One generation shall praise Thy works to another, and shall declare Thy mighty acts" (Psalm 145:4).

Our modern scientific generation almost idolizes new research, new gadgets, new discoveries. The God of eternity, however, is not so concerned that we develop new ideas as that we *not lose* what He has already given us. "For ever, O Lord, Thy Word is settled in heaven. Thy faithfulness is unto all generations: Thou hast established the earth, and it abideth" (Psalm 119:89, 90). Christ said: "That which ye have already hold fast till I come." "Hold that fast which thou hast, that no man take thy crown" (Revelation 2:25; 3:11).

The great principle of true education is given by Paul in II Timothy 2:2: "The things that thou has heard of me among many witnesses, the same commit thou to faithful men, who shall be able to teach others also." The great account of Christ's crucifixion especially, is to be taught forever. "They shall come, and shall declare His righteousness unto a people that shall be born, that He hath done this" (Psalm 22:31).

He Who Made the Stars

Seek Him that maketh the seven stars and Orion, and turneth the shadow of death into the morning, and maketh the day dark with night: that calleth for the waters of the sea, and poureth them out upon the face of the earth: The LORD is His name (Amos 5:8).

This striking exhortation is inserted in the midst of a prophetic rebuke by God of His people Israel. They were rapidly drifting into pagan idolatry, and Amos was trying to call them back.

His exhortation, given almost 3800 years ago, is more needed today than it ever was before. Modern pagan scientists have developed elaborate but absurdly impossible theories about the chance origin of the universe from nothing and the evolution of stars, planets and people from primordial hydrogen. But the mighty cosmos and its galaxies of stars—even the very constellations, such as Orion and the Pleiades (the "seven stars"), as well as the solar system—were *made*. All of these had to be *made* by an omniscient, omnipotent Creator, who had a glorious purpose for it all.

Similarly, the global evidences that waters once covered all the Earth's mountains (i.e., marine fossils and water-laid sediments at their summits) cannot possibly be explained—as evolutionary geologists try to do—by slow processes acting over æons of time. God the Creator had to call massive volumes of water forth from their original reservoirs and pour them out on the earth in His Flood judgment on a rebellious world.

All of these witness to the fact of creation and judgment, not to impotent "gods" personifying natural forces. Men urgently need to seek the true God of creation and salvation before judgment falls again, for "it is a fearful thing to fall into the hands of the living God" (Hebrews 10:31).

JANUARY 6

The Settled Word

For ever, O Lord, Thy Word is settled in heaven (Psalm 119:89).

There are yet quite a number of unsettled controversies among Bible scholars as to the original text of certain passages in both Old and New Testaments. In fact, a frequent objection raised to the doctrine of Biblical inerrancy is that, since all the original "autographs" have been lost, we can never really be *sure* of any passage.

It is interesting to speculate on what happened to those manuscripts directly inspired by God and penned by Moses, John, Paul and the others. It is strange that they all simply disappeared, with not a hint as to their history. If they had been preserved in a church or monastery somewhere, they would soon have become idolatrous objects of worship, so it is probably best they are gone.

But where did they go? The famous "ark of the covenant" similarly vanished at the time of the Babylonian invasion, and many fruitless searches have been conducted for it even in modern times. In this case, however, we do have a remarkable revelation. "And the temple of God was opened in heaven, and there was seen in His temple the ark of His testament" (Revelation 11:19). Evidently, the ark has been translated into heaven! We must realize that heaven is *a real place* in this eternal physical cosmos. Enoch and Elijah were translated there in their earthly bodies, and Christ is there in His physical resurrection body.

If, perhaps, angels somehow carried the original manuscripts of God's Word to heaven after enough copies had been made to assure its faithful transmission on earth, placing them there in the ark, like the tablets of the law when it was still on the earth, this would surely give added meaning to our wonderful text verse: "For ever, O Lord, Thy Word is settled in heaven!"

These Are Written

And many other signs truly did Jesus in the presence of His disciples, which are not written in this book: But these are written, that ye might believe that Jesus is the Christ, the Son of God; and that believing ye might have life through His name (John 20:30, 31).

The Gospel of John was written explicitly to lead people to salvation through faith in Christ. To do that, they must be shown that He was the very Son of the omnipotent God. This in turn required that certain great events in His human life become part of the *written* Word, the holy Scriptures.

John's Gospel was written after the Jewish dispersion in A.D. 70, and so was written especially with the pagan world of evolutionary humanism in view. Both Jew and Greek needed to know that Jesus was more than a great man, or even a wonder-worker, but the Creator Himself.

Therefore, John began his evangelistic appeal with a great affirmation of creation, starting with the very words of the only *real* record of *ex nihilo* creation in the ancient world—the Book of Genesis. "In the beginning was the Word . . . the Word was God. . . . All things were made by Him. . . . He was in the world, and the world was made by Him, and the world knew Him not" (John 1:1, 3, 10).

Then John described in detail seven great miracles of Christ, none of which could ever be duplicated by any sorcerer or magician. Solely by His own spoken word, He turned water into wine, healed a dying lad six miles away, gave perfect limbs to a life-long crippled man, created food for a multitude, walked on water, made perfect eyes for a man born blind, and restored a friend to life who had been dead four days. Finally, He arose from the dead Himself. Many have been those through the years who, on reading this Gospel, have said with Thomas, "My Lord and my God" (John 20:28)!

Forty Days

To whom also He showed Himself alive after His passion by many infallible proofs, being seen of them forty days, and speaking of the things pertaining to the Kingdom of God (Acts 1:3).

It is interesting how often the Scriptures refer to a forty-day period. There are nine different forty-day periods noted in Scripture (the phrase itself occurs seventeen times), and it may be noteworthy that forty days is one-ninth of the original (and prophetic) lunar/solar year of 360 days (note Genesis 7:11; 8:3, 4; Revelation 11:2, 3). Thus the total of the nine forty-day periods equals the ideal year.

The periods are as follows: (1) the intense rainfall at the Flood (Genesis 7:12, 17); (2) the first giving of the law (Exodus 24:18; Deuteronomy 9:9, 11); (3) the second giving of the law (Exodus 34:28; Deuteronomy 9:18, 25; (4) the searching of Canaan by the fearful spies (Numbers 13:25; 14:34); (5) the defiance of Israel by Goliath (I Samuel 17:16); (6) Elijah's journey to Horeb (I Kings 19:8); (7) Jonah's reluctant preaching in Nineveh (Jonah 3:4); (8) Christ's temptation in the wilderness (Matthew 4:2; Mark 1:13; Luke 4:2); (9) Christ's post-resurrection ministry (Acts 1:3).

Each of these periods was a time of great stress and intense testing for one or more of God's people, except the last. The final forty-day period, encompassing Christ's ministry to His disciples after His resurrection, was a time of triumph and great blessing. He had come victoriously through the most intense time of stress and testing that anyone could ever experience, and now He could show Himself alive eternally to His disciples and promise them the same victory. Forty days of testing, then forty days of triumph! Even a lifetime of testing is more than balanced by an eternity of blessing.

And Forty Nights

And the rain was upon the earth forty days and forty nights (Genesis 7:12).

There are nine forty-day periods in Scripture, but on only five of these the notation "and forty nights" is added. On the other four occasions (the spies in Canaan, Goliath's challenges, Jonah in Nineveh, and Christ's post-resurrection ministry), we can assume that the activity ceased at night. But on these five it continued unabated.

The first of these was the great Flood. The most intense rains ever experienced on the Earth poured torrentially, night and day. One can visualize the stress-filled nights for Noah's family, with the cries of the dying outside, and no light of the sun or moon to pierce the outer darkness. But, of course, they were all safe in God's specially designed ark.

Many years later, Moses twice spent forty days and forty nights in the awful presence of God on Mount Sinai, receiving the divinely-inscribed tablets, with the Ten Commandments and all the laws of God. The mountain was intermittently quaking and breathing fire and smoke while he was there, and the nights were surely more awesome even than the days, but God was there!

Elijah spent forty days and forty nights traveling back from Beersheba to Sinai, even though this relatively short journey would not normally require forty days. Evidently Elijah experienced great hardships and obstacles along the way, and many sleepless nights, but God met him again at Sinai, and it was worth it all.

Finally, the Lord Jesus (God Himself!) was "led up of the Spirit into the wilderness to be tempted of the devil . . . forty days and forty nights" (Matthew 4:1, 2). In weakened human flesh, without food or rest, this was a greater trial than any of the rest, but He was triumphant, and then the "angels came and ministered unto Him" (Matthew 4:11).

Ancient Times

I have considered the days of old, the years of ancient times (Psalm 77:5).

The Bible provides for us a fascinating perspective on the passage of time. Three thousand years ago, the psalmist was seeking to understand God's ways in *his* time, and each new generation seems to think that it is the "new wave," leading the world out of its past darkness into a new age of enlightenment.

There is need for scientific research, of course (in fact, this is implied in the "dominion mandate" of Genesis 1:26–28), but we need to keep in mind that *true* science is really "thinking God's thoughts after Him." The results of our scientific "discoveries" should always be to glorify the Creator and to draw men closer to Him, not lead them away from Him.

The same is true of history. We are merely the children of the ancient patriarchs, and our moral natures are the same as theirs, all contaminated by inherent sinfulness and the need for divine salvation. God dealt with them as He does with us, so that every later generation needs to study and learn from the generations of ancient times, and from God's inspired histories of them in the earliest books of the Bible—especially Genesis, as well as Exodus, Job and other ancient books. "For whatsoever things were written aforetime were written for our learning, that we through patience and comfort of the Scriptures might have hope" (Romans 15:4).

God is the same today as He was in Eden, on Mount Ararat, in Babel and Canaan and Sinai and Calvary. "LORD, Thou hast been our dwelling place in all generations. Before the mountains were brought forth, or ever Thou hadst formed the earth and the world, even from everlasting to everlasting, Thou art God" (Psalm 90:1, 2).

Scattered Abroad

Therefore they that were scattered abroad went every where preaching the word (Acts 8:4).

God has given two great commissions to His people, both of which would require worldwide effort to accomplish. Both, however, were so resisted that God Himself had to step in and force them to be obedient.

Immediately after the great flood, God gave the following command: "Be fruitful, and multiply, and replenish the earth" (Genesis 9:1). This was an extension of the Edenic mandate given to Adam in the beginning, a commission to fill the earth and exercise dominion over it, under God (Genesis 1:28). Noah's descendants, however, decided to stay in Babel and "make us a name, lest we be scattered abroad upon the face of the whole earth." As a result of this rebellion, "the LORD did there confound the language of all the earth: and from thence did the LORD scatter them abroad upon the face of all the earth" (Genesis 11:4, 9).

Over 2000 years later, the Lord gave His disciples another great worldwide commission. "Go ye into all the world, and preach the gospel to every creature" (Mark 16:15). Then followed the coming of the Holy Spirit, and soon "the number of the disciples multiplied in Jerusalem greatly" (Acts 6:7).

But they remained in Jerusalem, instead of spreading out to "the uttermost part of the earth" (Acts 1:8). Therefore God once again intervened and "there was a great persecution against the church which was at Jerusalem: and they were all scattered abroad. . . ." (Acts 8:1). Then, finally, began their full obedience to the great commission, for "they that were scattered abroad went everywhere preaching the word," and eventually some "of all nations, and kindreds, and people, and tongues" will stand in saving faith before the Lord (Revelation 7:9).

JANUARY 12

Lineage of the Savior

And Jacob begat Joseph the husband of Mary, of whom was born Jesus, who is called Christ (Matthew 1:16).

The lineage of Jesus Christ was remarkably prophesied, stage by stage, from the beginning of history. When sin first entered the world through Adam, the Lord promised a coming Savior; the "seed of the woman" (Genesis 3:15). Adam and Eve, had "sons and daughters" (Genesis 5:4); but it was only the line leading from Seth to Noah that would lead to Christ, for it was prophesied concerning Noah that he would "comfort us . . . because of the ground which the LORD hath cursed" (Genesis 5:29).

Of the three sons of Noah, God prophesied: "Blessed be the LORD God of Shem" (Genesis 9:26). In the line from Shem, God chose Abram, to whom He promised: "In thee shall all families of the earth be blessed" (Genesis 12:3). Abraham had eight sons, but it was to Isaac that God renewed the promise, and then He also renewed it to Jacob, instead of Esau (Genesis 26:4; 28:4; 35:9–12).

On his dying bed, Jacob blessed his twelve sons, but it was to Judah he gave the Messianic promise: "The scepter shall not depart from Judah, nor a lawgiver from beneath his feet, until Shiloh come; and unto Him shall the gathering of the people be" (Genesis 49:10). Then, out of the great tribe of Judah, God prophesied concerning David: "I will set up thy seed after thee . . . and I will establish His kingdom" (II Samuel 7:12). Much later, He predicted concerning the descendants of David in Bethlehem: "Though thou be little among the thousands of Judah, yet out of thee shall He come forth unto me that is to be ruler in Israel; whose goings forth have been from of old, from everlasting" (Micah 5:2).

At the proper time, the One who was prophesied from of old did come forth to be our Savior, fulfilling these and hosts of other marvelous prophecies.

Spiritual Entropy

I speak to your shame. Is it so, that there is not a wise man among you? no, not one that shall be able to judge between his brethren? (I Corinthians 6:5).

The word for "shame" in this verse is the Greek *entrope,* meaning "turning inward" or "inversion." It is used only one other time, in I Corinthians 15:34: "Awake to righteousness, and sin not; for some have not the knowledge of God: I speak this to your shame." Evidently this special variety of shame is associated with taking controversies between Christian brethren to ungodly judges and also with failing to witness to the non-Christian community. Instead of bringing the true wisdom of God to the ungodly, such "entropic Christians" were turning to worldly wisdom to resolve their own spiritual problems. This inverted behavior was nothing less than spiritual confusion!

The modern scientific term "entropy" is essentially this same Greek word. In science, entropy is a measure of disorder in any given system. The universal law of increasing entropy states that every system tends to disintegrate into disorder, or confusion, if left to itself. This tendency can only be reversed if ordering energy is applied to it effectively from a source outside the system.

This universal scientific law has a striking parallel in the spiritual realm. A person turning inward to draw on his own bank of power, or seeking power from an ineffective outside source, will inevitably deteriorate eventually into utter spiritual confusion and death. But when Christ enters the life, that person becomes a new creation in Christ Jesus (II Corinthians 5:17). Through the Holy Spirit and through the Holy Scriptures, "His divine power hath given unto us all things that pertain unto life and godliness" (II Peter 1:3). The law of spiritual entropy is transformed into the "law of the Spirit of life in Christ Jesus" (Romans 8:2).

The God of Heaven

And he said unto them, I am an Hebrew; and I fear the Lord, the God of heaven, which hath made the sea and the dry land (Jonah 1:9).

It was by these words that the prophet Jonah identified himself to the merchants of Tarshish as he was fleeing on their ship from the presence of the Lord. This special title, "the God of heaven," seems generally to have been used by the Jews when they were talking to men of other religions, stressing that their God was no mere tribal deity, but the true God who had created the very heavens.

The title was first used by Abraham, speaking to his servant: "And I will make thee swear by the Lord, the God of heaven, and the God of the earth . . . " (Genesis 24:3). At this time, the nation of Israel existed only in the promise of this God of heaven.

It also appears frequently in the books of Ezra and Nehemiah, first in the decree of Cyrus the Persian: "The Lord God of heaven . . . hath charged me to build Him an house at Jerusalem" (Ezra 1:2). Even though the Persians followed lesser gods, Cyrus knew that the one God of heaven was the Creator. The name then reappears several times in the book of Daniel, who was living in the palace of the heathen king of Babylon. Its final Old Testament occurrence is Daniel 2:44: "The God of heaven [shall] set up a kingdom, which shall never be destroyed."

In the New Testament it occurs only twice, both in Revelation. In one instance, John writes that the ungodly nations "blasphemed the God of heaven"; in the other, he says they "gave glory to the God of heaven" (Revelation 16:11; 11:13). In our own witnessing today, especially to those who don't know or believe the Bible, it is also good to stress that our God is not just the God of Judaeo-Christian tradition, but the Creator of all things.

Cursed Is the Ground

And unto Adam He said, Because thou hast hearkened unto the voice of thy wife, and hast eaten of the tree, of which I commanded thee, saying, "Thou shalt not eat of it: cursed is the ground for thy sake; in sorrow shalt thou eat of it all the days of thy life (Genesis 3:17).

The great curse which God placed on the ground because of man's deliberate rebellion against His word is worldwide and age-long. Until sin is removed, the curse cannot be removed.

In the new earth, after Christ returns and all unrepentant, unbelieving sinners have been cast with Satan into the lake of fire, then—and not until then—"there shall be no more curse" (Revelation 22:3).

The curse is not only on man ("unto dust shalt thou return"—Genesis 3:19), but also "the whole creation groaneth and travaileth in pain together until now" under "the bondage of corruption" (or "decay," Romans 8:22, 21). For the curse was placed on "the ground," that is, on the very material out of which God had formed Adam's body (Genesis 2:7). In fact, it was the "dust of the ground"—that is, the finest particles of matter—from which everything had been made.

Plants and animals, men and women, minerals and mountains, all may grow for a time, but all eventually decay and die, because God's curse is in the very dust of the ground from which they are formed. The principle has even come to be recognized by scientists as the "law of entropy," which has no known exception.

When Christ returns to reign in glory, however, the whole creation "shall be delivered from the bondage of corruption into the glorious liberty of the children of God" (Romans 8:21). Therefore, "we, according to His promise, look for new heavens and a new earth, wherein dwelleth righteousness" (II Peter 3:13).

JANUARY 16

Two Unbreakable Covenants

For this is as the waters of Noah unto me: for as I have sworn that the waters of Noah should no more go over the earth: so have I sworn that I would not be wroth with thee, nor rebuke thee (Isaiah 54:9).

The words of our text were written at least 1600 years after the great Flood went over the whole earth, yet it was still remembered as a unique event in history. Furthermore, another 2700 years have passed since Isaiah's time, yet God is still keeping His covenant with Noah; waters have never again gone over the earth.

The Noahic covenant was unconditional—God's promise to Noah in reward for His own unique obedience to God before the flood. Another judgment is coming, however, as the next verse warns. "For the mountains shall depart, and the hills be removed; but my kindness shall not depart from thee, neither shall the covenant of my peace be removed, saith the Lord that hath mercy on thee" (v. 10). A great earth-shaking judgment is coming, but there is also another covenant, no less sure and unconditional than that of Noah.

In context, the covenant of which God spoke was with the children of Israel. "In a little wrath I hid my face from thee for a moment; but with everlasting kindness will I have mercy on thee, saith the LORD thy Redeemer" (v. 8). This "Redeemer" is "the Holy One of Israel; The God of the whole earth shall He be called" (v. 5).

The Redeemer of Israel is thus also the God of the whole earth, and there is also a wonderful covenant He has made with all who appropriate His great work of redemption. "This is the covenant that I will make with them after those days, saith the Lord, I will put my laws into their hearts, and in their minds will I write them; And their sins and iniquities will I remember no more" (Hebrews 10:16, 17).

The Subjected Creation

For the creature was made subject to vanity, not willingly, but by reason of Him who hath subjected the same in hope (Romans 8:20).

Every creature of God that is—everything created by Him—has been subjected to "vanity," or futility. This is the great curse on the ground (Genesis 3:17) imposed thereon because of the primal rebellion of the man who had been given dominion over all the earth (Genesis 1:26).

Although we see the effects all around and even in us, certain idealistic theologians argue that Christ, by His resurrection, has already started the gradual triumph of life over death, righteousness over evil, and order over entropy.

But this is wrong. A whole generation after Christ's resurrection, Paul noted that "the whole creation groaneth and travaileth in pain together until now" (Romans 8:22). Then, after still another generation, Peter said that the devil was still freely walking about "seeking whom he may devour" (I Peter 5:8). Paul, just before his death, predicted that, "in the last days . . . evil men and seducers shall wax worse and worse" (II Timothy 3:1, 13).

The best-proved of all scientific laws, the law of increasing entropy, describes the tendency in all natural systems toward disorganization and death. Despite the resurrection, therefore, death is still the great enemy and will continue to be so until "death is swallowed up in victory" when Christ returns (I Corinthians 15:54).

Nevertheless, because of His death and resurrection, Christ has—in principle and sure prospect—"abolished death, and hath brought life and immortality to light through the gospel" (II Timothy 1:10). In the meantime, He commanded us to "occupy till I come" (Luke 19:13) that "we may have confidence, and not be ashamed before Him at His coming" (I John 2:28).

The Last Adam

And so it is written, The first man Adam was made a living soul; the last Adam was made a quickening spirit (I Corinthians 15:45)

In the great "resurrection chapter," Paul is quoting from Genesis 2:7: " . . . and man became a living soul." He also makes it clear that, contrary to the opinion of many liberal theologians, "Adam" was not merely a generic term for humanity in general, specifically indicating that Adam was "the first man." This also refutes the notion that there were any "pre-Adamite men," despite the claims of some who would compromise with evolutionary anthropology.

Just as there was a first Adam, so Jesus Christ was the last Adam. He was not the last man to be born, of course, but He was the second and last man whose body would be directly formed by God, as asserted in the same verse (Genesis 2:7) here cited by Paul. "That holy thing" (Luke 1:35) which Mary received in her womb, was conceived altogether miraculously. "Wherefore when He cometh into the world, He saith . . . a body hast thou prepared me" (Hebrews 10:5). "The first man is of the earth, earthy: the second man is the Lord from heaven: (I Corinthians 15:47).

Thus, with neither genetic mutations nor inherent sin in His perfect human body, this last Adam could become "the Lamb of God," whose body was "without blemish and without spot," able therefore to redeem lost men with His "precious blood," and thus to take "away the sin of the world" (John 1:29; I Peter 1:19).

But that is not all. He was also "made a quickening (that is, *resurrecting*) spirit." He was "put to death in the flesh, but quickened by the Spirit" (I Peter 3:18), and can now give eternal life to all who receive His life. "For as the Father raiseth up the dead . . . even so the Son quickeneth whom He will" (John 5:21).

Lifted Up from the Earth

And the flood was forty days upon the earth; and the waters increased, and bare up the ark, and it was lift up above the earth (Genesis 7:17).

This first occurrence in the Bible of the verb "lift up" is in a scene of judgment on a wicked world. The earth had been filled with such evil that God sent a global flood to destroy the old world and begin a new dispensation.

But there was an Ark of safety, and it bore all the battering of the storm for those who had entered the door in its side. The waters which buried the world merely lifted up the Ark above the earth and "eight souls were saved by water" (I Peter 3:20) from the sins of the old world.

Another greater judgment was yet to come, this one for the combined sin of the whole world and every age. Once again the judgment fell on one who would be lifted up from the earth, not this time by water but "by wicked hands" and "crucified and slain" (Acts 2:23).

Jesus said: "Now is the judgment of this world . . . And I, if I be lifted up from the earth, will draw all men unto me. This He said, signifying what death He should die" (John 12:31–33). The Ark of Noah, lifted up from the earth to save those who trusted their lives to it, is a type of the greater Ark of Safety, lifted up from the earth on the cross to die for the sin of the world and to save all who trust Him.

The Lord called Noah and all His house into the Ark, to shield them from judgment. Similarly, the Lord Jesus said: "I . . . will draw all men unto me," and Paul assures us that "there is therefore now no condemnation (or 'judgment') to them which are in Christ Jesus" (Romans 8:1). And as "the flood was forty days upon the earth" to assure the fulfillment of its purpose, so Jesus "showed Himself alive after His passion by many infallible proofs, being seen of them forty days" (Acts 1:3).

JANUARY 20

The Witness of the Creation

And unto the angel of the church of the Laodiceans write; These things saith the Amen, the faithful and true witness, the beginning of the creation of God (Revelation 3:14).

This salutation in the last of the seven church epistles in Revelation contains the last of four occurrences of the distinctive phrase, "the beginning of the creation." The glorified Christ here assumes this as one of His divine names. Even God's work of creation, long since completed (Genesis 2:1–3), had a beginning, and that beginning was Christ. "In the beginning was the Word . . . and . . . All things were made by Him." (John 1:1, 3).

The first two occurrences of this phrase also come from the lips of Christ. "From the beginning of the creation God made them male and female" (Mark 10:6). This assertion by the Creator, Jesus Christ, quoting Genesis 1:27, makes it unambiguously certain that Adam and Eve were created at the beginning of creation, not after the earth had already existed for 4.5 billion years. God also wrote this plainly on the tables of the law (Exodus 20:8–11). Those evangelicals who accept the geological ages evidently reject this clear statement of the creation's Creator!

Then Christ also referred to the end-time in the context of the beginning-times. "In those days shall be affliction, such as was not from the beginning of the creation which God created unto this time, neither shall be" (Mark 13:19).

The phrase is also used in Peter's very important prophecy concerning the scoffers of the end-times, who will argue (in willful ignorance) that "all things continue as they were from the beginning of the creation" (II Peter 3:3–4), thereby denying that there ever was a real creation or real Creator and thus rejecting Christ Himself. But He is also the "true witness" and the "Amen," and such denials will only be "unto their own destruction" (II Peter 3:16).

The Invisible God

No man hath seen God at any time; the only begotten Son, which is in the bosom of the Father, He hath declared Him (John 1:18).

God in His essential being is omnipresent. "Whither shall I go from Thy Spirit? or whither shall I flee from Thy presence?" (Psalm 139:7). This rhetorical question of David's has the obvious answer that one can never escape God's presence; He is present everywhere in His creation. Being present everywhere, He is necessarily invisible anywhere. He is "the King eternal, immortal, invisible, the only wise God" (I Timothy 1:17).

Yet, although God is omnipresent, He is also omnipotent, and He can therefore manifest Himself in tangible, visible form when He so chooses. This He has done at various times through the ages, as on the occasion when He, with two angels, appeared to Abraham in the form of three men (Genesis 18).

Our text resolves any apparent contradictions in these truths by noting that, when God manifests Himself visibly to man He does so in the person of His only begotten Son. The Lord Jesus Christ, in fact, is "the image of the invisible God, the firstborn of every creature" (Colossians 1:15). In some marvelous way beyond human comprehension, the omnipresent, infinite God, has on occasion taken on the appearance of human beings, in order to convey a specific revelation or accomplish some divine purpose. Such manifestations are called theophanies, and each has been implemented by the Son of God, in pre-incarnate form.

Finally, however, the only begotten Son of God became also the eternal Son of Man. "For the life was manifested, and we have seen it, and bear witness, and show unto you that eternal life, which was with the Father, and was manifested unto us" (I John 1:2).

The Blood of Abel

And to Jesus the mediator of the new covenant, and to the blood of sprinkling, that speaketh better things than that of Abel (Hebrews 12:24).

There are three references to the blood of Abel in the Bible, with each instance indicating that the shedding of Abel's blood by his brother Cain was a type of the shed blood of Christ. In fact, the very first reference to blood in the Bible (thus, the "law of first mention," a reference of foundational significance), is God's accusation to Abel's murderer: "The voice of thy brother's blood crieth unto me from the ground" (Genesis 4:10).

Abel was the first of multitudes through the centuries whose blood has been shed because of their witness for divine righteousness (note I John 3:12). This indictment of human wickedness reached its zenith in the spilling of the blood of the One who was perfectly righteous. "That upon you may come all the righteous blood shed upon the earth, from the blood of righteous Abel unto the blood of Zacharias" (Matthew 23:35, also Luke 11:50, 51).

But if the blood of Abel cries out for vengeance, along with "the blood of the saints; and with the blood of the martyrs of Jesus" (Revelation 17:6), the blood of Christ Himself, as our text assures us, speaks of better things than those called forth by Abel's blood. There was an old covenant, demanding blood for blood, with the atoning blood of animals substituting for that of sinners. "And Moses took the blood, and sprinkled it on the people, and said, Behold the blood of the covenant" (Exodus 24:8). But Jesus "is the mediator of the new testament . . . for the redemption of the transgressions that were under the first testament" (Hebrews 9:15), and with His blood, we have "our hearts sprinkled from an evil conscience . . . to serve the living God" (Hebrews 10:22, 9:14). Christ's blood was indeed the "blood of the everlasting covenant" (Hebrews 13:20).

The Dominion Mandate

And God blessed them, and God said unto them, Be fruitful, and multiply, and replenish the earth, and subdue it: and have dominion over the fish of the sea, and over the fowl of the air, and over every living thing that moveth upon the earth (Genesis 1:28).

This was God's first commandment to the man and woman He had created. They were to exercise dominion "over all the earth" (v. 26); not a despotic dominion, as some have insinuated, but a responsible stewardship.

In order to subdue the earth, we must first understand its processes. Thus, research is the foundational occupation for fulfilling the divine mandate. Then this knowledge must be applied in technology (engineering, medicine, agriculture, etc.). It must be implemented for use by all (business, commerce) and transmitted to future generations (education). The creation can also be described and praised in the humanities and fine arts. The dominion mandate thus authorizes all honorable human occupations, as a stewardship under God.

The mandate was reaffirmed to Noah after the Flood (Genesis 9:1–10), with the additional institution of human government, a change made necessary by the entrance of sin and death into the world. Thus all the occupations we now call the social sciences (law, civics, counseling, etc.) have been added to God's authorized vocations.

The tragedy is that leadership in practically all these fields has been taken over by secularists and humanists, so God's primeval commission has largely been subverted. Christians today need a renewed vision and commitment, not only to Christ's second great commission of evangelism, but also to His first mandate of responsible world stewardship. Therefore, "whatsoever ye do, do it heartily, as to the Lord, and not unto men" (Colossians 3:23).

The Philosophers

Then certain philosophers of the Epicureans and of the Stoics, encountered Him. And some said, What will this babbler say? other some, He seemeth to be a setter forth of strange gods: because he preached unto them Jesus and the resurrection (Acts 17:18).

The important ministry of Paul in Athens, the cultural center of the world of His day, was climaxed in this confrontation with two groups of philosophers, representing the spectrum of all humanistic evolutionary systems of past or present. The Epicureans were essentially atheists, devoted to the cultivation of pleasure as the chief aim of life. The Stoics were pantheists, dedicated to passive acceptance of whatever happens.

In all essentials these were no different than the evolutionary humanistic systems of the present day. Any philosophy that rejects special creation also must reject the atoning death and bodily resurrection of the Creator, so the Athenian philosophers regarded Paul's preaching as nothing but strange babbling.

Paul did not try to "dialogue" with them in the context of their own philosophies, but appealed rather to the evidence of creation, and their intuitive awareness, supported by the ancient traditions of the entire human race, that their "UNKNOWN GOD" was the "God that made the world and all things therein" (Acts 17:23, 24). Furthermore, this Creator God had demonstrated His identity to all men "in that He hath raised Him from the dead" (Acts 17:31).

Since these ancient pagan philosophies were essentially no different from either modern atheistic evolutionism, pantheistic Eastern evolutionism, or popular street-corner evolutionism—all rejecting or ignoring the God of the Bible—we might do well to emulate Paul's method of reaching them.

The Sceptre of Judah

The sceptre shall not depart from Judah, nor a lawgiver from between his feet, until Shiloh come; and unto Him shall the gathering of the people be (Genesis 49:10).

This is a remarkable Messianic prophecy, given by Jacob 1700 years before the first coming of Christ fulfilled it. Later prophecies would focus on His descent from David and then His birthplace in Bethlehem, but first one of the twelve sons of Jacob must be designated as His progenitor.

Remarkably, Jacob did not select either his first born son, Reuben, or his favorite son, Joseph. Nor did he choose Benjamin, the son of his favorite wife. He chose instead his fourth son, Judah, by divine direction.

Yet it was over 600 years before the tribe of Judah gained ascendancy over the others. The greatest leaders of Israel were from other tribes—Moses and Samuel from Levi, Joshua from Ephraim, Gideon from Manasseh, Samson from Dan, and Saul from Benjamin. Finally, David became king, and "the sceptre" was then held by Judah for a thousand years until Jesus was born in Bethlehem of Judea. Jesus' parents were both of Judah, both of the line of David, with both the legal and spiritual right to David's throne. But then, just 70 years after His birth, "the sceptre" (that is, leadership over the twelve tribes) departed from Judah with the worldwide dispersion of Israel, and no man since has ever held that right. It is still retained by Jesus, and will be reclaimed and exercised when He returns.

In the meantime, the prophecy stands as an unchallengeable identification of Jesus as the promised Messiah. Ancient Jewish commentators all recognized "Shiloh" as a name for Messiah. Since the sceptre has already departed, Shiloh has already come. When He returns, His people will, indeed, finally be gathered together "unto Him."

The Higher Law

Because that Abraham obeyed my voice, and kept my charge, my commandments, my statutes, and my laws (Genesis 26:5).

In the United States, the government should be a government of laws, rather than men, and our founding fathers established a Constitution, with its government of checks and balances, to safeguard this principle. Today, however, we have a great weight of both legislation and administrative regulations. Even our judges have become lawmakers themselves, assuming that the supposed "law" of evolution applies to the Constitution itself, adapting it to our "evolving" social policies.

The law of evolution is, of course, a pure fabrication, but there is indeed a higher law than even that of the Constitution. The founding fathers called it "the law of nature and of nature's God," or "the laws of divine providence." Studies of English jurisprudence, as codified particularly in the works of Blackstone and Rutherford, make it plain that the English common law was nothing more nor less than applied Biblical law. Our nation fundamentally was built on the framework of law established by the Creator in the Holy Scriptures, and has been greatly blessed because of this.

As a matter of fact, as our text shows, God's system of laws was established not only before Moses' time, but even before Abraham, and Abraham obeyed them. So did the ancient patriarch Job (note Job 23:12).

The courts of our country, however, have now seen fit to ban even the Ten Commandments from the schools, and God's laws are violated everywhere. Therefore, Christians have a greater responsibility now than ever before to do as our father Abraham did, obeying God's voice and His charge, with His commandments, statutes and laws.

The Creator of Israel

I am the LORD, your Holy One, the Creator of Israel, your King (Isaiah 43:15).

God is often referred to as the Holy One of Israel and as the King of Israel, but this reference to Him as Creator of Israel is unique. In the four other passages where God is named Creator, He is called "thy Creator" (Ecclesiastes 12:1), "Creator of the ends of the earth" (Isaiah 40:28), "the Creator, who is blessed for ever" (Romans 1:25) and "a faithful Creator" (I Peter 4:19). But in what sense has God become Israel's Creator?

Related to this truth is God's testimony in Isaiah 65:18: "Behold, I create Jerusalem a rejoicing, and her people a joy." Note also Isaiah 43:1: "But now thus saith the LORD that created thee, O Jacob, and He that formed thee, O Israel, Fear not: for I have redeemed thee, I have called thee by thy name; thou art mine."

It is obvious that God did not create the physical city of Jerusalem, for all its streets and walls were built by its inhabitants. Neither did He specially create the physical bodies of the Israelites nor the topography of the land of Israel. These testimonies apply rather to the spiritual creation of Israel in its special relation to God and to the world.

In one sense, of course, He even created physical Israel, for He created the marvelous process of human birth and the geological processes of the earth system, which He then providentially directed to eventually produce the people and the land of chosen Israel. There may also be an implied reference to the New Jerusalem, which will indeed be specially created (Isaiah 65:17).

In any case, God is Creator—not un-Creator. "I know that, whatsoever God doeth, it shall be forever" (Ecclesiastes 3:14). Israel, like the heavens and the earth, is forever, for God is her Creator.

JANUARY 28

The Lord Our Maker

O come, let us worship and bow down: let us kneel before the Lord *our Maker* (Psalm 95:6).

In the first chapter of Genesis, we are told that God was to "make man in our image" and also that He "created man in His own image" (Genesis 1:26, 27). Similarly, on the seventh day, God "rested from all His work which God created and made" (Genesis 2:3).

God is, therefore, both Creator and Maker of all things, including the image of God in man. These two terms are not synonymous, though they sometimes seem to be used interchangeably. "Creation" is calling into existence entities which previously had no existence. No one except God is ever the subject of the verb *create*. The work of *making*, on the other hand, is that of organizing created entities into complex systems.

It is interesting that God is called "Creator" five times in the Bible, whereas He is called "Maker" sixteen times. God *created* His image in men and women, but He also *made* them in that image. That is, He called into existence the spiritual component of man's nature, not shared in any degree by the animals. He also organized the basic material elements into complex human bodies, the most highly organized systems in the universe, and these were made in that image that God Himself would one day assume when He became an incarnate human being. In this way He is both Creator and Maker of His image in each person.

That image has been marred because of sin, but through the work of Christ, we have been "renewed in knowledge after the image of Him that created him" (Colossians 3:10), and our bodies will "be fashioned like unto His glorious body" (Philippians 3:21). Created and newly created, made and remade, let us humbly kneel before the Lord our Maker and Creator.

The River of God

Thou visitest the earth and waterest it: thou greatly enrichest it with the river of God, which is full of water: thou preparest them corn, when thou hast so provided for it (Psalm 65:9).

The inexhaustible river of God, watering the whole earth, is nothing less than the refreshing rains coming down from the heavens, "visiting" the earth on its amazing journey to the oceans, whence it flows back up to the skies again. This river incorporates all the rivers of earth, yet it is like no other river, for once it reaches the ocean, then it rises into the heavens, there to flow back over the thirsty ground and finally descend once more on its endless journey.

What a wonderful provision is this river of God! Without it, all life on earth would soon die. Far more valuable than gold, it continually "enriches" the earth on its regular visitations, "to satisfy the desolate and waste ground; and to cause the bud of the tender herb to spring forth" (Job 38:27).

Thereby does God also prepare corn, to feed man and beast. The word "corn" in this and other passages probably refers generically to any of the cereal grains, which provide the basic foodstuffs for people and animals all over the world. This is implied in the creation passage itself. "And God said, Behold, I have given you every herb bearing seed, which is upon the face of all the earth . . . And to every beast of the earth, and to every fowl of the air, and to every thing that creepeth upon the earth, wherein there is life, I have given every green herb for meat" (Genesis 1:29, 30).

This is God's wonderful life-giving river. "He watereth the hills from His chambers: the earth is satisfied with the fruit of thy works. He causeth grass to grow for the cattle, and herb for the service of man: that he may bring forth food out of the earth" (Psalm 104:13, 14). The Creator is also the Sustainer (Colossians 1:16, 17).

JANUARY 30

Singing Garments of Life

The pastures are clothed with flocks; the valleys also are covered over with corn; they shout for joy, they also sing (Psalm 65:13).

This is the concluding verse of the beautiful 65th psalm, climaxing a remarkable series of testimonies about God's providential care of His creation. In this final figure, the lands are pictured as clothed in beautiful, living garments—garments which shout and sing in joyful praise to their Maker.

The figure would be better appreciated in Biblical times, or in certain lands (e.g., New Zealand) today, where flocks of sheep are so abundant that they literally seem to cover the pasture lands in wool. The flocks first provide a metaphorical garment for the pastures, then literal clothing for men and women.

Similarly, the fertile valleys are everywhere arrayed in golden grain, which later provides food for both the animals and human beings.

And "the sounds of the earth are like music," as the song so eloquently expresses it. For those with ears to hear and eyes to see, praise is everywhere being offered up to our great Creator and faithful Sustainer, by the very creation itself.

Jesus also spoke of the beautiful garments of creation: "And why take ye thought for raiment? Consider the lilies of the field, how they grow; they toil not, neither do they spin: And yet I say unto you, That even Solomon in all his glory was not arrayed like one of these. Wherefore, if God so clothe the grass of the field, which today is, and tomorrow is cast into the oven, shall He not much more clothe you, O ye of little faith?" (Matthew 6:28–30).

The verse following our text, therefore, appropriately exhorts: "Make a joyful noise unto God, all ye lands. . . . All the earth shall worship thee" (Psalm 66:1, 4).

The Divine Designer

Who hath measured the waters in the hollow of His hand, and meted out heaven with the span, and comprehended the dust of the earth in a measure, and weighed the mountains in scales, and the hills in a balance? (Isaiah 40:12).

The answer to this rhetorical question can only be God, the divine Designer of all the intricate inter-relationships of His great creation. Four of the disciplines of natural science are implied here, and in each case a key principle of that science is anticipated.

The emphasis is on the precision of the divinely allocated quantities of each component. First, there is the precise balance of the waters of the earth, between the oceans, rivers, groundwater and atmospheric waters. Hydrology is the science of earth's waters, and life on earth is dependent on the fine tuning of the components of the hydrologic cycle. "He looketh to the ends of the earth . . . to make the weight for the winds; and He weigheth the waters by measure" (Job 28:24, 25). Also the atmospheric heaven has been carefully dimensioned in size and composition to make life possible, as formulated in the science of meteorology.

The "dust of the earth" is nothing less than the basic chemical elements, out of which all things are made. The accuracy with which elements combine with each other is based on their valences, and all of this is involved in the study of chemistry. The principle of isostasy ("equal weights") is the fundamental principle of the science of geophysics, involving the weights of mountains and hills, continents and ocean basins.

God does not deal in chance and caprice, even with inanimate physical systems such as mountains and waters.

Not even a sparrow can "fall on the ground without your Father" (Matthew 10:29).

FEBRUARY 1

Angels Round About

The angel of the L*ORD* *encampeth round about them that fear Him, and delivereth them?* (Psalm 34:7).

Since God's angels are normally unseen, we have little appreciation of how intimately they are involved in our lives. "Are they not all ministering spirits, sent forth to minister for them who shall be heirs of salvation" (Hebrews 1:14). As in our text, there may well be a protecting angel embracing and delivering us in times of danger. "For He shall give His angels charge over thee, to keep thee in all thy ways. They shall bear thee up in their hands, lest thou dash thy foot against a stone" (Psalm 91:11, 12).

Angels are sometimes called on to rout the enemies of God and His people. "Let them be confounded and put to shame that seek after my soul . . . and let the angel of the LORD chase them. Let their way be dark and slippery: and let the angel of the LORD persecute them" (Psalm 35:4–6).

Angels are intensely interested in the salvation and spiritual growth of believers, "which things the angels desire to look into" (I Peter 1:12). "For we are made a spectacle unto the world, and to angels, and to men" (I Corinthians 4:9). There are even occasions when "some have entertained angels unawares" (Hebrews 13:2).

There is "an innumerable company of angels" (Hebrews 12:22); beings of great power and wisdom (II Kings 19:35; II Samuel 14:20). They are not omnipotent, omnipresent or omniscient, of course, since they—like us—were created by God, simply to obey God. "Bless the LORD, ye His angels, that excel in strength, that do His commandments, hearkening unto the voice of His Word" (Psalm 103:20).

Finally, we shall be "carried by the angels" (Luke 16:22) into God's presence. Then we can better understand and thank them for all the many services rendered to us here on earth.

The Raging Seas

Thou rulest the raging of the sea: when the waves thereof arise, thou stillest them (Psalm 89:9).

There are few things in nature more fearsome or more uncontrollable by man than a mighty storm at sea. Only the One who created the waters of the sea can really control them.

But *He* can! "For He commandeth and raiseth the stormy wind, which lifteth up the waves thereof . . . He maketh the storm a calm, so that the waves thereof are still" (Psalm 107:25, 29).

One of the most striking demonstrations of the deity of Christ was in a storm on the sea of Galilee, when "He arose, and rebuked the wind and the raging of the water: and they ceased, and there was a calm" (Luke 8:24). Note also the experience of the mariners sailing to Tarshish, when they realized that the storm that was about to destroy them had been sent by the God of heaven because of Jonah. "So they took up Jonah, and cast Him into the sea and the sea ceased from her raging" (Jonah 1:15).

The Scriptures also compare opponents of the Gospel to a raging sea. "The wicked are like the troubled sea, when it cannot rest, whose waters cast up mire and dirt" (Isaiah 57:20). Similarly, Jude says that apostate teachers are like "raging waves of the sea, foaming out their own shame" (Jude 13).

Christ used this same figure to prophesy the turmoil of the ungodly nations of the world in the last days. "There shall be . . . upon the earth distress of nations, with perplexity; the sea and the waves roaring" (Luke 21:25). But just as God the Creator can calm the raging waves of the ocean, so God our Savior can speak peace to the nations and calm each troubled soul. As our text assures us, He rules the ragings of every sea, and stills them when the waves arise.

FEBRUARY 3

Men Can Be Like Animals

All we like sheep have gone astray; we have turned every one to his own way; and the Lord hath laid on Him the iniquity of us all (Isaiah 53:6).

Men have not evolved from animals; we have all been specially created in God's own image (Genesis 1:27). However, we often seem to "devolve" into animalistic behavior. As our text says, all of us are like stupid sheep, going our own way instead of God's way. "The ox knoweth his owner, and the ass his master's crib: but Israel doth not know, my people doth not consider" (Isaiah 1:3).

With some men it is even worse. The hypocritical Pharisees were compared by Christ to "a generation of vipers" (Matthew 23:33) and "false prophets" to "ravening wolves" (Matthew 7:15).

Apostate teachers in Christian churches are even worse than false prophets and hypocrites, for they teach their lies in the name of Christ. As Peter says: "It is happened unto them according to the true proverb, The dog is turned to his own vomit again; and the sow that was washed to her wallowing in the mire" (II Peter 2:22). In fact, he says they are "as natural brute beasts, made to be taken and destroyed," who must eventually "perish in their own corruption" (II Peter 2:12).

Now the dog and the sow, the sheep and the ox—even the viper—are just natural brute beasts, and their behaviors are instinctive, not volitional. But when men or women choose to behave like animals, they deserve the fate of animals. Many even claim an animal ancestry through evolutionary development to justify gross animalistic behavior, which, of course, has its own fitting reward. Nevertheless the Lord Jesus Christ has become "the Lamb of God" (John 1:29), and "the Lord hath laid on Him the iniquity of us all," so that He "taketh away the sin of the world."

Fiat Creation

Let them praise the name of the LORD: for He commanded, and they were created (Psalm 148:5).

Certain Christian intellectuals today are promoting the concept of what they call "process creation," a euphemism for theistic evolution. This is a contradiction in terms, however, for creation, by definition, is supernatural and instantaneous. The Bible makes this plain.

Our text is in one of the beautiful "hallelujah" psalms, in which the entire creation is exhorted to praise the Lord. The sun, moon and all the heavens are included, and then the testimony of our text is given. As soon as God commanded, they were created, not over long ages but immediately. God said "Let there be . . . " and so it was.

This is made especially emphatic in the 33rd psalm: "By the word of the Lord were the heavens made, and all the host of them by the breath of His mouth . . . For He spake, and it was done; He commanded, and it stood fast" (Psalm 33:6, 9). This is also the testimony in the great "faith" chapter, Hebrews 11. The very first object of faith is the following: "Through faith we understand that the worlds were framed by the word of God, so that things which are seen were not made of things which do appear" (Hebrews 11:3). That is, the things which are seen (sun, moon, stars, etc.) were not made out of pre-existing materials (things which appear), but by the spoken Word of God.

There is not any need at all to compromise either God's omnipotence or His inerrant Word by such devices as theistic evolution, progressive creation or process creation, for no natural "process" could ever generate the complex and beautifully organized systems of the creation. Compromising evangelical scientists and theologians who are intimidated by the ungodly philosophy of evolution should be corrected, not accommodated.

FEBRUARY 5

Creation and United Prayer

And when they heard that, they lifted up their voice to God with one accord, and said, Lord, thou art God, which hast made heaven, and earth, and the sea, and all that in them is (Acts 4:24).

When Christians can unite in acknowledging God as true omnipotent Creator, as did the early disciples, then they can pray in confidence, in spite of all the "threatenings" of those who are "gathered together against the Lord, and against His Christ" (Acts 4:26, 29). The God who called the infinite cosmos into existence, with all its creatures, can easily handle those who would seek to thwart His will.

But Christians do not speak with one accord today, even on this most basic of all truths—the fact of creation. Instead, many choose to dissemble and equivocate and compromise, inventing such self-contradictory concepts as theistic evolution, progressive creation, process creation and such like, wistfully seeking approval from those who deny that the God of the Bible created all things, and thereby doing great harm to the faith of many. Like the men-pleasers of old, who "loved the praise of men more than the praise of God" (John 12:43), they seek academic approval rather than Biblical authority and scientific factuality. Being of one accord with the intellectual establishment carries more weight to them than unity with Christian brethren who believe the Bible means what it says.

Nevertheless, when the Christians in any given place do pray with one accord, united on the basic truth of special creation as the foundation of all other truth, then the results will be as it was for the disciples cited in our text. "And when they had prayed . . . they spake the word of God with boldness. . . . and great grace was upon them all" (Acts 4:31, 33). There can be no real Christian unity until there is one accord on the foundation of Christian unity.

Christ the Creationist

For in those days shall be affliction, such as was not from the beginning of the creation which God created unto this time, neither shall be (Mark 13:19).

In predicting a future judgment on the unbelieving world, the Lord Jesus referred to "the beginning of the creation which God created," thus affirming the Biblical doctrine of supernatural, sudden creation. In the pagan world of His day, evolutionism was dominant almost everywhere.

The Epicureans, for example, were atheistic evolutionists. The Stoics, Gnostics, Platonists and others were pantheistic evolutionists. None of the extra-Biblical philosophers of His day believed in a God who had created all things, including even the universe itself.

But Christ was a creationist, and the much maligned "scientific creationists" of today are following His example and teaching. He even believed in *recent* creation, for He said, speaking of Adam and Eve, that "from the beginning of the creation God made them male and female" (Mark 10:6). The pagans all believed in an eternal cosmos, but Jesus said it had a beginning, and that man and woman were a part of that beginning creation, following which, "the Sabbath was made for man" (Mark 2:27).

He also believed that the "two accounts" of creation (Genesis 1 and 2) were complementary, not contradictory, for He quoted from both in the same context. "Have ye not read," He said, "that He which made them at the beginning made them male and female [from Genesis 1], And said, For this cause shall a man leave father and mother, and shall cleave to his wife: and they twain shall be one flesh? [from Genesis 2]" (Matthew 19:4–6).

There may be some Christians who are evolutionists, but there is no such thing as "Christian evolution," for Christ was a creationist!

FEBRUARY 7 ❧

The Voice of the Lord

❧

The voice of the LORD *is powerful; the voice of the* LORD *is full of majesty* (Psalm 29:4).

This solemn phrase, "The voice of the LORD," occurs seven times in Psalm 29, centered especially on the awful judgment of the great Flood in the days of Noah. "The voice of the LORD is upon the waters: the God of glory thundereth: the LORD is upon many waters" (v. 3). It occurs many other times in the Old Testament as well, with a wide variety of applications and circumstances.

The very first time it occurs, however (and this is also the first occurrence of "voice" in the Bible, indicating thereby that it is God's voice—not man's—which we must hear, if we seek guidance for life), is in the Garden of Eden immediately after man brought sin into the world. "And they heard the voice of the LORD God walking in the garden. . . . And the LORD God called unto Adam, and said unto him, Where art thou?" (Genesis 3:8, 9). Mankind is lost and separated from God, but God calls unto each of us, as He did to Adam, and we desperately need to hear His voice if our lives are to be fulfilled.

In contrast to this scene of alienation, the final occurrence of a "voice" in the Bible is a beautiful scene of reconciliation, when God again speaks to lost mankind, this time in glorious restoration of that broken fellowship. "And I heard a great voice out of heaven saying, Behold, the tabernacle of God is with men, and He will dwell with them, and they shall be His people, and God Himself shall be with them, and be their God" (Revelation 21:3).

To hear His voice *then*, however, we must first hear His voice *now* through His word. Jesus said: "He that heareth my word, and believeth on Him that sent me, hath everlasting life . . . the dead shall hear the voice of the Son of God: and they that hear shall live" (John 5:24, 25).

The Divine/Human Word

God, who at sundry times and in divers manners spake in time past unto the fathers by the prophets, Hath in these last days spoken unto us by His Son (Hebrews 1:1, 2).

The title of *the Word of God* is given both to Jesus Christ as the Living Word (John 1:1–3; Revelation 19:13), and to the Holy Scriptures as the Written Word (Ephesians 6:17; Hebrews 4:12; etc.). They are so perfectly synchronous that what is said of one can usually be applied also to the other.

Both are human, yet without error; both are divine, yet can be comprehended by man. "God was manifest in the flesh" (I Timothy 3:16). "Holy men of God spake as they were moved by the Holy Ghost" (II Peter 1:21). "In Him is no sin" (I John 3:5), "The Scripture cannot be broken," and "All Scripture . . . is profitable" (John 10:35; II Timothy 3:16).

Furthermore, each is eternal: "Jesus Christ the same, yesterday, and today, and for ever" (Hebrews 13:8). "For ever, O LORD, thy word is settled in heaven" (Psalm 119:89).

Each brings regeneration and everlasting life to all those who believe. "He saved us, by the washing of regeneration . . . through Jesus Christ our Savior" (Titus 3:5, 6). "God hath given to us eternal life, and this life is in His Son" (I John 5:11). "Being born again . . . by the word of God, which liveth and abideth for ever" (I Peter 1:23). "Search the Scriptures: for in them ye think ye have eternal life: and they are they which testify of me" (John 5:39).

Finally, judgment comes by both Christ and the Scriptures. "The Father . . . hath committed all judgment to the Son" (John 5:22). "The dead were judged out of those things which were written in the books" (Revelation 20:12). Both Christ and the Bible are vitally important to each Christian and must be studied, understood, known, loved, trusted, and relied upon in every human endeavor.

FEBRUARY 9

Jesus and the Flood

For as in the days that were before the flood they were eating and drinking, marrying and giving in marriage, until the day that Noah entered into the ark, And knew not until the flood came, and took them all away; so shall also the coming of the Son of man be (Matthew 24:38, 39).

The Lord Jesus Christ not only believed in the special, recent creation of all things by God (note Mark 10:6–8), but also in the worldwide flood of Noah's day, including the special preservation of life on the ark. The flood in which He believed was obviously not a "local flood," for He compared it to the worldwide future impact of His second coming.

Neither was it a tranquil flood, nor a selective flood, for Jesus said: "the flood came, and destroyed them all" (Luke 17:27). It is clear that He was referring to—and that He believed—the Genesis record of the great flood! There it says that the whole earth was "filled with violence" (Genesis 6:13) having first been filled with people, and that the resulting world-cleansing deluge was so cataclysmic that "every living substance was destroyed which was upon the face of the ground, both man, and cattle, and the creeping things, and the fowl of the heaven; and they were destroyed from the earth" (Genesis 7:23). Indeed, "the flood came and took [literally 'lifted'] them all away."

This is what Jesus said, and what He believed, and therefore, those who are truly His disciples must also believe this. The destructive effects of the flood can still be seen today, not only in the Biblical record, but also in the abundant evidences of cataclysmic destruction in the rocks and fossil graveyards all over the world. To refuse this evidence, as do many modern intellectuals, can only be because they "willingly are ignorant," as Peter said in referring to this testimony (II Peter 3:5).

Teaching Stones

Woe unto him that saith to the wood, Awake; to the dumb stone, Arise, it shall teach! Behold, it is laid over with gold and silver, and there is no breath at all in the midst of it (Habakkuk 2:19).

How foolish are those who worship idols—objects of wood and stone, with no life in them, not even when they are adorned in silver and gold. Can inanimate objects come to life and even become teachers? A child knows better.

But not college professors! All over the land, these proud purveyors of "science falsely so called" (I Timothy 6:20) are indoctrinating young minds with the absurd belief that inorganic substances can somehow first become simple living substances and then eventually organize themselves all the way up to being people. They would not, of course, suggest that sticks and stones could suddenly become human (neither did the ancient idolaters, for that matter). They just believe that time—lots of it—can magically develop people out of much simpler substances than even these ancient philosophers ever imagined. "In the beginning Hydrogen" is their arrogant notion.

But God will not be mocked in this way forever. Life can only come from life—ultimately from the living God! The wooden idol of the pagan is every bit as scientific as the evolutionary models of the modern intellectual; neither one can create life. "Their idols are silver and gold, the work of men's hands. They have mouths, but they speak not: eyes have they, but they see not. . . . They that make them are like unto them; so is every one that trusteth in them" (Psalm 115:4, 5, 8).

Only God can create life, and He can even cause stones to teach. "Speak to the earth, and it shall teach thee; . . . Who knoweth not in all these that the hand of the LORD hath wrought this?" (Job 12:8, 9).

FEBRUARY 11

God Remembers

And God remembered Noah, and every living thing, and all the cattle that was with him in the ark: and God made a wind to pass over the earth, and the waters assuaged (Genesis 8:1).

This verse contains the first mention of the beautiful word "remember" in the Bible, and it tells us that *God remembers!* During the awful cataclysm of the flood, the most devastating event thus far in the history of the world, God still remembered the faithful obedience of Noah, and He even remembered *every living thing!*

We may forget many things, but God remembers: "For God is not unrighteous to forget your work and labor of love, which ye have shewed toward His name" (Hebrews 6:10). Nor does He ever forget a promise. The first mention of "remember" in the New Testament is the Spirit-inspired testimony of Zacharias: "Blessed be the Lord God of Israel; for He hath visited and redeemed His people . . . to remember His holy covenant; The oath which He sware to our father Abraham" (Luke 1:68, 72, 73). That promise had been made 2000 years before, but God remembered.

God even remembers the sparrows; "not one of them is forgotten before God" (Luke 12:6). And He certainly remembers His own children: "For He knoweth our frame; He remembereth that we are dust" (Psalm 103:14).

Even after the children of Israel had gone deeply into idolatry He could still say, "I remember thee, the kindness of thy youth, the love of thine espousals, when thou wentest after me in the wilderness" (Jeremiah 2:2).

God remembers the evil as well as the good, of course. The one thing He chooses not to remember is the sinful past of those who have come to Christ for forgiveness. "And their sins and their iniquities will I remember no more" (Hebrews 10:17).

The Fire of God

For our God is a consuming fire (Hebrews 12:29).

Fire was considered by certain of the ancient pantheistic philosophers to have been the primeval element out of which all things had evolved, and this same myth is promulgated today by evolutionary cosmogonists in the form of their "Big Bang" theory. The fact is, however, that fire is a creation of God used both actually and symbolically as God's vehicle of judgment on sin.

It is significant that both the first and last references to fire in the Bible mention both fire and brimstone, used in flaming judgment on human rebellion against God. First, "the LORD rained upon Sodom and upon Gomorrah brimstone and fire from the LORD out of heaven" (Genesis 19:24). And finally, "the fearful, and unbelieving, and the abominable, and murderers, and whoremongers, and sorcerers, and idolaters, and all liars, shall have their part in the lake which burneth with fire and brimstone: which is the second death" (Revelation 21:8).

Our text is a reference to Moses' words to the tribes as they were preparing to enter the promised land after his death. Warning them against corrupting their faith through idolatry, he said: "For the LORD thy God is a consuming fire, even a jealous God" (Deuteronomy 4:24). Its New Testament context is a grave warning against rejecting God's word: "See that ye refuse not Him that speaketh. For if they escaped not who refused Him that spake on earth, much more shall not we escape, if we turn away from Him that speaketh from heaven" (Hebrews 12:25).

In this sense, God's word is also the fire of God. "His word was in mine heart as a burning fire shut up in my bones, and I was weary with forbearing, and I could not stay" (Jeremiah 20:9). It is better to be refined with the fire of God's word than to be consumed.

FEBRUARY 13

The Face of Jesus Christ

And they shall see His face; and His name shall be in their foreheads (Revelation 22:4).

This is the last reference in the Bible to the face of the Lord Jesus Christ, and a glorious promise it is, with its assurance that all His servants will finally see Him face to face!

Although they give us no specific description of His physical appearance (the only description of His appearance is in Revelation 1:13–16), the gospel writers do frequently mention His face.

On the Mount of Transfiguration, Peter, and James, and John saw how "His face did shine as the sun" (Matthew 17:2), as He spoke of His forthcoming death. Shortly after this, "He steadfastly set His face to go to Jerusalem" (Luke 9:51) to meet His death.

A few days after His entrance into Jerusalem, He was delivered into the hands of wicked men who took delight in desecrating that face which, in loving grief, had just wept over the city and its indifference to God. But first, in the garden just before His arrest, He "fell on His face" in agonizing prayer (Matthew 26:39).

Then the Roman soldiers began "to cover His face" (Mark 14:65), and to "spit in His face" (Matthew 26:67), and finally, "they struck Him on the face" (Luke 22:64). In fact, they abused Him so severely that "His visage was so marred more than any man, and His form more than the sons of men" (Isaiah 52:14).

But when He comes again, the Christ-rejecting world will cry out to the mountains to "fall on us, and hide us from the face . . . of the Lamb," "from whose face the earth and the heaven fled away" (Revelation 6:16; 20:11). All the redeemed, on the other hand, will rejoice forever in "the light of the knowledge of the glory of God in the face of Jesus Christ" (II Corinthians 4:6).

Milk and Honey

And I am come down to deliver them out of the hand of the Egyptians, and to bring them up out of that land unto a good land and a large, unto a land flowing with milk and honey (Exodus 3:8).

This is the first of no less than 18 references in the Old Testament to "milk and honey," plus four more referring to "butter and honey." The promised land of Canaan was repeatedly described as "a land flowing with milk and honey," symbolizing its fruitfulness. In ancient times, the pasturage was rich, sustaining large flocks of milk-producing goats and cattle, and the fields were verdant with many flowers, with a resulting abundance of wild bees depositing honey in great abundance in the rocks and trees.

Honey is often used symbolically for whatever is pleasant and delectable, while milk is used as a figure for necessary (rather than enjoyable) nourishment. Thus, the promised land was a land where both the necessities and the joys of life could be found in abundance.

Before the children of Israel entered the Promised Land, they had to spend forty years in a barren wilderness with neither milk, nor honey, nor other sustenance. Even there, however, the Lord graciously created manna each day for them, which provided both their necessary food and even some sweetness, for "the taste of it was like wafers made with honey" (Exodus 16:31).

Appropriately enough, both milk and honey are used in the Scriptures to picture God's word itself, in both its life-giving essentials and also its pleasant delights: "As newborn babes, desire the sincere milk of the word, that ye may grow thereby" (I Peter 2:2), we are commanded. Then there is also the testimony: "How sweet are thy words unto my taste! yea, sweeter than honey to my mouth!" (Psalm 119:103).

FEBRUARY 15

Creation and the Sciences

So God created man in His own image, in the image of God created He him; male and female created He them (Genesis 1:27).

The first chapter of Genesis is the foundational chapter of the Bible and, therefore, of all true science. It is the great creation chapter, outlining the events of that first week of time, when "the heavens and the earth were finished, and. . . . God ended His work which He had made" (Genesis 2:1, 2). Despite the evolutionists, God is not creating or making anything in the world today (except for special miracles as recorded in Scripture), because all His work was finished in that primeval week. He is now engaged in the work of conserving, or saving, what He first created.

There are only three acts of special creation—that is, creation out of nothing except God's omnipotent word—recorded in this chapter. His other works were those of "making" or "forming" the created entities into complex, functioning systems.

His first creative act was to call into existence the space/mass/time cosmos. "In the beginning God created the heaven and the earth" (Genesis 1:1). This is the domain which we now study in the *physical sciences*. The second is the domain of the *life sciences*. "God created . . . every living creature that moveth" (Genesis 1:21). It is significant that the "life" principle required a second act of direct creation. It will thus never be possible to describe living systems solely in terms of physics and chemistry.

The third act of creation was that of the image of God in man and woman. The study of human beings is the realm of the *human sciences*. Our bodies can be analyzed chemically, and our living processes biologically, but human behavior can only really be understood in terms of our relation to God, whose image we share.

Everlasting Contempt

And many of them that sleep in the dust of the earth shall awake, some to everlasting life, and some to shame and everlasting contempt (Daniel 12:2).

Some claim that the Old Testament knows nothing of a resurrection, but this promise of God clearly refutes such a notion. Not only will some be raised to everlasting life, but some to everlasting shame and contempt!

What a bitter end this will be for those who now look with contempt upon the Bible. The Hebrew word translated "contempt" is used only one other time, in the very last verse of Isaiah, but is there translated "abhorring." "And they shall go forth, and look upon the carcasses of the men that have transgressed against me: for their worm shall not die, neither shall their fire be quenched; and they shall be an abhorring unto all flesh" (Isaiah 66:24).

There is probably no doctrine of the Bible more hated by unbelievers than the doctrine of everlasting punishment. It was this teaching (not the imaginary evidence for evolution) that turned Charles Darwin away from God. Nevertheless, it was verified by Christ Himself. "It is better for thee to enter into the kingdom of God with one eye, than having two eyes to be cast into hell fire: Where . . . the fire is not quenched" (Mark 9:47, 48). Christ will say to the "goats" on His left hand, "Depart from me, ye cursed, into everlasting fire, prepared for the devil and his angels . . . these shall go away into everlasting punishment" (Matthew 25:41, 46). Paul also warned that those who "obey not the gospel . . . shall be punished with everlasting destruction from the presence of the Lord" (II Thessalonians 1:8, 9). Everlasting contempt, everlasting fire, everlasting punishment, everlasting destruction—these await all who reject God and His saving word, through Christ. How much better to "awake to everlasting life!"

FEBRUARY 17

True Science

The fear of the LORD is the beginning of wisdom: and the knowledge of the holy is understanding (Proverbs 9:10).

There is widespread propaganda being circulated today, emanating from the highest circles of establishment science and education, to the effect that Biblical Christian faith is either antagonistic to science or irrelevant to it. Therefore, these spokesmen argue, science must be taught on a purely naturalistic basis, with no reference whatever to God, or creation, or to the supernatural.

The Christian is thus forced to make a choice—the scientific establishment, or God. God's word makes it plain that "the fear of the LORD is the beginning of knowledge" (Proverbs 1:7) and "the fear of the LORD is the beginning of wisdom" (Proverbs 9:10). The New Testament, likewise, notes that in Christ "are hid all the treasures of wisdom and knowledge" (Colossians 2:3). Since Jesus Christ is the incarnate word of God, "and without Him was not any thing made that was made" (John 1:3), it is necessarily true that true science must be built on the knowledge of Him who created the world that scientists seek to study.

This is why science itself could only have developed—as indeed the leading historians of science recognize it did—in the context of the Christian world view. Practically all the founding fathers of modern science (Kepler, Newton, Boyle, Ray, Linnaeus, etc.) were men who believed in God, special creation, and the Bible. They did their science with the motivation that they were merely "thinking God's thoughts after Him."

When scientists try to eliminate God from His creation, using evolutionism as their explanation for the origin and history of the world, they are not building up science, but "science falsely so called" (I Timothy 6:20). True science always supports the Scriptures.

Hating Knowledge

How long, ye simple ones, will ye love simplicity? and the scorners delight in their scorning, and fools hate knowledge? (Proverbs 1:22).

This ancient question by the wise man, Solomon, was posed almost 3000 years ago and is still relevant today. "How long?" he asked. How long will men continue to scoff at true knowledge? "The fear of the LORD is the beginning of knowledge: but fools despise wisdom and instruction" (Proverbs 1:7).

The answer to your question, Solomon, would have been 3000 years at least! Peter prophesied "that there shall come in the last days scoffers . . . saying, Where is the promise of His coming?" (II Peter 3:3, 4), and Paul said "that in the last days perilous times shall come. For men shall be . . . boasters, proud, blasphemers . . . ever learning, and never able to come to the knowledge of the truth" (II Timothy 3:1, 2, 7).

Throughout history, men have scorned the true knowledge of God and His creation. Peter says they are "willingly ignorant" and Paul says they are "without excuse" (II Peter 3:5; Romans 1:20), but they "delight in their scorning" nonetheless.

It is remarkable that their hatred of God's true knowledge is cloaked in a robe of scientism and evolutionary pseudo-knowledge that even deceives many professing Christians. "Professing themselves to be wise, they became fools" (Romans 1:22), despising the true wisdom and instruction of God's word.

"To the law and to the testimony: if they speak not according to this word, it is because there is no light in them" (Isaiah 8:20). Those who scorn God's word have no light of their own, despite their scientific pretensions. "Wise men lay up knowledge: but the mouth of the foolish is near destruction" (Proverbs 10:14).

FEBRUARY 19

From Darkness to Light

And God said, Let there be light: and there was light. And God saw the light, that it was good: and God divided the light from the darkness (Genesis 1:3, 4).

The initial aspect of God's newly created world was one of darkness in the presence of the all-pervading waters. Since "God is light, and in Him is no darkness at all" (I John 1:5), the darkness had to be specially created (Isaiah 45:7) before God could then call for the light to appear in the darkness.

This would later serve as a striking picture of the entrance of light into the darkness of a soul born in sin. "For God, who commanded the light to shine out of darkness, hath shined in our hearts, to give the light of the knowledge of the glory of God in the face of Jesus Christ" (II Corinthians 4:6). The light enters our soul by His word. "The entrance of thy words giveth light" (Psalm 119:130).

This great theme, contrasting the darkness of the soul without Christ to the glorious light He brings when that soul receives Him by faith, is found often in Scripture. "[Christ] hath called you out of darkness into His marvelous light" (I Peter 2:9). "The darkness is past, and the true light now shineth" (I John 2:8). Jesus even called Himself that true light which divided the light from the darkness. "I am the light of the world" He claimed; "He that followeth me shall not walk in darkness, but shall have the light of life" (John 8:12).

And because we have received the true light, we should henceforth live in the light of His truth. "For ye were sometimes darkness, but now are ye light in the Lord: walk as children of light" (Ephesians 5:8). "Let us therefore cast off the works of darkness, and let us put on the armor of light" (Romans 13:12). God's light is good. In the Holy City "there shall be no night there" (Revelation 22:5).

Incorruptible Things

Forasmuch as ye know that ye were not redeemed with corruptible things, as silver and gold, from your vain conversation received by tradition from your fathers (I Peter 1:18).

Not all the wealth of the world can redeem a single soul, for all the gold and silver are merely corruptible elements in a world under "the bondage of corruption" (Romans 8:21). Everything in the physical creation is decaying and dying. In fact, one day all these "elements shall melt with fervent heat, the earth also and the works that are therein shall be burned up" (II Peter 3:10). Even the very seeds which transmit life are "corruptible seed" (I Peter 1:23), and all mankind is "corruptible man" (Romans 1:23). Modern science recognizes this universal principle of decay as one of its most basic laws—the law of increasing entropy.

Even in this corruptible world, however, some things are incorruptible. There is the "incorruptible . . . word of God, which liveth and abideth for ever" (I Peter 1:23). Even though "heaven and earth shall pass away," the words of Christ "shall not pass away" (Matthew 24:35).

We are redeemed, not by silver and gold, but "with the precious blood of Christ" (I Peter 1:19). God Himself is the "uncorruptible God" (Romans 1:23), and He has "begotten us again unto a lively hope by the resurrection of Jesus Christ from the dead, To an inheritance incorruptible and undefiled, and that fadeth not away" (I Peter 1:3, 4). We work not as others "to obtain a corruptible crown; but we an incorruptible" (I Corinthians 9:25).

Finally, these dying bodies will themselves be redeemed, "for the trumpet shall sound, and the dead shall be raised incorruptible, and we shall be changed. For this corruptible must put on incorruption, and this mortal must put on immortality" (I Corinthians 15:52, 53).

FEBRUARY 21

The Sin of Sodom

And the L*ORD* *said, Because the cry of Sodom and Gomorrah is great, and because their sin is very grievous* (Genesis 18:20).

These are strange times when men "call evil good, and good evil" (Isaiah 5:20). This has never been more obvious than in the sudden respectability of the ancient sin of the Sodomites, whose very name has been identified for thousands of years with the vice of homosexuality. Although human attitudes may change, God does not change, and His evaluation of sin remains the same. "With whom is no variableness, neither shadow of turning" (James 1:17).

We do well, therefore, to remind people today of what God has said about the sin of Sodom. Not only was it "great" and "grievous," as God said to Abraham, but also "wicked" and "exceeding" (Genesis 13:13), as well as "iniquitous" (Genesis 19:15). It was later called "bitter" (Deuteronomy 32:32), "flagrant" (Isaiah 3:9), and "horrible" (Jeremiah 23:14). In the New Testament period it was still called by Peter "ungodly," "filthy," and "unlawful" (II Peter 2:6–8).

Paul called the same sin "unclean," "vile," and "unseemly" (Romans 1:24, 26, 27), and those who practice it are called "dogs" in both Old and New Testaments (Deuteronomy 23:17, 18; Revelation 22:15).

Nevertheless we, like God, must love the sinner while hating the sin. Like any other sin, this can be forgiven and cleansed, and conquered by the grace of God. To the Corinthians, Paul wrote: "Be not deceived: neither fornicators, nor idolaters, nor adulterers, nor effeminate, nor abusers of themselves with mankind . . . shall inherit the kingdom of God. And such were some of you: but ye are washed, but ye are sanctified, but ye are justified in the name of the Lord Jesus, and by the Spirit of our God" (I Corinthians 6:9–11).

All Nations of Men

And hath made of one blood all nations of men for to dwell on all the face of the earth, and hath determined the times before appointed, and the bounds of their habitation (Acts 17:26).

This important truth was preached by Paul to the Greek intellectuals in Athens, reminding them (and us) that all nations are alike before God. Note that God has ordained distinct nations, not "races." Neither the word nor the concept of "race" ever appears in Scripture. All nations are of "one blood," and have all descended from Noah. "These are the three sons of Noah: and of them was the whole earth overspread" (Genesis 9:19).

Thus there is no Biblical basis for racism, or any notion that one race is intrinsically superior to any other. Racism has its basis in evolutionism—the idea that the so-called "races" have been evolving independently for 50,000 years or more. Racism has its roots in pre-Darwinian systems of evolutionary pantheism, but Darwin and most other evolutionists of the 19th century both in Europe and America were strong racists and gave it a pseudo-scientific sanction with their notions of struggle for existence and natural selection of the fittest.

Racist thought continued to dominate anthropology until the ardent evolutionist, Adolf Hitler, gave it a bad name with his Aryan racism in World War II. Modern evolutionists have now largely abandoned the racist ideas of Darwin, Huxley, Haeckel, et al., but evolutionary theory still naturally lends itself to such applications.

In any case, no Christian should harbor any concept of racial superiority, for we have been "renewed in knowledge after the image of Him that created [us]: Where there is neither Greek nor Jew . . . Barbarian, Scythian, bond nor free: but Christ is all and in all" (Colossians 3:10, 11).

Why?

Jesus answered and said unto him, What I do thou knowest not now; but thou shalt know hereafter (John 13:7).

In this scientific age, it is essential for us to remember that "science" can never answer any question beginning with "why." Scientific research seeks to answer questions of "what" and "how," and sometimes "where" and "when," but it can never deal with "why" questions. Such questions require a moral or theological answer.

Probably the most vexing of all such questions is: "Why do the righteous suffer?" Or, put another way: "Why is there evil in a world created by a God who is good?" The question becomes especially poignant when personal calamity comes and we ask, "Why did this happen to me?"

Many think the book of Job was written to answer such questions, for Job was one of the most godly men who ever lived, yet he suffered more than anyone. But God answered Job's searching questions only by pointing to the wonders of His Creation. God has made us for Himself, and He is "forming" us for His own holy purpose; that is all we need to know right now. "What I do thou knowest not now," said Jesus, "but thou shalt know hereafter" (John 13:7).

Yet even Jesus in His human suffering cried out on the cross: "My God, my God, why hast thou forsaken me?" (Matthew 27:46). We do know, at least in part, the answer to *this* question. "For He hath made Him to be sin for us, who knew no sin; that we might be made the righteousness of God in Him" (II Corinthians 5:21).

For answers to the other "why" questions, we may well have to await God's own time. Until then, "we know that all things work together for good to them that love God" (Romans 8:28), and we can say with Job: "Though He slay me, yet will I trust in Him" (Job 13:15).

Without Form and Void

I beheld the earth, and, lo, it was without form, and void; and the heavens, and they had no light (Jeremiah 4:23).

The language in this verse is clearly patterned after Genesis 1:2, the description of the primordial earth: "And the earth was without form, and void; and darkness was upon the face of the deep." That it is a metaphor, however, and not an actual reference to that primordial earth is evident from its context. The previous verse speaks of "my people" (that is, the people of Judah) and the following verse of "the mountains" (there were no mountains as yet at the time of Genesis 1:2).

Furthermore, the broader context makes it plain that the prophet is speaking of a coming judgment on the land of Judah because of the rebellion of its people against their God (verse 16 specifically mentions Judah, and verse 31 mentions Zion). The land is to be so devastated that the prophet compared its future appearance to the unformed and barren earth at its very beginning.

This ultimate fulfillment will be at Armageddon. The same Hebrew words (*tohu* for "without form," and *bohu* for "void") occur again in this context in an awesome scene of judgment described by Isaiah: "For the indignation of the Lord is upon all nations" (34:2), gathered together in the former land of Edom to fight against Jerusalem when Christ returns, "and He shall stretch out upon it the line of confusion [i.e., *tohu*] and the stones of emptiness [i.e., *bohu*]" (34:11). Instead of the regular surveyor's line and markers ordering the property boundaries, God's judgment will bring such disorder and barrenness to the land that it almost will seem to revert back to its primeval state at the beginning of time. "Nevertheless, we look for new heavens and a new earth" (II Peter 3:13), and *that* earth will be beautiful and bountiful with "no night there."

Breath and Spirit

Thus saith God the LORD, He that created the heavens, and stretched them out; He that spread forth the earth, and that which cometh out of it: He that giveth breath unto the people upon it, and spirit to them that walk therein (Isaiah 42:5).

God the Lord (*Elohim Jehovah*) is here identified as the Creator and organizer of all the universe, the heavens, and the earth, and all things therein. In context, He is also identifying Himself as the one sending forth "my servant," to be given as "a covenant of the people, for a light unto the Gentiles" (Isaiah 42:1, 6), the coming Messiah of Israel.

He who does all these things also gives every person born both breath and spirit. The "breath" (Hebrew, *neshumah*) is that "breath of life" which God breathed into Adam's nostrils when He created him at the beginning. Even those who do not believe in God must depend on Him for their very breath, since "He giveth to all life, and breath, and all things." Therefore, He is "not far from every one of us: For in Him we live, and move, and have our being" (Acts 17:25, 27, 28).

He also gives each person a spirit (Hebrew, *ruach*), a word used first of all in reference to the "Spirit of God" (Genesis 1:2). It is this attribute in particular that constitutes the created "image of God" in man (Genesis 1:27). The higher land animals all possess "the breath of life," along with man (Genesis 7:21, 22), but only men and women are created in the image of God, each with an eternal spirit.

Man's breath and spirit are closely related, and sometimes the words are used almost interchangeably. When the breath departs from a person's body at death, the spirit also departs with it, but the latter "shall return unto God who gave it" (Ecclesiastes 12:7). The breath also will be activated again on the coming resurrection day.

Things to Keep

And He said unto him, Why callest thou me good? there is none good but one, that is, God: but if thou wilt enter into life, keep the commandments (Matthew 19:17).

The two main Greek words for "keep" in the New Testament both mean more than just "obey," though this meaning is certainly included. They also mean "guard" and "preserve." We are thus told by Christ, in our text above, to guard and obey God's commandments.

The same urgent command to *keep* what God has given is applied to many other entities in Scripture. For example, Paul stresses that we are to "keep that which is committed to thy trust, avoiding profane and vain babblings, and oppositions of science falsely so called" (I Timothy 6:20). In other words, false science (evolution) and vain babbling (humanistic philosophies) will seek to destroy the tenets of God's truth, so we must always be diligent to guard and protect these truths.

Each person is also urged to "keep himself unspotted from the world" and to "keep thyself pure" (James 1:27; I Timothy 5:22). The forces of darkness make perpetual attacks against the spiritual and moral integrity of the Christian, so we must constantly be alert to protect ourselves against their enticements.

Then we must also endeavor "to keep the unity of the Spirit in the bond of peace" (Ephesians 4:3), and to "keep yourselves in the love of God" (Jude 21), for the enemy will continually try to sow discord and bitterness among God's people.

There are many verses which stress the keeping of His commandments (e.g., John 14:15) and the keeping of His words (e.g., I John 2:5). Finally, in the very last chapter of the Bible, the Lord sums it all up, as it were, when He promises: "Blessed is he that keepeth the sayings of the prophecy of this book" (Revelation 22:7).

The Heaven of Heavens

But will God in very deed dwell with men on the earth? Behold, heaven and the heaven of heavens cannot contain thee; how much less this house which I have built! (II Chronicles 6:18).

This intriguing phrase, "the heaven of heavens," is found at least five times in the Bible. Our text is taken from the prayer of Solomon at the dedication of the beautiful temple he had built as a dwelling for God. Solomon understood that God was infinite and omnipresent, yet it was somehow possible for Him to be also in a finite place for a finite time.

But what is this "heaven of heavens?" Can the heavens themselves have a heaven? Whatever it is, it is part of God's creation, and He rules over all. "Behold, the heaven and the heaven of heavens is the LORD's thy God, the earth also, with all that therein is" (Deuteronomy 10:14).

There is, of course, the atmospheric heaven in which the birds "fly above the earth in the open firmament of heaven" (Genesis 1:20). There is also the sidereal heaven, containing "the stars of the heaven," the number of which God compared to "the sand which is upon the sea shore" (Genesis 22:17). Scientists know fairly well the outer boundary of the atmospheric heaven, but the boundary of the starry heaven, billions of light-years from the earth, has not yet been reached by their telescopes.

Nevertheless, it must have a boundary, for when Christ went back to the Father after His resurrection, He "ascended up far above all heavens, that He might fill all things" (Ephesians 4:10). Perhaps this divine realm beyond the stars is "the heaven of heavens," the "third heaven," where Paul "was caught up into paradise" (II Corinthians 12:2, 4), and where Christ, having ascended, has entered "into heaven itself, now to appear in the presence of God for us" (Hebrews 9:24).

Christ-Made Men

For He hath made Him to be sin for us, Who knew no sin; that we might be made the righteousness of God in Him (II Corinthians 5:21).

Many men would boast of being "self-made" men, but no Christian can do this. Everything we are that is truly worthy and eternal was made in us by God, through Jesus Christ. Our text is clear on this. We have been made righteous in Christ, but this was only because God made Him to be sin for us.

When He made us righteous in Christ, He also "made us accepted in the Beloved" (Ephesians 1:6). Furthermore, we were "made nigh by the blood of Christ" (Ephesians 2:13). The contexts of these passages make it abundantly clear that our being made righteous, accepted in Christ, and nigh to God, is all of grace; we did nothing to merit such privileges.

This is not all. At the same moment, He also has "made us meet ['fit'] to be partakers of the inheritance of the saints in light" (Colossians 1:12). That we in our poverty should be made joint-heirs with Christ, once again, is only by His unmerited grace. "Being justified by His grace, we should be made heirs according to the hope of eternal life" (Titus 3:7).

In promise now, and in full reality later, He has "made us kings and priests unto God and His Father" (Revelation 1:6). Positionally, we even share His throne, for He "hath raised us up together, and made us sit together in heavenly places in Christ Jesus" (Ephesians 2:6).

Without Him, we are nothing; but in Him we have all things. He is "made unto us wisdom, and righteousness, and sanctification, and redemption" (I Corinthians 1:30). Truly, in salvation as well as in creation, "it is He that hath made us, and not we ourselves" (Psalm 100:3).

The Winds of the World

The wind goeth toward the south, and turneth about unto the north; it whirleth about continually, and the wind returneth again according to his circuits (Ecclesiastes 1:6).

This is one of the Bible's many scientific insights, long before the process was discovered in the modern science of meteorology. The basic circulation of the atmosphere (which generates the winds of the world) is "toward the south" near the ground, which then "turneth about unto the north" aloft. The heated air near the equator expands and rises, then flows north to replace the colder, heavier air which has descended to the ground in the polar regions.

This simple north-south-north cycle is complicated, however, by the earth's rotation. Further complexities are introduced by the different topographical features of the surface (oceans, mountains, etc.), but the end result is a general circulation of the whole atmosphere, which "whirleth about continually, and . . . returneth again according to his circuits."

None of this was understood at all until very modern times, but this ancient verse in Ecclesiastes corresponds beautifully to modern science. In fact, it was not even known until recent times that air had weight, but the patriarch Job had noted about 4000 years ago that "[God] . . . seeth under the whole heaven; To make the weight for the winds" (Job 28:24, 25), and this fact is essential to the atmospheric circulation.

This is only one of many scientific principles implied in the Bible ages before men discovered them in their scientific research. In contrast, there are no demonstrable scientific errors in the Bible. This is not really surprising, for the same God who wrote the Word made the world! In Jesus Christ "are hid all the treasures of wisdom and knowledge" (Colossians 2:3).

The Rivers and the Sea

All the rivers run into the sea; yet the sea is not full; unto the place from whence the rivers come, thither they return again (Ecclesiastes 1:7).

As the ancients observed the mighty Nile and Euphrates, and other great rivers flowing into the ocean, they could not help but wonder why the sea level never rose. They knew that many of the waters in the rivers came from rainfall, especially during floods, but they had only quaint notions, at best, as to where the rains originated. Not until the days of modern science did men discover that rainfall actually comes from the oceans, via evaporation and atmospheric transportation.

But the Bible writers somehow seemed to know about the true nature of the hydrologic cycle thousands of years in advance of modern science. The rivers come from the place where they return—that is, the sea.

But how do the waters of the sea ever rise into the sky? "He maketh small the drops of water: they pour down rain according to the vapor thereof; Which the clouds do drop and distill upon man abundantly" (Job 36:27, 28). Water droplets are made very small by the process of evaporation, so they can be carried aloft by the uprushing air forces over warm waters; later they "distill upon man abundantly."

There are other references in Scripture to different phases of this great hydrologic cycle, but one of the most significant is Isaiah 55:10–11: "For as the rain cometh down, and the snow from heaven, and returneth not thither, but watereth the earth. . . . So shall My word be that goeth forth out of My mouth: it shall not return unto Me void, but it shall accomplish that which I please." The waters return to the skies only after doing their good work on the lands. Just so, the life-giving Word of God returns to Him, not void, but full of the spiritual fruit for which He sent it.

MARCH 2

Eyes and Ears

The hearing ear, and the seeing eye, the Lord *hath made even both of them* (Proverbs 20:12).

One of the most amazing testimonies to human perversity is the phenomenon of evolutionary naturalism. The very idea that such complex physiological mechanisms as eyes and ears with the intricate nervous system that conveys their messages, and the magnificently organized brain that receives and uses them, could develop by natural processes, could only arise in hearts in desperate rebellion against God.

The very laws of science as well as the instinctive testimony of human reason make such notions absurdly foolish. No evolutionist has any evidence or natural explanation as to how such devices ever arose by chance, for all living organisms are marvels of complex engineering design. It is far more likely that a skyscraper or an airplane could evolve by chance processes than could the wing of a butterfly or the petals of a rose, not to mention the human brain and its mysterious thought processes.

And if only God could design the eye, and the ear, and the brain, we can be sure He sees all we do, hears all we say, and knows all our thoughts. "Understand, ye brutish among the people: and ye fools, when will ye be wise? He that planted the ear, shall He not hear? He that formed the eye, shall He not see? He that chastiseth the heathen, shall not He correct? He that teacheth man knowledge, shall not He know?" (Psalm 94:8–10).

Belief in evolution is nothing but rebellious folly, yet evolution is taught as sober fact in schools and colleges everywhere. No one has ever seen it happen, and no one knows how it could work. It is nothing but an attempt to get away from God, for only God can make a hearing ear and a seeing eye!

The Unseen Angels

For He shall give His angels charge over thee, to keep thee in all thy ways (Psalm 91:11).

God has created "an innumerable company of angels" (Hebrews 12:22) and there are many references to them in both Old and New Testaments, but few living men or women have ever actually seen angels—or, at least, recognized them as such. We may "have entertained angels unawares" (Hebrews 13:2), for they can assume the appearance of men on occasion, but normally they are invisible to human eyes.

Nevertheless, they are *there!* Furthermore, they are "all ministering spirits, sent forth to minister for them who shall be heirs of salvation" (Hebrews 1:14). God has given them charge over us—that is, over each believer "that dwelleth in the secret place of the most High" (Psalm 91:1). They "excel in strength, that do His commandments, hearkening unto the voice of His word" (Psalm 103:20).

Wide is the variety of His commandments with respect to angelic ministry to believers. "The angel of the Lord encampeth round about them that fear Him, and delivereth them. . . . They shall bear thee up in their hands, lest thou dash thy foot against a stone" (Psalms 34:7; 91:12).

Not only physical protection but also guidance and encouragement are angelic ministries. When a believer dies, angels translate his spirit to the Lord's presence (Luke 16:22; II Corinthians 5:8), and we can look forward then to meeting and thanking them personally as we come to understand better all their ministries on our behalf during our lifetime. They are keenly concerned with our salvation and spiritual progress, "which things the angels desire to look into" (I Peter 1:12). Finally, "when the Son of man shall come in His glory," He will bring "all the holy angels with Him" (Matthew 25:31) as He judges the world.

MARCH 4

The Opened Heavens

And I saw heaven opened, and behold a white horse; and He that sat upon him was called Faithful and True, and in righteousness He doth judge and make war (Revelation 19:11).

This is the final climactic reference in the Bible to God's opened heavens. Sometimes, as in this verse, heaven is opened in judgment; sometimes in blessing. Sometimes it is the atmospheric heaven that is open; sometimes the heaven of heavens where stands the throne of God.

The first such mention refers to the world-destroying Flood of Noah's day when "the windows of heaven were opened" (Genesis 7:11). The second mention, however, speaks of blessing. God had "opened the doors of heaven, and had rained down manna upon them to eat" (Psalm 78:23, 24). The windows of heaven rained down the waters of *death,* while the doors of heaven rained down the bread of *life!*

Ezekiel also saw the heavens opened in judgment (Ezekiel 1:1), but God told Malachi, "Bring ye all the tithes into the storehouse . . . and prove me now . . . if I will not open you the windows of heaven, and pour you out a blessing, that there shall not be room enough to receive it" (Malachi 3:10).

At the baptism of Jesus the heavens were opened and men heard the great testimony of the Father concerning His beloved Son (Matthew 3:16; Mark 1:10; Luke 3:21). Jesus promised Nathanael: "Hereafter ye shall see heaven open" (John 1:51), and Stephen and Peter actually saw the heavens open (Acts 7:56; 10:11).

Finally, the Apostle John reported that "a door was opened in heaven" (Revelation 4:1), and he saw the Lord on His throne. Thus there are twelve specific references (four in the Old testament, eight in the New) to heaven's opened windows.

Things Not Seen

By faith Noah, being warned of God of things not seen as yet, moved with fear, prepared an ark to the saving of his house: by the which he condemned the world, and became heir of the righteousness which is by faith (Hebrews 11:7).

The little phrase "things not seen" is used three times in the New Testament, and interestingly enough, these refer to the past, present, and future works of God with respect to the things that *are* seen.

At the beginning of the "faith chapter" of Hebrews occur these remarkable words. "Now faith is . . . the evidence of things not seen. . . . Through faith we understand that the worlds were framed by the word of God, so that things which are seen were not made of things which do appear" (Hebrews 11:1, 3). That is, the material things of this present world were not made of pre-existing materials; they were supernaturally *created* by the word of the Creator! These things which are now seen provide evidence (or better, the "conviction") of the things not seen—that is, of God's creative work completed in the past.

The "processes" that are now seen (as distinct from the "materials") date especially from the time of the great Flood. The "things not seen as yet" by Noah—that is, the present atmospheric circulation, the present hydrological cycle, the present seasonal changes, and many other key phenomena of the present order, all were instituted in the days of Noah when "the world that then was, being overflowed with water, perished" (II Peter 3:6).

Finally, "we look not at the things which are seen, but at the things which are not seen: For . . . the things which are not seen are eternal" (II Corinthians 4:18). Just as surely as the materials and processes of the present world once were unseen, but now are easily seen, so the future eternal world will soon be clearly seen when Christ returns.

MARCH 6

King of Peace

And Melchizedek king of Salem brought forth bread and wine: and he was the priest of the most high God (Genesis 14:18).

The mysterious king Melchizedek was at least a type—if not an actual pre-incarnate appearance—of Christ. As such, it is appropriate that he is called the "King of Salem," or "King of peace," and that this is the first mention of the word "peace" (Hebrew, *Shalem,* or *Shalom*) in the Bible. He is also called "King of righteousness" (Hebrews 7:2), because his name is a combination of two Hebrew words carrying this meaning.

Thus, Melchizedek—that is, in principle, Jesus Christ—is king of both peace and righteousness, for neither can really exist without the other. True peace can be founded only on true righteousness, for "there is no peace, saith the LORD, unto the wicked" (Isaiah 48:22). Similarly, God had promised: "O that thou hadst hearkened to my commandments! then had thy peace been as a river, and thy righteousness as the waves of the sea" (Isaiah 48:18).

Peace and righteousness go together. No armistice or peace treaty will ever be permanent (always there is a new "Pearl Harbor Day" ahead) unless founded on righteousness, and this will never be until Christ returns, for He is both the "Prince of Peace" and "the righteousness of God" (Isaiah 9:6; II Corinthians 5:21). The nations of the world have been at war with God—and therefore with each other—ever since sin entered the world. When He does return, there will finally be permanent peace and eternal righteousness. "In His days Judah shall be saved, and Israel shall dwell safely: and this is His name whereby He shall be called, THE LORD OUR RIGHTEOUSNESS" (Jeremiah 23:6).

We may well honor those who have fought and died for peace, but real and permanent peace can only be attained through the King of Peace.

Judging Error

Now I beseech you, brethren, mark them which cause divisions and offenses contrary to the doctrine which ye have learned; and avoid them. For they that are such serve not our Lord Jesus Christ, but their own belly; and by good words and fair speeches deceive the hearts of the simple (Romans 16:17, 18).

In order to *mark* and *avoid* those professing Christian teachers and leaders who are promoting doctrinal heresy, thus causing divisions among Christian believers, it is obvious that we must exercise sound Biblical discernment and judgment. This judgment must be based on "the doctrine which ye have learned" from God's Word. "To the law and to the testimony: if they speak not according to this Word, it is because there is no light in them" (Isaiah 8:20).

Such decisions are not to be based on supposed scholarship or tolerance or eloquence, for such teachers "by good words and fair speeches deceive the hearts of the simple." Instead, we must know and apply God's Word, the Holy Scriptures. We must be like the Bereans, who, when they heard new teachings, "searched the Scriptures daily, whether those things were so" (Acts 17:11).

It is sadly true today that many who call themselves Christians have compromised with the pseudo-scientific world view of evolutionary humanism that controls all secular schools and colleges, hoping thereby to avoid the "offense of the cross" (Galatians 5:11), and to remain on good terms with "the princes of this world" and "the wisdom of this world" (I Corinthians 2:6).

They do this for their own personal gain or prestige, however, not serving Christ, "but their own belly" (Romans 16:18). Those who are "simple" Bible-believing Christians are, therefore, not to be "deceived" by their "good words," but to "mark" and "avoid" them.

MARCH 8

The Complex Cosmos

He hath made the earth by his power, He hath established the world by His wisdom, and hath stretched out the heavens by His discretion (Jeremiah 10:12).

This verse gives a fascinating insight into God's primeval creation of the universe, especially on the first four days of His week of creative work. The "earth" refers to the geosphere, or the inorganic components of the globe, the "world" to its biosphere, especially the plant life, and the "heavens" to the atmosphere and astrosphere.

God's "power" refers to the tremendous energy or force required to organize the complex systems and physico-chemical processes which govern the earth. The "wisdom" of God speaks of the skillful planning by which He set up the plant biosphere and the hydrologic systems to maintain it. His "discretion" is the infinite intelligence necessary to spread out the infinite cosmos filled with innumerable stars and clusters of stars, all individually distinct from all others.

The infinite, complex, highly energized universe could never in all eternity have evolved itself out of primeval chaotic nothingness, as evolutionists delude themselves into believing. The universal law of entropy now operates in such a way as to dissipate its energy and disintegrate its complexity, as it heads downward towards chaos and death. It is absurd to think that the cosmos could have "organized" itself by the same processes which are now "disorganizing" it.

The two preceding verses say it well. "But the Lord is the true God, He is the living God, and an everlasting king: . . . The gods that have not made the heavens and the earth, even they shall perish from the earth, and from under these heavens" (Jeremiah 10:10, 11). We do well, therefore, to trust Him in all things. "I am the LORD," says He, "the God of all flesh: is there anything too hard for me?" (Jeremiah 32:27).

The Wisdom of This World

Where is the wise? where is the scribe? where is the disputer of this world? hath not God made foolish the wisdom of this world? (I Corinthians 1:20).

The scholars and scientists and intellectuals of this world may be held in great esteem by men, but to God, their humanistic reasonings are foolishness. In fact, the evolutionary philosophy which dominates the "wisdom of this world" has led to our modern amoral culture, to racism, to imperialism, to communism, Nazism, to New Age pantheism, humanism, atheism, abortionism, and to all manner of evil and foolish beliefs and practices.

Yet many modern evangelicals feel they must accommodate the wisdom of this world in their own schools and churches, forgetting that "the world by wisdom knew not God" (I Corinthians 1:21). God has warned us not to follow "the wisdom of this world, nor of the princes of this world, that come to nought" (I Corinthians 2:6). Why should we waste precious time in teaching our students or our congregations the wisdom of this world that not only is false and harmful, but is soon coming to nought? The only valid reason at all for doing so is to teach them what's wrong with it, so that they can "be ready always to give an answer to every man that asketh" (I Peter 3:15).

Above all, they must not accommodate the wisdom of this world in their own world view. God has gravely warned against the evolutionary philosophy of the world (II Peter 3:3–6) in these sobering words: "Seeing ye know these things before, beware lest ye also, being led away with the error of the wicked, fall from your own steadfastness" (II Peter 3:17).

Therefore, "if any man among you seemeth to be wise in this world, let him become a fool, that he may be wise. For the wisdom of this world is foolishness with God" (I Corinthians 3:18, 19).

MARCH 10

The Unequal Yoke

Be ye not unequally yoked together with unbelievers: for what fellowship hath righteousness with unrighteousness? And what communion hath light with darkness? (II Corinthians 6:14).

This is one of the definitive statements in Scripture on the doctrine of Christian separation. Not only should believers refrain from practicing evil teaching and error; they should not join in any formal association with those who do such things, nor should they enter into a binding relationship of any kind with non-Christians.

There may be a question regarding the full scope of this prohibition, though it probably would not apply to civic clubs, professional societies and such like, with no religious connotations. The context of this verse implies an association of Christians with pagan idolaters, compromising God's Word with the immoral pantheism of the Greek religions.

The "unequal yoke" seems, therefore, to be one involving an actual "fellowship" and "communion" in some kind of religious or quasi-spiritual union with unbelievers, and this is forbidden, for how "can two walk together except they be agreed?" (Amos 3:3). In the modern scene, ancient Greek pantheism has now become one form or another of evolutionary humanism. Thus the prohibition would at least apply to membership in secret lodges or fraternities with a pseudo-religious structure and purpose, as well as membership in liberal churches or cults in the so-called New-Age orbit. It clearly must also include marriage or partnership or other formal unions with individuals who, as unbelievers in Christ, are either knowingly or unknowingly affected by such pagan beliefs or practices. Instead of such an unequal yoke, we should be joined only to Christ and His followers, for, said He: "My yoke is easy, and My burden is light" (Matthew 11:30).

Moses or Miracle

And he said unto him, If they hear not Moses and the prophets, neither will they be persuaded, though one rose from the dead (Luke 16:31).

This is the testimony of Abraham, in Christ's parable of the rich man in Hades, concerning the type of evidence needed to induce repentance in the hearts of those still on earth. There are many today who would seek a sign before they believe God's Word. Even then, however, said Jesus, they won't believe if they are unwilling to believe the Scriptures, especially the writings of Moses. "For had ye believed Moses, ye would have believed Me: for he wrote of Me. But if ye believe not his writings, how shall ye believe My words?" (John 5:46, 47). Those who refuse to believe the historicity of the words of Genesis can hardly believe in Christ.

Certain well-meaning Christian apologists today argue that the Genesis record of early history is too controversial, so we should emphasize Christ's miracles instead, especially His resurrection, to lead men to Christ. These are indeed powerful evidences, for one can argue effectively that Christ's bodily resurrection is the best-proved fact of history.

Nevertheless, Christ asserted—and experience confirms—that those who reject the Mosaic account of creation and the other foundational events of history will not believe in the resurrection either, regardless of the evidence. The early apostles indeed preached the resurrection to those who already believed in creation and the Scriptures (e.g., Acts 17:2, 3) but they preached first the creation, *then* the resurrection to those who did not (e.g., Acts 17:18–31).

Therefore, according to Christ Himself, people will not truly repent unto salvation, even when faced with overwhelming evidence of His resurrection, unless they are first willing to believe the holy Scriptures, especially the records of Moses in the first book of the Bible.

MARCH 12

That Old Serpent

And he laid hold on the dragon, that old serpent, which is the Devil, and Satan, and bound him a thousand years (Revelation 20:2).

This prophetic vision given to John leaves no doubt as to the identity of the serpent in the Garden of Eden. That "old serpent" (literally, "that primeval serpent") who deceived our first parents into rebelling against the word of God, is none other than the Devil, or Satan, often viewed in Scripture as typified by a "great dragon" (Revelation 12:9), the fearsome animal of ancient times, probably the dinosaur.

His ultimate doom is sure—he will be bound a thousand years, then finally "cast into the lake of fire . . . tormented day and night for ever and ever" (Revelation 20:10). At present, however, he is not bound, for "your adversary the devil, as a roaring lion, walketh about, seeking whom he may devour" (I Peter 5:8). We must be sober and vigilant, "lest Satan should get an advantage of us: for we are not ignorant of his devices" (II Corinthians 2:11).

His devices are manifold, but all are deceptive (he was the most "subtle" of all God's creatures, Genesis 3:1), malevolent, and designed to turn us away from the true Christ. "But I fear, lest by any means, as the serpent beguiled Eve through his subtlety, so your minds should be corrupted from the simplicity that is in Christ" (II Corinthians 11:3).

He is the great deceiver. He can appear as a fire-breathing dragon or a roaring lion, deceiving us into fearing and obeying him instead of God. He can also be "transformed into an angel of light" (II Corinthians 11:14), deceiving us into trusting the feigned words of his false teachers (II Peter 2:1–3) instead of the Holy Scriptures of the God of creation. Our recourse against his deceptions is to "put on the whole armor of God, that ye may be able to stand against the wiles of the devil" (Ephesians 6:11).

Made in Christ

But of Him are ye in Christ Jesus, Who of God is made unto us wisdom, and righteousness, and sanctification, and redemption (I Corinthians 1:30).

The Greek word *ginomai,* translated "is made" in this verse, is most fascinating. It is rendered many different ways—"become," etc., as well as "be made." Most often it is simply translated "be." It basically means "begin to be," or "be caused to be." It is even applied to the work of Christ in calling the universe into being. "All things were made by Him; and without Him was not any thing made that was made" (John 1:3). "Things which are seen were not made of things which do appear" (Hebrews 11:3).

It is frequently used also to denote the marvelous work of Christ in and on the believing Christian. As our text says, He becomes wisdom to us who lack wisdom; He is made our righteousness, although we were sinners; we who are unholy receive our sanctification in Him; and when we were lost, He became our redemption. "But as many as received Him, to them gave He power to become [same word, *ginomai*] the sons of God" (John 1:12). All that Christ is, we are made, through His great sacrifice for us.

Note some of the other things we are made, in Christ, by His grace. We are "made nigh by the blood of Christ" (Ephesians 2:13). We are "made heirs according to the hope of eternal life" (Titus 3:7). "We are made partakers of Christ" and also "made partakers of the Holy Ghost" (Hebrews 3:14; 6:4).

In fact, when we receive Christ, old things pass away and "all things *are become* [same word] new" (II Corinthians 5:17). These wonderful attributes are given to us and appropriated right now by faith, and will be accomplished in full perfection when Christ returns and "we shall see Him as He is" (I John 3:2).

MARCH 14

Savor of Life or Death

For we are unto God a sweet savor of Christ, in them that are saved, and in them that perish: To the one we are the savor of death unto death; and to the other the savor of life unto life. And who is sufficient for these things (II Corinthians 2:15, 16).

It is remarkable how the very same testimony can have such dramatically opposite effects on its recipients. A lecture on the scientific evidences of creation, for example, or on the inspiration of the Bible, will be received with great joy and understanding by some, provoke furious hostility in some, and generate utter indifference in others. This seems to be true of any message—written or verbal, or simply demonstrated in behavior—which has any kind of Biblically spiritual dimension to it. It is like the pillar of cloud in the wilderness, which "came between the camp of the Egyptians and the camp of Israel; and it was a cloud and darkness to them, but it gave light by night to these: so that the one came not near the other all the night" (Exodus 14:20). A Christian testimony draws and wins the one, repels and condemns the other. Some there are who "loved darkness rather than light, because their deeds were evil" (John 3:19).

Thus the wonderful message of the Gospel yields two diametrically opposite results. "He that believeth on the Son hath everlasting life: and he that believeth not the Son shall not see life; but the wrath of God abideth on him" (John 3:36). Christ came to bring both unity and division. "Behold I lay in Sion a chief corner stone, elect, precious. . . . Unto you therefore which believe He is precious: but unto them which be disobedient. . . . a stone of stumbling, and a rock of offense, even to them which stumble at the word" (I Peter 2:6–8).

But the wonderful thing is this: whether a true testimony generates life or condemns to death, it is still "unto God a sweet savor of Christ."

The Sin of the Devil

Now I know that the Lord is greater than all gods; for in the thing wherein they dealt proudly He was above them (Exodus 18:11).

This is the first mention in the Bible of the sin of pride, and it appropriately refers to the primeval sin of the "gods"—that is, the supposed deities of the heathen.

Led by Lucifer, a great host of the created angels had rebelled against their Creator, seeking also to be "gods" like Him. Lucifer, later to be called Satan (i.e., "Adversary") thought he could become the highest of all. "O Lucifer . . . thou hast said in thine heart, I will . . . exalt my throne above the stars of God . . . I will be like the most High. Yet thou shalt be brought down to hell . . . " (Isaiah 14:12–15).

Satan's sin—and that of the other self-proclaimed "gods"—was that of "being lifted up with pride . . . the condemnation of the devil" (I Timothy 3:6). But they shall all, with him, eventually "be brought down to hell," and the "everlasting fire, prepared for the devil and his angels" (Matthew 25:41).

This was also the sin of Adam and Eve, for Satan had seduced them with the promise, "ye shall be as gods" (Genesis 3:5).

It is also the sin of all humanists and evolutionary pantheists, from Adam's day to our day, for they seek to do away with God and make "gods" out of "corruptible man . . . worshiping the creation more than the Creator" (Romans 1:23, 25).

But "pride goeth before destruction, and an haughty spirit before a fall" (Proverbs 16:18). Our Lord of creation is "above all gods," even in that "thing wherein they dealt proudly." The sin of pride was the very first sin and is still the most difficult sin to overcome, but "God resisteth the proud, and giveth grace to the humble" (I Peter 5:5).

The Meaning of "Day"

And God called the light Day, and the darkness He called Night. And the evening and the morning were the first day (Genesis 1:5).

Many people today, professing to believe the Bible, have compromised with the evolutionary philosophy which dominates our society by accepting its framework of geological ages. This system interprets the rocks and fossils in terms of a supposed 4.6-billion-year history of the earth and life, culminating in the evolution of early humans about a million years ago. In order to justify this compromise, they usually say that the "days" of creation really correspond to the geological ages, arguing that the Hebrew word for "day" (*yom*) does not have to mean a literal solar day.

Oh, yes it does—at least in Genesis Chapter One! God, knowing that the pagan philosophers of antiquity would soon try to distort His record of creation into long ages of pantheistic evolution (as in the Babylonian, Egyptian, Greek and other such ancient cosmogonies), was careful to define His terms! "*God called the light Day,*" and that was the first Day, with its evening and morning. All subsequent days have followed the same pattern—a period of darkness (night), then a period of light (day).

One may quibble about the exact length if he insists (e.g., equatorial days versus polar days), but there is no way this definition can accommodate a geological age. This is the very first reference to "day" (or *yom*) in the Bible, and this is given as an actual statement of the meaning of the word.

This ought to settle the question for anyone who really believes the Bible. One may decide to believe the evolutionary geologists if he wishes, instead of God, but he should at least let God speak for Himself. *God* says the days of creation were literal days, not ages. "In six days the Lord made heaven and earth" (Exodus 31:17).

Be Fruitful and Multiply

And God blessed them, and God said unto them, Be fruitful, and multiply, and replenish the earth, and subdue it: and have dominion over the fish of the sea, and over the fowl of the air, and over every living thing that moveth upon the earth (Genesis 1:28).

This "dominion mandate," as it has been called, was the very first command of God to the first man and woman. It applies to the whole earth, all its processes and all its creatures. To subdue the earth and control it implies the development of science and technology, commerce and education—indeed every honorable human vocation. As God's first "great commission," it applies to all people, and has never been withdrawn. God even expanded it to Noah after the Flood (Genesis 9:1–7), twice repeating the command to "be fruitful and multiply."

In order to really subdue and exercise dominion over the earth, a large population would be necessary. Despite all the concern in modern times about population growth, God's command has never yet been fully accomplished. Vast areas of the earth are still barren and undeveloped.

Furthermore, the great majority of humans are oblivious of the dominion mandate and live their lives utterly without concern for the will and purpose of their Creator. Therefore, He has given another Great Commission to those who *do* love God, trusting Him as both Creator and Savior, and this also involves the whole world. Jesus said to His disciples: "I have chosen you, and ordained you, that ye should go and bring forth fruit, and that your fruit should remain" (John 15:16). That is, we who are His disciples are also to be fruitful and multiply spiritually, as well as physically. Then, in the age to come, the first great Mandate will also finally be fulfilled, "and the earth shall be full of the knowledge of the LORD, as the waters cover the sea" (Isaiah 11:9).

MARCH 18

As in the Days of Noah

And as it was in the days of Noah, so shall it be also in the days of the Son of man. They did eat, they drank, they married wives, they were given in marriage, until the day that Noah entered into the ark, and the flood came, and destroyed them all (Luke 17:26, 27).

This is an important passage, a prophecy from Christ Himself. It makes it certain that Jesus, the Son of God, believed that Noah was a real man, that he really did build an ark, and that the great Flood (Greek *kataklusmos*) was a devastating worldwide cataclysm that "destroyed them all"). The description of the Genesis Flood (Genesis 6–9) is so clear and graphic that the Lord must be impatient with those modern compromising evangelicals who try to accommodate evolutionism with their "local flood" or "tranquil flood" theories. The global nature of the Flood, in fact, is analogous to the global impact of Christ's return.

Furthermore, said Christ, world conditions at the time of His coming would be similar to those in Noah's day. This means that the earth would be "filled with violence" in that day (Genesis 6:11). One thinks of World Wars I and II, regional wars and revolutions in every part of the world, millions of unborn babies murdered, crime-filled streets, bursting prisons, genocides in many nations, as well as unspeakable violence portrayed daily on movie and television screens everywhere.

It also means that human wickedness would be "great in the earth" (Genesis 6:5). Think of the overt and almost universal promiscuity, aggressive homosexuality, serial marriages, the drug plague, child abuse, atheism and pantheism abounding and, especially, utter indifference to God and His Word. No age since Noah has been more like his age than our age. "Even thus shall it be in the day when the Son of man is revealed" (Luke 17:30).

The Stars Forever

And they that be wise shall shine as the brightness of the firmament; and they that turn many to righteousness as the stars for ever and ever (Daniel 12:3).

The setting of this beautiful verse is after the resurrection of the saved to everlasting life and the unsaved to eternal shame (v. 2). Its glorious promise to those who are "wise" and who "turn many to righteousness" through Jesus Christ is that of "shining" forever, like the stars.

Evolutionary astronomers believe that stars evolve through a long cycle of stellar life and death, but this idea contradicts God's revelation that He has created this physical universe to last forever. Speaking of these stellar heavens, the majestic 148th Psalm, centered on God's creation, says that God "hath also stablished them for ever and ever: He hath made a decree which shall not pass" (Psalm 148:6).

It is true that, because of sin, "the whole creation groaneth . . . until now" (Romans 8:22), and the heavens "shall wax old as doth a garment: . . . and they shall be changed" (Hebrews 1:11, 12). In fact, the earth and its atmospheric heaven (not the sidereal heaven) one day will "pass away" (Matthew 24:35), and then will be transformed by God into "new heavens and a new earth" (II Peter 3:13) which will never pass away.

But the infinite cosmos of space and time, created in the beginning by God, was created to last forever, and God cannot fail in his purposes. "I know that, whatsoever God doeth, it shall be forever: nothing can be put to it, nor any thing taken from it: and God doeth it, that men should fear before Him" (Ecclesiastes 3:14).

The stars are innumerable, each one unique, each one with a divine purpose, and they will shine forever. We can never reach them in this life, but in our glorified bodies, we shall have endless time to explore the infinite heavens.

MARCH 20

God Spared Not

For if God spared not the natural branches, take heed lest He also spare not thee (Romans 11:21).

God is patient and long-suffering, but unrepentant sin inevitably brings unsparing judgment. First of all, "God spared not the angels that sinned, but cast them down to hell, and delivered them into chains of darkness, to be reserved unto judgment" (II Peter 2:4). These fallen angels not only followed Lucifer in his primeval rebellion but also possessed the very bodies of the ungodly in Noah's day.

When worldwide evil and violence in the world followed the sin of the angels, "God spared not the old world, . . . bringing in the flood upon the world of the ungodly" (II Peter 2:5). Then, from the remnant that survived the flood, He eventually chose Israel to be His peculiar people.

But when Israel finally rebelled and long persisted in their sin, as our text says, "God spared not the natural branches" and grafted in the believing Gentiles. To a considerable degree, we here in America have inherited God's special blessing, but now His Word is warning us, too: "Take heed lest He also spare not thee." We have departed far from the faith of our fathers and, like Noah's world, our world is rapidly filling with violence and is fast heading for judgment.

God spared not the fallen angels, He spared not the wicked antediluvians, then He spared not the chosen people Israel, and soon, when his patience ends, He will spare not the whole Gentile world.

But for those who repent and desire His forgiveness and salvation, God "spared not His own Son, but delivered Him up for us all" (Romans 8:32). In order to spare us, Christ died for us, now lives for us, and soon will come for us! "What shall we then say to these things?" . . . He that spared not His own Son, . . . how shall He not with Him also freely give us all things?" (Romans 8:31, 32).

Dividing Light from Darkness

And God said, Let there be light: and there was light. And God saw the light, that it was good: and God divided the light from the darkness (Genesis 1:3, 4).

Initially, the created cosmos was in darkness—a darkness which God Himself had to create ("I form the light, and create darkness," Isaiah 45:7). But then the dark cosmos was energized by the Spirit's moving, and God's light appeared. The darkness was not dispelled, however, but only *divided* from the light, and the day/night sequence began which has continued ever since.

This sequence of events in the physical creation is a beautiful type of the spiritual creation, "a new creature" (II Corinthians 5:17). Like the cosmos, each individual is born in spiritual darkness, but "God, who commanded the light to shine out of darkness, hath shined in our hearts, to give the light of the knowledge of the glory of God in the face of Jesus Christ" (II Corinthians 4:6). We are now "partakers of the inheritance of the saints in light," because He "hath delivered us from the power of darkness" (Colossians 1:12, 13).

However, the light in the primeval darkness resulted only in a division of night and day. The night still comes, but God has promised that, in the coming Holy City, "there shall be no night there" (Revelation 22:5).

Just so, even though we have been given a new nature of light, the old nature of darkness is still striving within, and we have to be exhorted: "For ye were sometimes darkness, but now are ye light in the Lord: walk as children of light" (Ephesians 5:8). Nevertheless, "the path of the just is as the shining light, that shineth more and more unto the perfect day" (Proverbs 4:18). When we reach that city of everlasting light, all spiritual darkness will vanish as well, for "there shall in no wise enter into it any thing that defileth" (Revelation 21:27), and we shall be like Christ.

MARCH 22

The Two Greatest Weeks

Rejoice greatly, O daughter of Zion; shout, O daughter of Jerusalem: behold, thy King cometh unto thee: He is just, and having salvation; lowly, and riding upon an ass; and upon a colt the foal of an ass (Zechariah 9:9).

The two greatest events in all history are the creation and the redemption of the world. Each of these events involved a great divine Week of work and a Day of rest. Day by day throughout the coming week, culminating on Easter Sunday, we will, in these pages, briefly compare the events of the seven days of Creation Week and Redemption Week.

The First Day of Creation Week involved the very creation of the universe itself (Genesis 1:1). An entire cosmos responded to the creative fiat of the Maker of heaven and earth. Initially, this space-mass-time (i.e., heaven, earth, beginning) continuum was created in the form of basic elements only, with no structure and no occupant (v. 2)—a static suspension in a pervasive, watery matrix (II Peter 3:5). When God's Spirit began to move, however, the gravitational and electromagnetic force systems for the cosmos were energized. The waters and their suspensions coalesced into a great spherical planet, and at His Word, visible light was generated (v. 3).

In a beautiful analogy, on the first day of Redemption Week, the Creator King of the universe entered His chosen capital city (Matthew 21:1–9) to begin His work of redemption, as He had entered His universe to begin His work of creation. All the basic components of creation were there to acknowledge their Creator. The stones would have cried out to Him (Luke 19:39, 40), the branches of the palm trees provided a carpet for Him (John 12:13; Mark 11:8), the ass's colt became His chariot (see our text, Zechariah 9:9), and the common people sang His praises (Matthew 21:9). "Behold, thy King cometh unto thee!"

Preparation of the Father's House

And He taught, saying unto them, Is it not written, My house shall be called of all nations the house of prayer? but ye have made it a den of thieves (Mark 11:17).

As we continue to compare the corresponding days of Creation Week and Redemption Week, we must note that the chronology of the latter has been the subject of much disagreement among authorities. Details are uncertain, but we can at least consider this possible additional dimension to the understanding and harmony of the two weeks.

Having created and activated the earth on the First Day, God next provided for it a marvelous atmosphere and hydrosphere in which, later, would live the birds and fishes. No other planet is equipped with air and water in such abundance; the earth was uniquely planned for life! The hydrosphere, on the Second Day, was further divided into waters below and waters above "the firmament," equipped to maintain a perfect climate worldwide.

Paralleling the primeval provision of life-sustaining air and water, on Day Two of Redemption Week, the Lord entered again into the city and into the temple, which He had called His Father's house (John 2:16). As He approached the city, He cursed the barren fig tree (Mark 11:12–14) and then, in the temple, overthrew the tables of the money-changers (Mark 11:15). Both actions—the cursing of the fig tree and the cleansing of the temple—symbolize the purging of that which is barren or corrupt in the Creator's kingdom. He had created a world prepared for life, but mankind had made it unfruitful and impure. As physical life must first have a world of pure air and water, so the preparations for a world of true spiritual life require the purifying breath of the Spirit and the cleansing water of the Word, preparing for the true fruit of the Spirit and the true temple of God's presence, in the age to come.

MARCH 24

The Sea and the Mountains

Whosoever shall say unto this mountain, Be thou removed, and be thou cast into the sea; and shall not doubt in his heart, but shall believe that those things which he saith shall come to pass; he shall have whatsoever he saith (Mark 11:23).

On the Third Day of Redemption Week, the sight of the withered fig tree led to an instructive lesson on faith in God, the Lord Jesus assuring the disciples that real faith could even move mountains into the sea. In parallel, on the Third Day of Creation Week, He had literally called the mountains up out of the sea (Genesis 1:9, 10)!

It was also on this day that the Lord rebuked the Jewish leaders with two parables about a vineyard (Matthew 21:28–43). They had been placed in charge of God's vineyard on the earth, and had failed. Like the fig tree, there was no fruit for God from their service, and they must be removed.

Likewise, on Day Three of Creation, the entire earth had supported an abundance of fruit to nourish every living creature (Genesis 1:11, 12). It had been placed in man's care (1:28–30; 2:15), but he had failed. Before the earth can become a beautiful garden again (Revelation 22:2), it must be purged, and the faithless keepers of the vineyard banished.

This Third Day of Passion Week was climaxed with His great discourse on the Mount of Olives, in which the Lord promised He would come again some day in power and great glory (Matthew 24). He then spent the night with His disciples there on the mountain, no doubt remembering the first mountains. Also, the little Garden of Gethsemane—on its slopes—would bring to mind the beautiful Garden of Eden and the verdant world He had planted everywhere that same day. Now, because of what He was about to do in Jerusalem, the ground would some day be cleansed of its Curse and the world made new again.

The Lights of the World

And God made two great lights; the greater light to rule the day, and the lesser light to rule the night: He made the stars also (Genesis 1:16).

On the Fourth Day of Creation Week, the Lord Jesus had formed the sun and the moon and all the stars of heaven. There had been "light" on the first three days, but now there were actual lights! Not only would the earth and its verdure be a source of beauty and sustenance to man, but even the very heavens would bring joy and inspiration to him. Furthermore, they would guide his way, and keep his time.

But instead of the stars of heaven turning man's thoughts and affections toward his Creator, they had been corrupted and identified with a host of false gods and goddesses. Furthermore, instead of creating a sense of awe and reverence for His majesty, they had bolstered the humanistic belief that the earth is insignificant and meaningless in a vast, evolving cosmos. Perhaps thoughts such as these troubled the mind of the Lord that night as He lay on the mountain gazing at the lights He had long ago made for the darkness.

When morning came and Day Four of Redemption Week began, He returned to Jerusalem, where many were waiting to hear Him. He taught in the temple (Luke 21:37, 38), but the synoptic gospels do not record His teachings. This lack is probably supplied in the apparently parenthetical record of His temple teaching as given only in John's Gospel (12:20–50), because there He twice compared Himself to the lights He had made. "I am come a light into the world, that whosoever believeth on me should not abide in darkness." "Yet a little while is the light with you. Walk while ye have the light, lest darkness come upon you" (John 12:46, 35). He who was the True Light must become darkness, in order that, in the new world, there would never be night again (Revelation 22:5).

MARCH 26

The Lamb of God

Purge out therefore the old leaven, that ye may be a new lump, as ye are unleavened. For even Christ our passover is sacrificed for us (I Corinthians 5:7).

The Fifth Day of Redemption Week was the annual day for the Passover Supper. We know nothing of His words during that day, but perhaps this Scriptural silence is for the purpose of emphasizing the greater importance of these preparations for the Passover.

Multitudes of sacrificial lambs and other animals had been slain and their blood spilled through the centuries, but this would be the last such acceptable sacrifice. On the morrow, the Lamb of God would take away the sin of the world (John 1:29). He would offer one sacrifice for sins forever (Hebrews 10:12). With the blood of His cross, He would become the great Peace Maker, reconciling all things unto the Maker of those things (Colossians 1:16, 20).

As the Lord thought about the shedding of the blood of that last Passover Lamb on that Fifth Day of Holy Week, He must also have thought of the Fifth Day of Creation Week, when He had first created animal life (Genesis 1:21). This had been His second great act of creation—this creation of the entity of conscious animal life (the first act of *ex nihilo* creation had been the creation in Genesis 1:1 of the physical elements). In these living animals, the "life" of the flesh was in their blood, and it was the blood which would later be accepted as an atonement for sin (Leviticus 17:11). Note that the words "creature," "soul," and "life" are all translations of the same Hebrew word *nephesh*. Surely the shedding of the innocent blood of the lamb that day would recall the far-off day when the "life" in that blood had first been created. And because He, the Lamb of God, was about to become our Passover (note our text for the day), death itself would soon be swallowed up in victory and life (I Corinthians 15:54).

The Groaning Creation

For we know that the whole creation groaneth and travaileth in pain together until now (Romans 8:22).

On the Sixth Day, man had been created in God's image and likeness—the very climax and goal of creation (Genesis 1:26, 27). But on this Sixth Day, God, made in the likeness of man, finished the even greater work of redemption.

Under the great Curse, the whole creation had long been groaning and travailing in pain. But now, the Creator, Himself, had been made the Curse (Galatians 3:13; Isaiah 52:14), and it seemed as though the Creation also must die. Though He had made heaven and earth on the First Day, now He had been lifted up from the earth (John 3:14) and the heavens were silent (Matthew 27:46). Though He had made the waters on the Second Day, He who was the very Water of Life (John 4:14), was dying of thirst (John 19:28).

On the Third Day, He had made the dry land, but now the "earth did quake, and the rocks rent" (Matthew 27:51). He had also covered the earth with trees and vines on that Third Day, but now the True Vine (John 15:1) had been plucked up and the Green Tree (Luke 23:31) cut down. He had made the sun on the Fourth Day, but now the sun was darkened (Luke 23:45) and the Light of the World (John 8:12) was burning out. On the Fifth Day, He had created life, and He, Himself, was life (John 11:25; 14:6), but now the life of His flesh, the precious blood, was being poured out, and He had been brought "into the dust of death" (Psalm 22:15). On the Sixth Day, He had created man and given him life, but now man had rejected Him and was putting Him to death.

The creation has been groaning and travailing in pain ever since Adam's sin, but its Creator has paid the price for its redemption, and therefore, it will someday "be delivered from the bondage of corruption into the glorious liberty of the children of God" (Romans 8:21).

It Is Finished!

When Jesus therefore had received the vinegar, He said, It is finished: and He bowed His head, and gave up the ghost (John 19:30).

"On the seventh day God ended His work which He had made" (Genesis 2:2). Furthermore, "every thing that He had made . . . was very good" (Genesis 1:31).

And so is His work of salvation! "Jesus knowing that all things were now accomplished, that the Scripture might be fulfilled . . . said, It is finished" (John 19:28, 30). The emphasized words ("accomplished," "fulfilled," "finished") are all the same in the Greek original.

When all the relevant Scriptures had been fulfilled and the price of reconciliation ("the blood of His cross," Colossians 1:20) fully paid, He could finally shout the great victory cry (Matthew 27:50), "It is finished!" As the finished creation was "very good," so is our finished salvation. The salvation which Christ our Creator thus provided on the cross is "so great" (Hebrews 2:3) and "eternal" (Hebrews 5:9), that the hope thereof is "good" (II Thessalonians 2:16).

Then, finally, having finished the work of redemption, Christ rested once again, on the Seventh Day. As He had rested on that first Seventh Day, now He could rest again, His body sleeping in Joseph's tomb.

He had died quickly, and the preparations for burial had been hurried (Luke 23:54–56), so that He could be buried before the Sabbath. On the third day (that is, the first day of the new week), He would rise again, as He had said (Matthew 16:21, et al.). His body rested in the tomb all the Sabbath Day, plus part of the previous and following days, according to Hebrew idiomatic usage, "three days and three nights" (Matthew 12:40)—but death could hold Him no longer. He arose from the dead, and is now "alive forevermore" (Revelation 1:18).

Resurrection and Creation

And He is before all things, and by Him all things consist. And He is the head of the body, the church: who is the beginning, the firstborn from the dead; that in all things He might have the preeminence (Colossians 1:17, 18).

The two greatest miracles in all history were the Creation of the World and the Resurrection of its Creator. In the devotional studies for the past week, we have noted the remarkable parallels between the Week of Creation and the Week of Redemption, with both these incomparable work weeks completed with a day of divine rest.

But then, that One who was "before all things" became also "the firstborn from the dead." Only the Creator could redeem His lost creation, cursed and dying because of sin, by Himself taking the Curse and dying for sin. God, however, cannot die (in the sense of ceasing to exist), for He is Life itself. His mortal body could sleep in the grave, and His holy Spirit suffer the anguish of hell, but it was inevitable that He must conquer sin and death. The omnipotent Creator cannot possibly fail in His purpose in creation. In all things, He must have the preeminence, for it is only by Him that things exist at all!

Therefore, as Creation is the foundation of all true science, so the Resurrection is the centrality of all true history. All real facts of science support the primeval Creation, and the best-proved fact of history is the Resurrection. As the great Apostle preached long ago in the very center of all human wisdom and culture, in Athens, "God that made the world and all things therein, seeing that He is Lord of heaven and earth . . . hath appointed a day, in the which He will judge the world in righteousness by that man whom He hath ordained; whereof He hath given assurance unto all men, in that He hath raised Him from the dead" (Acts 17:24, 31).

Alive with Christ

Now if we be dead with Christ, we believe that we shall also live with Him: Knowing that Christ being raised from the dead dieth no more; death hath no more dominion over Him (Romans 6:8, 9).

The bodily resurrection of Jesus Christ from the dead both guarantees the future bodily resurrection of the believer and associates us positionally with Him now. Since He died for our sins, we, in effect, were "dead with Christ." Therefore, when He defeated death and hell, and revived His own dead body in immortal power, He broke any dominion of death over Him or over those who were, positionally, with Him.

This is one of the grandest Scriptural themes of the Christian life. We were dead with Christ, but now God "hath quickened us together with Christ" (Ephesians 2:5). Not only have we been "made alive" (I Corinthians 15:22) with Him, but we have also been "raised" with Him up from the grave and then into heaven where we are "seated" with Him on His throne! "[God] hath raised us up together, and made us sit together in heavenly places in Christ Jesus" (Ephesians 2:6).

This means also that we have been glorified with Him and are actually reigning with Him. "The Spirit [Himself] beareth witness with our spirit, that we are the children of God: . . . that we may be also glorified together" (Romans 8:16, 17).

But if all this is only true in position, what meaning does His resurrection life have on our daily lives now? Simply this—that, knowing these truths gives us the incentive and power to live them. "If [or, literally, 'Since'] ye then be risen with Christ, seek those things which are above, where Christ sitteth on the right hand of God. Set your affection on things above, not on things on the earth. For ye are dead, and your life is hid with Christ, in God" (Colossians 3:1–3). "For we also are weak in Him, but we shall live with Him by the power of God toward you" (II Corinthians 13:4).

Thou Hast Rejected Knowledge

My people are destroyed for lack of knowledge: because thou hast rejected knowledge, I will also reject thee, that thou shalt be no priest to Me: seeing thou hast forgotten the law of thy God, I will also forget thy children (Hosea 4:6).

This lament over the ancient apostasy of Israel embodies an age-long principle which surely applies to those nations today which once professed Christianity, but are now dominated by humanism. Our own nation is experiencing an awful scourge of moral anarchy among our children and young people, and the reason why is because their parents and grandparents have largely "forgotten the law of thy God."

America—particularly its intellectual leadership—has "rejected knowledge," so its people are being "destroyed for lack of knowledge." This ignorance exists despite an abundance of supposed actual knowledge (i.e., "science") in our educational institutions, for such facts are almost universally taught in a secular context, and our teachers have forgotten that "the fear of the LORD is the beginning of knowledge" (Proverbs 1:7).

Even in evangelical and fundamentalist churches and schools today, there is often too little emphasis on *knowledge,* and too much on *experience*. Christian faith is not "feeling"; it is volitional commitment to a true intellectual understanding of the person and work of the Lord Jesus Christ. "Except ye repent, ye shall all likewise perish," said Christ (Luke 13:5). The Greek word for "repent" means "change your *mind!*" One can only believe right if he first thinks right, and this requires true knowledge.

Listen again to Hosea's warning: "The LORD hath a controversy with the inhabitants of the land, because there is no truth, nor mercy [i.e., 'kindness'], nor knowledge of God in the land" (Hosea 4:1). "They have sown the wind, and they shall reap the whirlwind" (Hosea 8:7).

"Wise" Fools

As the thief is ashamed when he is found, so is the house of Israel ashamed; . . . Saying to a stock, Thou art my father; and to a stone, Thou hast brought me forth: for they have turned their back unto me, and not their face (Jeremiah 2:26, 27).

Indeed, the leaders of Israel *should* have hidden their faces from God! The very idea of repudiating the God who had created them, redeeming them from death, and then establishing them as a great nation, in favor of a vain evolutionary, pantheistic polytheism rampant among their heathen neighbors, is preposterous. God's people should have tried to lead these pagan evolutionists back to the Creator, instead of adopting their own utterly impotent cosmogony. They surely had sense enough to know that wooden images and stone idols could never generate living human beings!

But this ancient delusion is highly sophisticated and realistic, compared to our modern "scientific" evolutionism. Modern "inflationary" cosmogonists actually believe that the entire ordered universe evolved out of a "quantum fluctuation in a primeval state of nothingness." Modern "origin-of-life" biochemists have faith that dead chemical elements in a primordial soup generated complex living cells against infinitely impossible odds. And modern physical anthropologists credulously insist that chattering chimpanzee-like "hominids" were miraculously transmuted into intelligent, spiritual human beings—all in spite of the fact that true science utterly repudiates every aspect of this impossible evolutionary fantasy.

Paul, speaking of the ancient evolutionists, commented as follows: "Professing themselves to be wise, they became fools" (Romans 1:22). Yet these early idolaters never carried their anti-creationism to such absurd reductionist extremes as do their modern descendants. The Bible calls them fools.

A Holiday for Atheists

The fool hath said in his heart, There is no God. Corrupt are they, and have done abominable iniquity: there is none that doeth good (Psalm 53:1).

There are many religious holidays, and April 1 would be a good holiday for atheists, humanists, pantheists, and others who deny the reality of an omnipotent, personal Creator God. The Word of God has made it plain that such a faith is the faith of a fool (the Hebrew word, *nabal,* means both "stupid" and "wicked").

It is obvious that no one could ever prove atheism to be true, for it is impossible to prove a universal negative. In fact, there is such overwhelming evidence of designed order and complexity in the universe, especially in the marvelous structures of living organisms, that one must exercise an enormous amount of credulity to make himself believe that it all just happened! This is the New Testament testimony as well: " . . . they are without excuse: . . . Professing themselves to be wise, they became fools" (Romans 1:20–23).

Both ancient pagans and modern evolutionists have "changed the truth of God into a lie, and worshipped and served the creature [same as 'creation'] more than the Creator" (Romans 1:25), and this is inexcusable. The anomaly is that they usually boast of such folly as "intellectual" and "scientific," when it is nothing but "abominable iniquity," as our text calls it. They insist that their viewpoint is alone suitable for the public schools, claiming that since creationism implies a Creator, it is necessarily religious, and therefore not scientific. But they have rejected God purely and simply because "they did not like to retain God in their knowledge" (Romans 1:28). Their knowledge, no matter how copious and complex, is foolishness, without God. "The fear of the LORD is the beginning of knowledge: but fools despise wisdom and instruction" (Proverbs 1:7).

APRIL 3

Promotional Geography

Lift not up your horn on high: speak not with a stiff neck. For promotion cometh neither from the east, nor from the west, nor from the south. But God is the judge: He putteth down one, and setteth up another (Psalm 75:5–7).

National politics, city politics, office politics, all are alike in two respects. One who seeks promotion to higher office manages somehow to "lift up his horn on high" and also to persuade some kind of constituency (often geographical, but possibly professional or some other) to back him as its representative. But this isn't the way it should work in God's service. Promotion does not come from a geographical election, and God is not pleased with those who "toot their own horn" or speak arrogantly concerning their own qualifications. "And seekest thou great things for thyself? seek them not" (Jeremiah 45:5).

Jesus said: "He that is greatest among you shall be your servant. And whosoever shall exalt himself shall be abased; and he that shall humble himself shall be exalted" (Matthew 23:11, 12). "Before destruction the heart of man is haughty, and before honor is humility" (Proverbs 18:12).

As far as governmental offices are concerned, it is well to remember that—whether in a democracy, monarchy, or dictatorship—"the powers that be are ordained of God" (Romans 13:1), and sometimes, for His own good reasons, "the most High ruleth in the kingdom of men, and giveth it to whomsoever He will, and setteth up over it the basest of men" (Daniel 4:17).

God is the ultimate Judge, and it is His will that we pray "for kings, and for all that are in authority" (I Timothy 2:2) and submit ourselves "to every ordinance of man for the Lord's sake" (I Peter 2:13). "Humble yourselves therefore under the mighty hand of God, that He may exalt you in due time" (I Peter 5:6).

The Origin and Destiny of Nations

And the nations of them which are saved shall walk in the light of it: and the kings of the earth do bring their glory and honor into it (Revelation 21:24).

This somewhat enigmatic verse assures us that, even in the eternal ages, God still has a place and purpose for distinct nations. Presumably, they will all speak the same "pure language" (Zephaniah 3:9), but they will continue to be recognized as nations.

The nations were originally established after the confusion of tongues and dispersion of the families at Babel (Genesis 11:9). There seem to have been 70 families there, and these became the 70 original nations, as listed in the Table of Nations in Genesis 10. There were three basic streams of nations (Semitic, Japhetic, and Hamitic) and although there has been much mixing and proliferation, these three basic streams of nations (*not* "races") are still roughly distinct.

In his day, as God was about to establish Israel as His chosen nation, Moses said: "Remember the days of old . . . When the Most High divided to the nations their inheritance, when He separated the sons of Adam, He set the bounds of the people according to the number of the children of Israel" (Deuteronomy 32:7, 8). This may be a reference to the 70 souls in the original family of Israel (Genesis 46:27), and probably also to Israel's home at the hub of the world's nations.

God has a purpose for each nation as is evident from Paul's sermon: "God . . . hath made of one blood all nations of men for to dwell on all the face of the earth, and hath determined the times before appointed, and the bounds of their habitation; That they should seek the Lord" (Acts 17:24, 26, 27).

Old nations have disappeared because they refused to seek the Lord, and new nations have risen, proliferating now into over 150 nations and 3000 languages, but each has had a time, and place, and purpose in the sovereign plan of God.

APRIL 5

The Teaching Universe

The heavens declare the glory of God; and the firmament sheweth His handywork. Day unto day uttereth speech, and night unto night sheweth knowledge (Psalm 19:1, 2).

This familiar psalm, extolling God's creation (vv. 1–6) and God's word (vv. 7–14), begins with a beautiful summary of the testimony of the physical universe. "The heavens" and "the firmament" are synonymous (Genesis 1:8), both being equivalent to our modern scientific concept of space. The "glory of God" refers to His infinite power, or energy, and "His handiwork" implies the infinite variety and complexity of physical systems, or matter, in the universe. This interaction of matter and energy occurs everywhere throughout space, but also has to operate and be understood in the context of time, "day unto day" and "night unto night."

The entire marvelous complex of space/time/matter/energy is continually "uttering speech" and "showing knowledge," teaching men and women of all times and places that there is a great Creator God who made it all. "The invisible things of Him from the creation of the world are clearly seen" (Romans 1:20).

The boundless space, the endless time, the infinite energies, and the innumerable complexities of the matter of the universe all unite in irrefutable testimony to the God of creation. The most fundamental principle of science, as well as the most universal rule of human experience, is the Law of Cause and Effect, stating that no effect can transcend its cause. Thus the great Cause of the universe must be infinite, eternal, omnipotent, and omniscient. And since we, as living, feeling persons are able to think about all this, that Cause must also be a living, feeling, thinking person. This is the great lesson engraved on the textbook of the universe for all to read and learn. The whole creation, indeed, declares the glory of God.

The True God

Whatsoever is commanded by the God of heaven, let it be diligently done for the house of the God of heaven: for why should there be wrath against the realm of the king and his sons? (Ezra 7:23).

This decree, given to Ezra the scribe by Artaxerxes, the emperor of Persia, is one of many rather surprising acknowledgments in Scripture by pagan idolaters that the true God is the God of heaven. Abimelech of the Philistines and Pharaoh in Egypt are also examples (Genesis 21:22; 41:38). Balaam, the false prophet of Mesopotamia, recognized that the God of Israel was omnipotent (Numbers 22:38). Nebuchadnezzar, the mighty king of Babylon, was forced to "praise and extol and honor the King of heaven, all whose works are truth, and His ways judgment" (Daniel 4:37).

However, the nations of the world and their leaders long ago "changed the glory of the uncorruptible God into an image made like to corruptible man, and to birds, and fourfooted beasts, and creeping things," preferring to worship and serve the creature more than the Creator. They are "without excuse," since the very creation reveals the Creator (Romans 1:20, 23, 25). They instituted the religion of pantheism, replacing the Creator with nature, denying any real creation, and this soon led to polytheistic idolatry, the worship of natural systems and forces in nature, personified as various gods and goddesses.

Nevertheless, they have always known in their hearts that there really is a God of heaven who created all things and who, therefore, will someday come in great wrath against all who reject Him. This is no less true for today's modern evolutionary pantheists than for the idolatrous evolutionary pantheists of antiquity, for they are all guilty of the same foolish sin. "For all the gods of the nations are idols: but the LORD made the heavens" (Psalm 96:5).

APRIL 7

The Creator of Marriage

Have ye not read, that He which made them at the beginning made them male and female, And said, For this cause shall a man leave father and mother, and shall cleave to his wife: and they twain shall be one flesh? . . . What therefore God hath joined together, let not man put asunder (Matthew 19:4–6).

With these clear statements, the Lord Jesus settled forever (for those who believe His words) the question of human origins and the historicity of the Genesis account of creation. God created Adam and Eve as a full-grown man and woman in the beginning, united as husband and wife—not a population of primates slowly evolving into people over millions of years. The multitude of skeptical scientists and liberal theologians who have insisted that the "two" accounts of creation in the first two chapters of Genesis contradict each other here stand sharply rebuked by the Creator, Himself, for Christ quoted specifically from both Genesis 1:27 and 2:24, thus accepting both of them as valid, historical, and complementary accounts of the same event.

Furthermore, He who is the heavenly Bridegroom confirmed the Genesis teaching that the first and most basic of all human institutions was the home, and that marriage was designed by its Creator to be monogamous and permanent.

Although modern evangelicals may have differing opinions concerning acceptable criteria for divorce and remarriage, it is obvious that "from the beginning it was not so." The ideal marriage is even used by Paul as a picture of the loving, permanent union of Christ and His Church (Ephesians 5:25–27). God, in His grace, does forgive sin when it is confessed and forsaken—even sin against the marriage covenant—but this does not eliminate the accompanying suffering and heartbreak. How much better to follow God's creative purpose in all things, especially concerning marriage and the home.

The Truth and the Lie

Who changed the truth of God into a lie, and worshipped and served the creature more than the Creator, who is blessed forever. Amen (Romans 1:25).

The truth above all other truths is that God is Creator, and thus deserves eternal worship and blessing by His creatures. The lie that is greater than all other lies is that some creature—some created being or entity—is greater than its Creator, and as such is to be worshipped more than God.

The Lord Jesus Christ has made it plain that Satan, the Devil, was the father of lies. "When he speaketh a lie, he speaketh of his own: for he is a liar, and the father of it" (John 8:44). He is the one who seeks to turn men away from the Creator, because he, himself, wants to be worshipped as God.

This has been his basic lie all through the ages. "Ye shall be as gods," he told Eve (Genesis 3:5), and the deception of humanism has persisted in many guises and in every nation from that time to this. All of ancient paganism, as well as its modern varieties, perpetuates this lie in its denial of a personal, omnipotent Creator. But modern "scientific" evolutionism, with its absolute denial of supernatural creation and its veneration of man as the pinnacle of the cosmic process of evolution, has been by far his most successful variation of this ancient lie.

This modern form of the ancient apostasy, which has already generated such would-be man/gods as Hitler, Lenin, and Mao, will eventually culminate in the Man of Sin, who, "as God sitteth in the temple of God, shewing himself that he is God" (II Thessalonians 2:3, 4), and who will be worshipped by the whole world (Revelation 13:8). Let any who are now tempted to accept this ancient/modern lie of evolutionism heed God's warning: "Because they received not the love of the truth, that they might be saved . . . God shall send them strong delusion, that they should believe a [actually 'the'] lie: That they all might be damned" (II Thessalonians 2:10–12).

The Father of Lights

Every good gift and every perfect gift is from above, and cometh down from the Father of lights, withWhom is no variableness, neither shadow of turning (James 1:17).

God, Himself, is both Author and Finisher of everything we have that is good. This, of course, is the testimony concerning His creation in the beginning, which was both "very good," and "finished" (Genesis 1:31; 2:1). The unique name "Father of lights" seems to suggest a remarkable scientific insight. Since light is the most basic form of energy, and yet is equivalent also to all other forms, and since literally *everything* in the physical universe is energy in *some* form, it is singularly appropriate to speak of the totality of all God's good and perfect gifts in creation as "lights." And, since all these energies are not now being created (only "conserved"), their original source can only be from the *Father* of lights!

There even seems to be a hint of both of the two great laws of science here: energy conservation as well as energy deterioration. The term "variableness," used only here, means literally "transmutation." Just as God is immutable, the total amount of His created "lights" is conserved—neither created nor destroyed. The Second Law states that, in all energy conversions (that is, in everything that happens), the entropy of the universe increases. "Entropy" means "in-turning," coming from two Greek words, *en* and *trope*—the second of which is used in this verse. Entropy is a measure of disorganization, and its inexorable increase is a result of God's curse on the creation following man's rebellion. Thus, although the total energy of the universe is conserved (by the First Law), the available energy is decreasing (by the Second Law). Nevertheless, God Himself is not bound by this law which He has imposed, for a time, on His creation. With Him is not even a "shadow" of any "turning" (*trope*). God never changes, and His purposes can never be defeated!

Dinosaurs and the Bible

Behold now behemoth, which I made with thee; he eateth grass as an ox. Lo now, his strength is in his loins, and his force is in the navel of his belly. He moveth his tail like a cedar. . . . His bones are as strong pieces of brass; his bones are like bars of iron. He is the chief of the ways of God (Job 40:15–19).

In this remarkable passage, the Lord has been urging Job and his three philosophizing friends to consider all the marvelous evidences of God's power and wisdom in nature. Finally he calls their attention to "behemoth" (from a Hebrew word meaning "gigantic beast"), the greatest land animal God ever made—"chief of the ways of God."

Commentators who have tried to identify a living animal as behemoth have called it either an elephant or a hippopotamus, but it is obvious that neither of these animals "moveth his tail like a cedar." The other descriptions are also inappropriate. It should be obvious that the behemoth is an extinct animal, very probably a great dinosaur. This would be obvious, were it not for the widespread evolutionary delusion that dinosaurs became extinct 70 million years ago, with man evolving only about a million years ago. Modern creation scientists, however, have published many well-documented evidences that dinosaurs existed contemporaneously with early humans up to relatively recent times, and that these supposed evolutionary eons of time are pure fiction. Early men, such as Job, could, indeed, marvel at this gigantic creature of God, and also rejoice in God's ability to control the great problems of life as well as His sincere concern with every individual need of His people.

It is also worth noting that there are several references to dragons in the Bible, as well as in ancient traditions everywhere, and it is likely these also reflect the memories of dinosaurs retained by early tribes after the Flood.

All Things

But to us there is but one God, the Father, of whom are all things, and we in Him; and one Lord Jesus Christ, by whom are all things, and we by Him (I Corinthians 8:6).

This small but comprehensive phrase—"all things"—occurs over 150 times in the New Testament, and reveals some slight glimpse of the greatness of God's power and majesty. In the context of this particular verse, Paul is refuting the evolutionary pantheists of his day, stressing that *all* things in the universe were *"of"* the Father, and *"by"* the Son. "God . . . created all things by Jesus Christ" (Ephesians 3:9; see also Revelation 4:11; Colossians 1:16; John 1:3). Furthermore, when He first created all things, "God saw every thing [same as 'all things' in the Hebrew] that He had made, and, behold, it was very good" (Genesis 1:31).

He is now "upholding all things by the word of His power" (Hebrews 1:3), and every day He "giveth to all life, and breath, and all things" (Acts 17:25). Even though sin has brought God's temporary curse upon "the whole creation" (Romans 8:22), He has "made peace through the blood of His cross, by Him to reconcile all things unto Himself" (Colossians 1:20).

Therefore He has promised "That in the dispensation of the fulness of times He might gather together in one all things in Christ" (Ephesians 1:10), and then He will "make all things new" (Revelation 21:5), and "all things shall be subdued unto Him" (I Corinthians 15:28).

In view of the comprehensive power of our Creator and Savior, we who are "in Christ" should never doubt or fear. "He that spared not His own Son, but delivered Him up for us all, how shall He not with Him also freely give us all things?" (Romans 8:32). "And we know that all things work together for good to them that love God" (Romans 8:28). "For of Him, and through Him, and to Him, are all things: to whom be glory forever. Amen" (Romans 11:36).

The Creator of Darkness

I form the light and create darkness; I make peace and create evil, I the LORD do all these things (Isaiah 45:7).

This seems at first to be a confusing verse. How could a God of holiness create evil and darkness? Actually, the word translated "evil" (Hebrew *ra*) does not mean "sin," but "affliction." God pronounced the great curse on the ground "for man's sake" (Genesis 3:17), that the sorrows and pains of life might cause him to know his need of redemption. All of these physical evils will be forever removed—even the curse itself—in the new earth, when sin has been removed.

The same is the case with darkness: Since "God is light, and in Him is no darkness at all" (I John 1:5), it was necessary for Him to create darkness if there was to be a distinction between day and night. The latter would be necessary for at least the probationary period of man's tenure on earth, for he would need nightly rest as well as daily food, for his responsibilities as steward over God's creation. Further, there must be a background of heavenly darkness in order for the sun and moon and stars to serve their function of indicating "signs and seasons and days and years" (Genesis 1:14).

Thus the darkness enveloping the primeval earth at its creation (Genesis 1:2) was not at all a judgment on the earth because of the fall of Satan, as some have taught. Like everything else in the primeval creation, it was "very good" (Genesis 1:31)—created for specific and beneficent divine purposes. The evil connotations of darkness came later, when evil men and devils found they could better promote their deceptions under cover of darkness. However, God's light is even then always available to dispel the darkness when needed and desired. "For God, who commanded the light to shine out of darkness, hath shined in our hearts, to give the light of the knowledge of the glory of God in the face of Jesus Christ" (II Corinthians 4:6).

APRIL 13

Lord of Hosts

And this man went up out of his city yearly to worship and to sacrifice unto the LORD of hosts in Shiloh. And the two sons of Eli, Hophni and Phinehas, the priests of the LORD, were there (I Samuel 1:3).

This majestic name of God, "Lord of hosts" (Hebrew *Jehovah Sabaoth*) occurs almost 240 times in the Bible, first of all in our text above. It is noteworthy that Elkanah, the father of Samuel, understood this name of God better than did the wicked priests, the two sons of Eli. The name occurs only once in the New Testament, speaking of oppressed laborers crying to "the Lord of sabaoth" (James 5:4).

A similar name, "God of hosts," occurs nine times, the first in Psalm 80:7: "Turn us again, O God of hosts, and cause thy face to shine; and we shall be saved." The combined name "LORD God of hosts" is used about 25 times, first in II Samuel 5:10: "And David went on, and grew great, and the LORD God of hosts was with him."

In all these 270 or so references, the name is used to emphasize the mighty power of God and His great host of angels "that excel in strength, that do His commandments" (Psalm 103:20). Not only is God Himself omnipotent and omniscient (after all, He is the Creator of all things!), but He has "an innumerable company of angels" (Hebrews 12:22) at His call. Occasionally some of these mighty hosts have actually been seen by men, as in the days of Elisha (II Kings 6:17), and at the birth of Christ (Luke 2:13).

There is evidently an angelic hierarchy among these heavenly hosts. There are the cherubim and seraphim (Genesis 3:24; Isaiah 6:2), for example, as well as "Michael the archangel" (Jude 9). However, the great "Captain of the host of the LORD" (Joshua 5:14) is none other than the Lord Jesus Christ. He, and He alone, is the true "Lord of hosts."

Pseudo-Science

O Timothy, keep that which is committed to thy trust, avoiding profane and vain babblings, and oppositions of science falsely so called (I Timothy 6:20).

The "science falsely so called," of which Paul warned Timothy, can be nothing less than the age-old philosophy of evolutionary humanism. This anti-God belief has appeared in many guises throughout history, but has always been characterized by a worship of the creation instead of the Creator (note Romans 1:25). It was especially true of gnosticism (the Greek word for "science" in this verse was *gnosis*). Its proponents claimed to be more "scientific" than others, and to possess "knowledge" not shared by laymen. But it was mere "pseudo-science" (literal translation) and Timothy was warned not to compromise with it. Instead, he was urged to guard carefully the faith in the true God, who is the only Creator and Redeemer of the world, not even entering into dialogue with these empty philosophizers.

The apostle's sober warning surely applies at least as urgently today. Multitudes, even of professing Christians, have embraced or compromised with one of the deadly modern forms of this philosophy. These appear in many guises—Darwinism, Marxism, occultism, socialism, nazism, existentialism, and numerous others—but all are one in their hatred of creationism and salvation through the death and resurrection of Christ. All are based on evolution, which is the example *par excellence* of pseudo-science, promoted everywhere in the name of science, but without a shred of scientific evidence supporting it.

The antidote for *false* science is *true* science, and in Jesus Christ "are hid all the treasures of wisdom and knowledge" (Colossians 2:3). Therefore, "grow in grace, and in the knowledge of our Lord and Savior Jesus Christ" (II Peter 3:18).

APRIL 15

Christ at Creation

When He prepared the heavens, I was there: when He set a compass upon the face of the depth: When He established the clouds above; when He strengthened the fountains of the deep (Proverbs 8:27, 28).

This chapter contains a beautiful description of some of God's works during Creation Week, when God, in Christ, was creating and making all things. Christ Himself, personified as the divine Wisdom, the Word of God, is speaking.

Verse 27 speaks of His pre-existence, before the creation of the space/time universe itself. At first the "earth" matter was "without form," with only a great "deep" of water. Then God "set a compass" on the face of the deep, activating the gravitational forces which brought it into spherical form. The Hebrew word for "compass" means "sphere." It is the same word used in Isaiah 40:22, where it is said that God "sitteth upon the circle [i.e., 'sphere'] of the earth."

Then God "established the clouds above." The word for "clouds" means "thin mists," undoubtedly referring to the great water canopy "above the firmament" (Genesis 1:7). Finally, He strengthened the fountains of the deep, locking them under the "foundations of the earth" (v. 29). The same strong fountains of the deep would later be broken up at the time of the great Flood. When the earth was finished, He "rejoiced in the habitable part of His earth" (v. 31).

In all these and the other mighty works of creating and making all things, the Lord Jesus Christ assures us "I was there!" That further assures us, of course, that through all the ages to come, He *will* be there.

This remarkable eighth chapter of Proverbs concludes with the following exhortation, more relevant today than ever: "For whoso findeth me findeth life, and shall obtain favor of the LORD. But he that sinneth against Me wrongeth his own soul: all that hate Me love death" (Proverbs 8:35, 36).

The Angelic Shout

When the morning stars sang together, and all the sons of God shouted for joy (Job 38:7).

The phrase "shouted for joy" in this verse is actually a single word (*ruwa*) in the Hebrew, and it can carry a number of meanings. It is most frequently translated simply "shout," as when the army of Joshua surrounding Jericho shouted, and the walls fell down (Joshua 6:20). In Psalm 100:1, it is translated "make a joyful noise." It can refer to a shout of alarm, or shout of triumph, as well as a shout of joy, but it always refers to a loud shout. In fact, it comes from a root meaning "to split"—a noise that would split eardrums or shatter glass.

In the context of Job 38, the Lord is reminding Job and his friends of the great primeval event of creation. When the earth—which is destined eventually to house God's throne in the eternal ages to come—was established on solid foundations (on the third day of Creation), a resounding noise like mighty thunder—or, better, a gigantic angelic anthem—echoed throughout the universe. An "innumerable company of angels" (Hebrews 12:22), identified in the poetic structure of the Hebrew parallelism in our text as both "morning stars" and "sons of God," shouted exultantly and sang in unison when the solid earth appeared.

This was before the creation of man and woman. The angels probably were created on the first day of Creation Week, immediately after the creation of the universe, itself. Even though Satan and other angels later rebelled against God, most of the angels still obey Him, and one day, we ourselves will actually hear them singing His praises and shouting for joy when He returns to earth (I Thessalonians 4:16; Revelation 4:9–11; 5:11–14; Psalm 148:1–6).

Therefore, "Praise ye Him, all His angels: Praise ye Him, all His hosts" (Psalm 148:2). Someday, we shall join them in a "joyful noise" at God's throne.

APRIL 17

The Unknown Creator

He was in the world, and the world was made by Him, and the world knew Him not (John 1:10).

This verse is surely one of the saddest, most poignant, verses in all the Word of God. In the Lord Jesus Christ, our Creator/Redeemer, "we live, and move, and have our being" (Acts 17:28). The atoms of our bodies are sustained by Him, (Hebrews 1:3), yet multitudes ignore Him, ridicule Him, and take His name in vain. What presumption! What foolishness!

Once He even entered visibly into the world He had created, so that people actually could *hear* His words of life and *see* His works of love. But they wilfully refused to acknowledge Him, and then hung Him on a cross to die.

The height of irony and the depth of foolishness are reached when those whose very minds and bodies were created by Christ refuse even to admit the fact of creation. In effect, they turn Psalm 100:3 upside down and claim: "It is not He that hath made us—it is we ourselves!" Not only do modern men deny His creation, they also reject His salvation, thinking they can save themselves.

It is important to note that John 1:10 specifically refers to the refusal of the "world" to know Him as its Creator. It was made by Him, but would not acknowledge His work of creation. How then could the world ever "receive" Him as its Savior (v. 11). Only its Creator could ever become its Savior, since no one else in all creation was both deserving and capable of such a mission.

Even more inexcusable than those who rejected Him when He was here in the world are those who reject Him today. With all the marvelous evidences of creative design in nature, as revealed by modern science, plus the unanswerable evidences of His own bodily resurrection from the dead, it is wicked foolishness for modern men and women still to reject Him as their Creator and Savior.

Fables and Endless Genealogies

Neither give heed to fables and endless genealogies, which minister questions, rather than godly edifying which is in faith: so do (I Timothy 1:4).

The "fables and endless genealogies" of which the Apostle Paul warns could not have been Jewish traditions and patriarchal family records, as many have taught. Timothy was pastor of a Gentile church (Ephesus) and his father was a Gentile, so that such Jewish heresies would not have been a problem either to Timothy or his church. On the other hand, his childhood home, in Lycaonia, and, especially, his recent ministry in Ephesus, had been in centers of intense pagan idolatry, replete with all kinds of nature myths personifying the various forces of nature as a pantheon of immoral gods and goddesses, combined with an evolutionary pantheism involving endless cycles of æons in an eternal universe.

Since *all* Scripture is profitable for everyone (II Timothy 3:16, 17), these fables must refer to a far more serious and permanent danger than that. The myths of which Paul warns in the first verses of this letter must be the same as the "profane and vain babblings . . . of science falsely so called" which he condemns in the last verses (I Timothy 6:20). In light of both the evolutionary paganism of Paul's day and the evolutionary humanism predicted for the last days (see for example II Timothy 3:1–13), it becomes clear that Paul's reference to "fables and endless genealogies" is merely first-century terminology for the twentieth-century mythology of multi-billion-year particles-to-people evolutionism.

The tragedy is that many 20th-century Christians and Christian leaders have indeed "given heed" to this renewal of ancient evolutionary pantheistic paganism, and their teachings have "ministered questions" which lead many into apostasy. If a Christian life is to become a "godly edifice," it must be established on a godly foundation.

The Enduring Work of God

Whatsoever God doeth, it shall be for ever: nothing can be put to it, nor any thing taken from it: and God doeth it, that men should fear before Him (Ecclesiastes 3:14).

God is both omniscient and omnipotent. He has the wisdom to know what is best to do, and the power to do it; therefore, He makes no mistakes, and never needs to go back and revise or redirect something He started. What He does is forever!

This fundamental principle has many profound implications. It anticipates the basic scientific law of conservation, the most important and universal law of science. The basic physical entities which comprise and organize all natural processes—energy, mass, momentum, electric charge—are all "conserved" throughout nature, being neither created nor destroyed in the present natural order of things.

The same applies to the basic kinds of plants and animals—evolutionists to the contrary notwithstanding. "After its kind" is the universal law of reproduction, and there is not the slightest evidence in the real data of biology that this law has ever been violated, or even *could* be violated.

And it also applies to the created cosmos, as a whole. Many Scriptures (e.g., Psalm 148:1–6) assure us that the sun, moon, and stars, as well as the renewed earth, will continue to function through all the endless ages to come. Nothing can defeat God's primeval purposes in creating them.

Most of all, it applies to our great salvation: "I give unto them eternal life; and they shall never perish" (John 10:28). "The mercy of the Lord is from everlasting to everlasting upon them that fear Him" (Psalm 103:17). "His dominion is an everlasting dominion, which shall not pass away" (Daniel 7:14). "My salvation shall be for ever" (Isaiah 51:6). "The word of our God shall stand for ever" (Isaiah 40:8).

This remarkable principle of universal conservation is given "that men should fear before Him."

The Gods Shall Perish

Thus shall ye say unto them, The gods that have not made the heavens and the earth, even they shall perish from the earth, and from under these heavens (Jeremiah 10:11).

This is a unique verse. Jeremiah, the second longest book in the Bible, is written in Hebrew, except for this one verse! Why would Jeremiah make this remarkable exception here?

This verse was written in Aramaic, which was the official language of the great Babylonian empire—the world's chief nation at that time. The Babylonians, as prophesied by Jeremiah, were soon to be used as a weapon in God's hand, to punish His chosen people, carrying them into exile and captivity, and the main reason for such punishment was apostasy. They had corrupted the worship of the true Creator God with the teachings and idols of the Babylonians and all the other nations around them who had rejected God.

Jeremiah had repeatedly condemned this apostasy, showing that God's people were to be punished by the very nations whose religious philosophies had so attracted them.

But those nations needed also to understand that this was not because of their own strength nor the merits of their own gods. Thus, Jeremiah appropriately inserted a special word to be conveyed to the Babylonians, in their own official tongue. Only the true God, who *made* the heavens and the earth, is in *control* of the heavens and the earth.

The same type of warning, delivered in the "official" language of the modern world ("science?"), is needed even more today than it was in Jeremiah's day. Today's "gods"—Marx, Darwin, etc.—are even less deserving of trust than Zeus or Baal, and yet professing Christians have gone after them in droves. It is urgent that we call them back to the true Creator and Savior, Jesus Christ, urging them—before God's judgment falls once again, through pagan nations—to repudiate every vestige of evolutionary humanism.

APRIL 21

The Seventh Day

For in six days, the LORD *made heaven and earth, the sea, and all that in them is, and rested the seventh day; wherefore the* LORD *blessed the sabbath day, and hallowed it* (Exodus 20:11).

God's Word is omnipotent, and He could just as well have created an entire universe, fully populated and functioning, in an instant of time. Instead, He chose to do it in six days, with a seventh day to be set aside as a day of rest and remembrance of His completed, "very good," creation. Since that time, it has been the universal practice among monotheists—those who believe in one Creator God—to measure time in seven-day weeks, with one of those days observed as a day of rest and worship of the Creator.

This divine assertion was inscribed with "the finger of God" on a table of stone (Exodus 31:18), clearly settling, once and for all, the ancient question of the age of the cosmos, at least for those who really believe in the inerrant perspicuity and authority of the Holy Scriptures. Not only did the Lord precisely equate the six days of man's work week with the six days of His own work week, He then pronounced it all "very good" and "sanctified" the seventh ("sabbath") day (Genesis 1:31; 2:3). This would have been an unthinkable thing for Him to say if there were, at that time, a great mile-deep graveyard, consisting of the fossil remains of dead animals from the so-called geological ages, extending all around the globe. These fossils must all be dated as post-Eden, after human sin and God's curse brought death into the world (Romans 5:12).

In the meantime, those who still believe in God and creation should certainly continue to remember Him by observing every seventh day as a day of rest and worship in honor of their Creator, who has now also become their Redeemer and who will soon come again to reign as eternal King.

Before the World Began

In hope of eternal life, which God, that cannot lie, promised before the world began (Titus 1:2).

There are some things that God, even in His omnipotence, cannot do. He cannot fail in His ultimate purpose in creation, for one thing. He cannot do wrong, or be wrong, for what He does is right and what He says is true, by definition. And God cannot lie, so whatever He has promised, He will perform.

One of His most glorious promises is that of eternal life, for this promise was made even before He made the world, including space and time. But how could anything take place *before* time began? The same word is used in II Timothy 1:9, " . . . His own purpose and grace, which was given us in Christ Jesus before the world began." Similarly, Romans 16:25 speaks of "the revelation of the mystery which was kept secret since the world began."

Our very minds are locked in space and time, and therefore, we cannot even conceive of anything "beyond" space, or "before" time. Nevertheless, God is the Creator, and even "the worlds (that is, the "*aeons,*" the space/times) were framed by the Word of God" (Hebrews 11:3). He *created* time and space and all the phenomena that exist in time and space, and the fact that we cannot *comprehend* this simply confirms the Scriptures. "Who hath directed the Spirit of the LORD, or being His counsellor hath taught Him?" (Isaiah 40:13). "Such knowledge is too wonderful for me; it is high, I cannot attain unto it" (Psalm 139:6).

But what we cannot understand, we simply *believe,* for God cannot lie. Even though the worlds had a beginning, and our lives each had a beginning, the world will never end, and our lives will never end, for God will never end! We receive, by faith, His immutable promise of everlasting life, given us in Christ Jesus, according to His own purpose and infinite grace, before the world began.

APRIL 23

The Brightness of the Glory

Who being the brightness of His glory, and the express image of His person, and upholding all things by the word of His power, when He had by Himself purged our sins, sat down on the right hand of the majesty on high (Hebrews 1:3).

This verse constitutes one of Scripture's most magnificent declarations of the person and work of the Lord Jesus Christ. Let us examine the one phrase—"the brightness of His glory."

The word for "brightness" is used only this one time in the Bible, and means, literally, "out-radiating." The word picture conveyed is of the energy outflow from the sun. The sun constitutes a tremendous generator of energy, more than adequate to sustain all processes on earth. However, these energies would be utterly useless for any such noble purpose if they could not somehow be transmitted from sun to earth. They are transmitted, however, through the remarkable radiant energy known as sunlight, or solar radiation.

It is this figure which the writer is using. As the sun's rays are to the sun itself, so is Christ to the Godhead. He is "the Light of the world" (John 8:12). It is He, whose "goings forth" have been "everlasting" (Micah 5:2). His glorified countenance is "as the sun shineth in his strength" (Revelation 1:16). The Lord Jesus Christ is the life-giving radiation of the ineffable glory of the Eternal One, from whose face one day the very heaven and earth will flee away (Revelation 20:11). "But unto you that fear My name shall the Sun of righteousness arise with healing in His wings [or 'outspreadings']" (Malachi 4:2).

And through this One who mediates God to us, we can enter boldly into His presence. "For God, who commanded the light to shine out of darkness, hath shined in our hearts, to give the light of the knowledge of the glory of God in the face of Jesus Christ" (II Corinthians 4:6).

In the Days of Thy Youth

Remember now thy Creator in the days of thy youth, while the evil days come not, nor the years draw nigh, when thou shalt say, I have no pleasure in them (Ecclesiastes 12:1).

Here is the wisest counsel a young person can receive. Though it was first written many years ago, it is more relevant than ever, today, when young people are being bombarded daily with the propaganda and practices of evolutionary humanism. They urgently need to realize that despite these pressures, they are *not* products of chance, with pleasure their only aim in life. They are special creations of God, with a high and holy purpose destined for them by their Creator.

If they will only recognize this fact, acknowledging God, in Christ, as Creator and Savior while they are young, trusting and obeying His Word as they mature, they can anticipate a life of fulfillment and true happiness. "I have been young, and now am old"; David said, "yet have I not seen the righteous forsaken, nor his seed begging bread" (Psalm 37:25).

If they refuse their Creator in the days of their youth, however, then it will become increasingly difficult to remember their Creator as the years go by. Few are converted in later life. They can only anticipate the bitterness and regrets of old age and death, as described so vividly in the verses following our text. Under the figure of a decaying house symbolizing their aging bodies, the forlorn picture is drawn of fading eyesight, trembling hands, buckling knees, sleepless nights, easy irritability, increasing senility, and other aspects of approaching death—all with no pleasure in them, because they long ago had forgotten their Creator. Remember *now* thy Creator, young man, young woman! *Now* is the accepted time, *now* is the day of salvation (II Corinthians 6:2). Therefore, "let no man despise thy youth; but be thou an example of the believers, in word, in conversation, in charity, in spirit, in faith, in purity" (I Timothy 4:12).

APRIL 25

In Him Is No Darkness

This then is the message which we have heard of Him, and declare unto you, that God is light, and in Him is no darkness at all (I John 1:5).

Light is the most fundamental and important form of energy, and energy includes every phenomenon in the physical universe. It is appropriate for John to affirm that God *is* light, because everything created must reflect the character of its Creator. The term "light," therefore, has come to be applied not only to light in the physical sense, but also to that which is true in the intellectual realm, and holy in the moral realm as well.

In terms of truth and genuine knowledge, "the entrance of thy words giveth light" (Psalm 119:130). "In thy light shall we see light" (Psalm 36:9). Without the true God's truth, there is only darkness. "The god of this world hath blinded the minds of them which believe not, lest the light of the glorious gospel of Christ, who is the image of God, should shine unto them" (II Corinthians 4:4). The Bible also speaks of light as moral holiness. "For ye were sometimes darkness, but now are ye light in the Lord: walk as children of light. . . . And have no fellowship with the unfruitful works of darkness, but rather reprove them" (Ephesians 5:8, 11).

There are still other analogies: "In Him was life; and the life was the light of men" (John 1:4). Not only is light symbolic of life itself, but it also depicts God's daily guidance for our lives. "I am the Light of the world: he that followeth Me shall not walk in darkness, but shall have the light of life" (John 8:12). Since there is no darkness in God, "if we walk in the light as He is in the light" (I John 1:7), there remains no just excuse for any darkness in our own lives. "For God, who commanded the light to shine out of darkness, hath shined in our hearts, to give the light of the knowledge of the glory of God in the face of Jesus Christ" (II Corinthians 4:6).

An Unlikely Testimony

And the LORD opened the mouth of the ass, and she said unto Balaam, What have I done unto thee, that thou hast smitten me these three times? (Numbers 22:28).

This tale of a donkey talking has been the object of great ridicule by skeptics. That it is not an allegory or fable, however, but a real historical event, was confirmed in the New Testament by the Apostle Peter (II Peter 2:15, 16).

There is no naturalistic explanation for it, of course, but to insist that the event was impossible is simply to deny the power of God. Such miracles of creation are very rare, however, and there must always be a good reason when God intervenes in the laws which normally govern His creation.

One reason, in this case, obviously, was to rebuke the prophet Balaam, who was resisting God's will simply for monetary gain. Balaam's voice itself would soon also have to be constrained and controlled by God to force him to do God's will (Numbers 22:38; 23:16, 26; 24:13), blessing Israel instead of pronouncing the curse for which he was to have been paid by the Moabites, who were desperately trying to keep God's people out of the promised land. The Moabites also needed an unforgettable rebuke. They were descendants of Lot, who had known the true God, but they now had become apostate (Numbers 25:1–3), determined to thwart God's purposes.

There may be another, more universal reason: God is concerned about His animal creation, caring even for every sparrow (Matthew 10:29). The animals have been placed under man's dominion, but they are for his service, his instruction, and his enjoyment—not for his abuse.

Thus Balaam's ass was providentially allowed by God to rebuke not only Balaam but also anyone who would unnecessarily abuse one of his specially and beautifully designed animal subjects. Most Christians need to be much more sensitive to this concern of God.

APRIL 27

O Praise the Lord

O praise the L*ORD, all ye nations: praise Him, all ye people. For His merciful kindness is great toward us: And the truth of the Lord endureth forever. Praise ye the* L*ORD* (Psalm 117:1, 2).

Psalm 117 is especially noteworthy for two reasons: First, it is the middle chapter of the Bible, and, secondly, it is the shortest chapter in the Bible, consisting of only the two verses cited above. Thus, it is significant and appropriate that its theme be that of universal and everlasting praise. The very purpose of human language is that God might communicate His Word to us, and that we might respond in praise to Him.

The word "nations" in verse 1 refers specifically to Gentiles, while "people" seems to refer to all tribes of people. Two different Hebrew words for praise are used, so that the verse could be read: "Praise the LORD, all ye Gentile nations; extol Him all ye peoples of every tribe." In any case, the sense of the exhortation is to urge everyone to praise His name.

"Merciful kindness" is the same Hebrew word as "lovingkindness," even more commonly rendered simply as "mercy" or "kindness." Whichever is preferred, the significant point is that it has been *great* toward us. This word (Hebrew *gabar*) is not the usual word for "great," but is a very strong word meaning to "triumph" or "prevail." An example of its use is in the story of the great Flood. "And the waters prevailed exceedingly upon the earth" (Genesis 7:19). In fact, it is used four times in this account of the "overwhelmingly mighty" waters of the Flood (Genesis 7:18–20, 24).

In other words, God's merciful kindness has prevailed over our sin and the awful judgment we deserve in a manner and degree analogous to the way in which the Deluge waters prevailed over the ancient evil world.

God's mercy and truth are eternal, and this will be the great theme of our praise throughout all the ages to come.

God's Infinite Universe

For as the heavens are higher than the earth, so are My ways higher than your ways, and My thoughts than your thoughts (Isaiah 55:9).

Since God's ways are infinite and His thoughts utterly beyond human comprehension, this verse tells us plainly that the height of the heavens is also infinite.

This means that modern relativistic cosmologies that involve a finite universe, or bounded universe, are bound to be wrong. They are all based on esoteric mathematical models, not on measurement or observation. Space, according to God's Word, is infinite and unbounded, just as its Creator is infinite and almighty. Our minds, operating in space as they do, cannot even comprehend the idea of an end, or limit, to space. What could be *beyond* any supposed boundary of space, except more space?

This fact also means that speculations about the location of the center of the universe are pointless. It is impossible even to *define* the center of infinite space. *Any* point could, with equal geometric propriety, be chosen as the center, since space extends infinitely in all directions from *that* point!

In the eternal ages to come, however, the new earth can at least be defined as the center of God's interest in the universe. The holy city will rest on the earth, and "the throne of God and of the Lamb shall be in it" (Rev. 22:3).

Meanwhile, we can rejoice that such an infinite God is directly concerned with each of us. It is absurdly foolish for us to question Him, or His ways, or His thoughts. What He does is right, simply by definition! It is our great privilege simply to believe and trust His Word and His ways. "O the depth of the riches both of the wisdom and knowledge of God! How unsearchable are His judgments, and His ways past finding out! . . . For of Him, and through Him, and to Him, are all things: To whom be glory forever. Amen" (Romans 11:33–36).

APRIL 29

Dark Waters and Thick Clouds

And He rode upon a cherub, and did fly: And He was seen upon the wings of the wind. And He made darkness pavilions round about Him, dark waters, and thick clouds of the skies (II Samuel 22:11, 12).

This mysterious passage in David's song of deliverance (also in Psalm 18) is usually classified by commentators as mere poetic hyperbole. However, it may also be taken literally, if we only assume that David was translated by the Holy Spirit (who "spake by me"—II Samuel 23:2) far back in time to the great Flood, seeing in vision the Lord in great power unleashing the mighty waters of judgment on a corrupt world, yet delivering Noah through it all. A similar vision was experienced by David when he wrote Psalm 29, which speaks explicitly of the Noahic Flood (Hebrew *mabbul,* v. 10).

In our text above, the Hebrew word for "wind" is the same as "spirit," so this phrase could refer to "the wings of the Spirit." In the Bible's first reference to "the Spirit of God" (Genesis 1:2), He is seen as "moving" in the presence of the primeval waters, the word being the same as that for the fluttering movement of the wings of a great bird. This vibrating motion implies the generating of mighty waves of energy, flowing out from the Spirit to energize the newly created cosmos of Genesis 1:1. Similarly, the divine energy emanates again from the Spirit here at the Flood, but this time in destructive rather than creative power.

The references to waters and darkness in these and nearby verses may well refer to the condensation and precipitation of the extensive vapor canopy suggested by the "waters above the firmament" (Genesis 1:7), when great torrents of rain suddenly poured through "the sluiceways of heaven," continuing at highest intensity for forty days, then at lesser intensity for 110 more days, until the "thick clouds" were emptied and the great Flood covered the whole earth.

Death and Spilled Water

For we must needs die, and are as water spilt on the ground, which cannot be gathered up again; neither doth God respect any person: yet doth He devise means, that His banished be not expelled from Him (II Samuel 14:14).

The inevitability of death is here compared to spilt water disappearing into the ground. The comparison is quite incisive.

Both processes are examples of "irreversible processes," operating (as do all *real* processes) in accordance with the universal law of increasing entropy, or increasing disorganization, also known as the Second Law of Thermodynamics. This best-proved law of science observes that every real system or process in nature—unless artificially constrained otherwise—tends to go down to disorder, randomness, decay, and death. All this explicitly contradicts the anti-scientific theory of evolution, despite the modern-day slavish commitment of most "intellectuals" to evolutionism—a "science falsely so called" (I Timothy 6:20), if there is such a thing! No one has ever been able to see evolution in action, for this simple reason: nature works in the opposite direction.

Only a miracle of creation, requiring the divine intervention of the Creator, Himself, could suspend or reverse the law of entropy (or make natural evolution possible) in any given system or process. Gathering spilled water back up from the ground into its container, or restoring the dead back to life, is no more improbable than evolving an ape into a man.

Only the Creator can create life from death, and the bodily resurrection of Jesus Christ after three days in the grave (as certainly proved historically as any other fact of history!), is proof positive that Jesus Christ is the Creator (note John 1:1–3; 20:30, 31). And He *does* devise means whereby lost and dying sinners—through the work of Christ—can be brought back to Him and given everlasting life.

MAY 1

Lift Up Your Eyes

Lift up your eyes on high, and behold who hath created these things, that bringeth out their host by number: He calleth them all by names by the greatness of His might, for that He is strong in power; not one faileth (Isaiah 40:26).

Our text makes three majestic statements about the cosmos, each reflecting true scientific insight, as well as the work of each person of the divine Trinity, in turn: The Omnipresent Father of all purpose, order, structure, and design in the universe has "brought out" an infinite "host" of organized systems in the cosmos—galaxies, stars, planets, animals, and people. All are capable of description mathematically, "by number," and thus all bear witness to their great Designer. One of the two basic laws of science, the Second Law of Thermodynamics, describes the universal fact that chance processes never generate organization or complexity, so that special creation by God is the only legitimate explanation for the "numbered" host of heaven.

The Son is the Omniscient Word of information, description, and meaning. Every system in the cosmos is not only numbered, but named! That is, in the mind of its Creator, it has a function, and has been coded to fulfill its purpose. The Second Law states that systems never code themselves, but rather always tend to distort the information originally programmed into them. Only an omniscient Creator could thus implement the divine purpose for every created entity.

Finally, the Holy Spirit is the omnipotent Energizer who activates and empowers every system. The Second Law says that energy becomes less available as time goes on, so that only the Creator could provide the energy to activate the designed, programmed cosmos in the beginning.

When we finally look up and really "behold Who hath created these things," we must see God the Creator—Father, Son, and Holy Spirit.

Pride Goes Before Destruction

Pride goeth before destruction, and an haughty spirit before a fall (Proverbs 16:18).

This is the middle verse of the entire book of Proverbs, and, in view of the obviously structured original verse divisions throughout the book, it may well have been divinely designed as such. In any case, the sin of pride is so deadly, it is appropriate that a solemn warning concerning it should be placed here right at the heart of God's Book of true wisdom.

The sin of pride was the primeval sin of Satan: "Thine heart was lifted up because of thy beauty, thou hast corrupted thy wisdom by reason of thy brightness" (Ezekiel 28:17). It was the sin by which Satan led Adam and Eve to fall. "Ye shall be as gods" (Genesis 3:5), he had said. It is always the "easily besetting" sin of Christian leaders, especially those who have assumed such leadership prematurely. "Not a novice, lest being lifted up with pride he fall into the condemnation of the devil" (I Timothy 3:6). Even Jesus was thirty years old before He began to teach.

Though pride is not named as such in the Ten Commandments, in reality it is implied in the very first one. "Thou shalt have no other gods before Me" (Exodus 20:3). The essence of all false religion is evolutionary humanism—worshipping and serving the creature more than the Creator (Romans 1:25). Pride and unbelief are two sides of the same coin. When men and women refuse the Word of their Creator, it is fundamentally because they want to be their own "gods," as did Adam and Eve. Human pride is the hidden root of humanism, and of evolutionism, and of "every high thing that exalteth itself against the knowledge of God" (II Corinthians 10:5). It is the very essence of the sin nature which we have inherited from our first parents. How carefully we need to guard against this secret sin of pride. If we do not, it will inevitably lead to humiliation and defeat.

The Grace of God in Creation

> *He left not Himself without witness, in that He did good, and gave us rain from heaven, and fruitful seasons, filling our hearts with food and gladness* (Acts 14:17).

There is abundant evidence of the mighty power and wisdom of God in the vast cosmos and the tremendously complex world. "For the invisible things of Him from the creation of the world are clearly seen, being understood by the things that are made, even His eternal power and Godhead; so that they are without excuse" (Romans 1:20).

But, in addition to such evidence of His wisdom and power, there is also wonderful evidence of the grace of God in nature. Although "the whole creation groaneth and travaileth in pain together until now" (Romans 8:22), laboring under the awful curse on the ground imposed by God when Adam sinned (Genesis 3:17), it has been so subjected "in hope," with God's promise of ultimate deliverance from the "bondage of corruption," and "we are saved by hope" (Romans 8:21, 24).

This goodness of God is evidenced in the daily victory of light over darkness, the annual return of spring after winter, and, especially, the oft-repeated triumph of life over death. Although individuals die, new souls are born; life goes on, and always, there is hope. Man must eat his bread in the sweat of his face as he labors to wrest a living from the cursed ground, but God does send the rain and the fruitful seasons, and the food is grown. Though he must eat of it in sorrow all the days of his life, somehow God nevertheless fills his heart with food and gladness. And all of the labor and sweat and sorrow is "for thy sake" (Genesis 3:17), urging man to return to God for both his daily bread and his eternal salvation. How foolish is the man who receives all these gifts of God's grace without acknowledging their source. "Despisest thou the riches of His goodness . . . not knowing that the goodness of God leadeth thee to repentance?" (Romans 2:4).

Who Is Jesus Christ?

In the beginning was the Word, and the Word was with God, and the Word was God. The same was in the beginning with God. All things were made by Him; and without Him was not any thing made that was made (John 1:1–3).

It is remarkable how many names and titles are associated with Jesus Christ (meaning "Anointed Savior") in the first chapter of John's Gospel. In verse 9, He is called "the true Light, which lighteth every man that cometh into the world." He is "the only begotten of the Father, full of grace and truth" in verse 14 and "the only begotten Son, which is in the bosom of the Father" in verse 18. John the Baptist called Him "the Lord" in verse 23, "the Lamb of God, which taketh away the sin of the world," in verse 29, and "the Son of God," in verse 34. The disciples then called Him "Master" in verse 38 and "Messiah" in verse 41, as well as "Jesus of Nazareth" in verse 45. Nathanael acknowledged Him as "King of Israel" in verse 49, and Jesus called Himself "the Son of man" in verse 51.

But the very first title ascribed to Him by John, as he introduced his Gospel, was simply "the Word" (v. 1), from a word hard to translate in its fullness. In the New Testament, it is rendered by "word," "reason," "communication," "doctrine," "speech," and many others. With reference to Christ, it tells us that He is always the One who reveals, speaks for, manifests, explains, and incarnates the Heavenly Father.

John 1:1 even takes us back before Genesis 1:1, where we learn that the pre-incarnate Christ created all things (note Colossians 1:16). "In the beginning," He was, before He created! And all things were made by Him. "By the Word of the LORD" were the heavens made; "and all the host of them by the breath of His mouth" (Psalm 33:6).

As the eternal, omnipotent Word of God, the pre-incarnate Christ spoke all things into being. Our Lord was personal Savior; Jesus Christ is the Word; and the Word is God!

The Incarnate Wisdom

The L*ORD* *possessed me in the beginning of His way, before His works of old. I was set up from everlasting, from the beginning, or ever the earth was* (Proverbs 8:22, 23).

The book of Proverbs repeatedly extols the virtues of true wisdom, founded on the fear of the Lord. In the eighth chapter, however, beginning at verse 22, the theme changes, retreating far back in time to the week of creation itself, and even before. The statements in the next ten verses, especially, must be of an actual divine Person. From the New Testament perspective, especially with John 1:1–14 as the definitive exposition, it becomes clear that the divine Wisdom of Proverbs 8:22–31 is none other than the incarnate Word of John's prologue.

The Lord Jesus Christ, indeed, fits perfectly, all the statements in this particular section of Proverbs, which then gives marvelous new insight into the events of creation and the divine fellowship in the Godhead before the creation. Note that in these first two verses, the Lord's "ways" were prior to His "works," and that He "possessed" His Son "from everlasting." This is the profound doctrine of "eternal generations," whereby the Son is "brought forth" continually from the Father, forever manifesting Him in His creation.

The New Testament makes it plain that Jesus Christ is, indeed, the incarnate Wisdom of God. He is the "Word" by whom all things were made (John 1:1–3). He is "the Truth" (John 14:6) and "the Light" (John 8:12), by whom alone men can come to God and follow Him. He is called "the power of God, and the wisdom of God" in I Corinthians 1:24 and He called Himself "the wisdom of God" in Luke 11:49.

All of the vaunted knowledge of the world's thinkers and scientists is empty and futile apart from the Lord Jesus Christ, the living Word of God, for in Him alone are found "all the treasures of wisdom and knowledge" (Colossians 2:3).

Evolution and the Woman

For the man is not of the woman; but the woman of the man. Neither was the man created for the woman; but the woman for the man (I Corinthians 11:8, 9).

In spite of the overwhelming scientific evidence against evolution, "Christian evolutionists" still argue (or, at least, allow) that evolution could be God's method of creation.

Such a fence-straddling position is logically untenable, however, and gravely dangerous spiritually. There are numerous Biblical and theological reasons why evolution, under any guise, must be unequivocally repudiated by Bible-believing Christians, and one of the most obvious is the unique Biblical account of the formation of the body of the first woman. By no stretch of the imagination or device of spiritualizing exposition can this account be harmonized with the assumed evolution of human beings from some earlier group of hominids.

God "formed man of the dust of the ground" (Genesis 2:7). Many theistic evolutionists have asserted that this phrase could be applied to the long process of evolution, as imagined by modern paleoanthropologists. This, of course, is fantasy, not exegesis. But whatever argument might be made for this strange interpretation, there is simply no way at all for the record of Eve's subsequent formation out of Adam's side (Genesis 2:21, 22) to be so interpreted. All they can do with this passage is to ignore it, trying to pass it by with some comment about woman being close to man's heart, or some other explanation. It is not only clearly spelled out in Genesis, but is confirmed by the Apostle Paul, both here and in I Timothy 2:13. The Lord Jesus Christ, Himself, quoted from the Genesis account of the creation of man and woman (Matthew 19:4–6) as literal history. Both man and woman are special creations of God, with no evolutionary connection whatever, to any kind of animal ancestry.

MAY 7

The Beginning of the Creation

For in those days shall be affliction, such as was not from the beginning of the creation which God created unto this time, neither shall be (Mark 13:19).

The phrase "from the beginning of the creation" or equivalent, occurs at least six times in the New Testament, indicating, beyond question, that the world was created at a definite beginning-point of time, All other cosmogonies, on the other hand, are evolutionary cosmogonies, which deny a real beginning for the space/time cosmos at all.

What almost seems a redundancy in our text is the phrase "the creation which God created." Evidently the Lord thought it vital to stress the fact of divine creation, especially as the great last-days "affliction" draws near.

That the "creation" mentioned in this verse refers explicitly to the cosmos, is evident from the parallel passage in Matthew 24:21, where the same prophecy is rendered as follows: "For then shall be great tribulation, such as was not from the beginning of the world to this time." Here, "world," is actually the Greek *kosmos,* referring to the ordered universe of heaven and earth. Thus, according to the Bible, the entire universe (including even time itself) came into existence at the "beginning," when God created it, as recorded in Genesis 1:1.

Note especially the significance of Mark 10:6 in this connection: "But from the beginning of the creation God made them male and female." Jesus was here quoting from the account of the creation of Adam and Eve (Genesis 1:27), and included what seemed an almost-incidental confirmation that God created them, not after many billions of years of cosmic evolution, but from the very *beginning* of creation! Man and woman were not divine afterthoughts, as evolution would imply, but were the very reason why God created the universe in the first place.

The Everlasting Gospel

And I saw another angel fly in the midst of heaven, having the everlasting gospel to preach unto them that dwell on the earth, and to every nation, and kindred, and tongue, and people, Saying with a loud voice, Fear God, and give glory to Him; for the hour of His judgment is come: And worship Him that made heaven, and earth, and the sea, and the fountains of waters (Revelation 14:6, 7).

When the Lord Jesus returned to heaven after His resurrection, He left the disciples with the Great Commission to "preach the Gospel to every creature" (Mark 16:15). Unfortunately, over the centuries, there has developed much misunderstanding concerning the content of the Gospel ("good tidings") and many have preached "another gospel" (Galatians 1:6) which can never save. This false gospel wears many faces, but inevitably, at its heart will be found the false hope of evolutionary humanism, glorifying man instead of God, "worship[ping] and serv[ing] the creature more than the Creator" (Romans 1:25).

We can be sure that the Gospel preached in our text is the true Gospel—in fact, it is called specifically the everlasting Gospel! And its great burden is to call people everywhere back to faith in the one true Creator God, who made all things in heaven and earth. The Lord Jesus Christ must be accepted, first of all, as God and Creator, before it can be meaningful to present Him as Savior and Lord. Otherwise, we preach "another gospel" and "another Jesus"—neither of which are even real!

The true Gospel must also present Christ as the sin-bearing, crucified, resurrected Savior (I Corinthians 15:1–4), and as the coming King of kings and Lord of lords (Matthew 4:23; I Timothy 6:15; Revelation 19:16). But it must first of all present Him as omnipotent and offended Creator. Then only, like the angel, do we truly proclaim the everlasting Gospel.

Contend for the Faith

Beloved, when I gave all diligence to write unto you of the common salvation, it was needful for me to write unto you, and exhort you that ye should earnestly contend for the faith which was once delivered unto the saints (Jude 3).

Jude long ago addressed a problem in his day which is still very real in our day, among Christians. It is easier and more comfortable just to teach and preach about the blessings of our common salvation than it is to contend for the faith, but the latter is more "needful." The word conveys the idea that he was so constrained, evidently by the Holy Spirit, as actually to be in distress about this compelling need. Similarly, his exhortation to "earnestly contend" does not mean to "be argumentative," but rather, to "agonize with intense determination." It is one word in the Greek, *epagonizomai* (literally, "agonize over"). Defending and contending for the faith is serious, urgent business, for the adversaries are many.

That which we are to defend is "the faith"—the whole body of Christian truth, wherever it is under attack. It would, of course, be especially important to contend for the doctrine of special creation, which is the foundation of all others, and which is the doctrine perpetually under the most concerted and persistent attack by the adversary and his hordes.

That faith has been, long ago, "once delivered" to the saints. The sense of these words is "once for all turned over for safekeeping." The Lord has entrusted us with his Word, completed and inscripturated, and we must keep it, uncorrupted and intact, for every generation until He returns, preaching and teaching all of it to every creature, to the greatest extent we possibly can.

Finally, note that the safeguarding of the faith was not merely to specially trained theologians or other professionals, but to "the saints." Every Christian believer is commanded to "earnestly contend for the faith."

Saving Faith and True Creation

Through faith we understand that the worlds were framed by the word of God, so that things which are seen were not made of things which do appear (Hebrews 11:3).

This is the very first object and example of faith in the Bible's great "faith chapter," Hebrews 11. This fact strongly argues that any truly meaningful and effective faith must be founded, first of all, on the revealed fact of special creation—creation *ex nihilo*—not creation through some protracted, naturalistic, imaginary process of evolution. All of the "worlds" (Greek, *aion*—that is, the "space/times"—the continuum of space and time which constitutes the physical cosmos) were simply called into existence by God's omnipotent word. "He spake, and it was done" (Psalm 33:9). In no way did He have to start with some chaotic form of matter already in existence. Jesus Christ—the Word of God (John 1:14)—created space and time as well as matter. "By Him were all things created" (Colossians 1:16). "Without Him was not any thing made that was made" (John 1:3).

Right at the end of the previous chapter, the apostle asserts that "the just shall live by faith" (10:38) and concludes by speaking of those "who believe [literally, 'have faith'] to the saving of the soul" (v. 39). Following immediately then is his definition of faith, and after that the great progression of objects and examples of faith in Hebrews 11. Heading the list of these, of course, is faith in the special creation of all things by the Word of God. The necessary conclusion is that a "living" faith and "saving" faith must be founded, first of all, on the fact of supernatural creation of all things by God in the beginning. This is not all, of course, but it is the foundation!

Evolution is also based on faith, but it is contrary both to Scripture and to true science. "Theistic evolution" is a false faith, and those Christians who believe such things should carefully examine their hearts in the light of God's Word.

MAY 11

The Virtuous Woman

Who can find a virtuous woman? for her price is far above rubies (Proverbs 31:10).

The famous passage on "the virtuous woman" (Proverbs 31:10–31) is often used on Mother's Day, so the description of the attributes of such a woman is already well known. But it is not so well known that these 22 verses were originally put together in the form of an acrostic, with each verse starting, in turn, with the successive 22 letters of the Hebrew alphabet. It is as though the compiler of Proverbs wanted to conclude the book with a special tribute to his own mother (v. 1), and to imply in so doing that it would exhaust all the resources of human language!

However, the translators have done something of a disservice by using the word "virtuous," which tends to make us think primarily today simply of moral purity. This woman was far more than just that. The Hebrew word, when used as an adjective or adverb describing a woman, was always translated "virtuous" (Ruth 3:11; Proverbs 12:4; 31:10) or "virtuously" (Proverbs 31:29). When used in reference to men, however (as it is far more frequently), it is always translated by such words as "strong, "valiant," "worthy," etc. Its most common translation is "army." Thus, an ideal woman is a strong, brave, industrious, trustworthy woman, worth an entire army to her husband and her children and her nation. This is woman as God intended woman to be. She is, most especially, a godly woman. "Favor is deceitful, and beauty is vain; but a woman that feareth the Lord, she shall be praised" (v. 30).

"Her children arise up, and call her blessed; her husband also, and he praiseth her" (v. 28). This verse is usually acknowledged on Mother's Day, but let us remember that "Honor thy . . . mother" (Exodus 20:12), means every day of the year as well!

The Mother of Us All

And Adam called his wife's name Eve; because she was the mother of all living (Genesis 3:20).

Sarah, Abraham's wife, was called the mother of all "the children of promise" (Galatians 4:28), and the wife of Noah was the mother of all post-flood mankind, but Mother Eve, alone, was "the mother of all living." "Adam was first formed, then Eve," Paul said in I Timothy 2:13, and so-called "Christian evolutionists" have never yet been able to explain God's unique formation of Eve's body in any kind of an evolutionary context.

Eve, as our first mother, experienced all the great joys and great sorrows that all later mothers would know. She evidently had many "sons and daughters" (Genesis 5:4), and probably lived to see many generations of grandchildren. With Adam, she had even known paradise, but sin had entered their lives when they rebelled against God's Word, and God had to say: "In sorrow thou shalt bring forth children" (Genesis 3:16). The greatest sorrow was no doubt when Cain slew Abel, and as with another mother whose Son's innocent blood was shed many years later, it was like a sword piercing her own soul (Luke 2:35).

Nevertheless, as near as we can tell, after her first great sin, Eve trusted God's Word henceforth, and received His forgiveness and salvation. Later, as the mother of Seth, she taught him and her grandson, Enos, about the Lord and all His promises. "Then began men to call upon the name of the LORD" (Genesis 4:26).

Most Christian believers are looking forward to seeing their own mothers again someday—restating their love and appreciation for all they did in bearing them, and in caring, teaching, and praying for them. But it will be a wonderful experience to meet our first mother, also, as well as Sarah, Hannah, Mary, and all the other godly mothers of old.

MAY 13

When the Earth Trembled

Then the earth shook and trembled; the foundations of heaven moved and shook, because He was wroth (II Samuel 22:8).

The terrible scenes depicted in verses 8–17 of this chapter (essentially the same as Psalm 18:7–16), go far beyond even any poetic license that David might properly use to describe his own personal deliverance from his enemies. They do, however, make sense in connection with the great earthquake and mid-day darkness at the scene of Christ's crucifixion (Matthew 27:45, 51), thus helping to confirm that this, indeed, is one of the Messianic psalms.

But they seem to go beyond even this, for the physical convulsions experienced around the cross were only a foretaste of those that will soon occur when "He ariseth to shake terribly the earth" (Isaiah 2:19). In that great coming day of judgment, God will "shake the heavens, and the earth, and the sea, and the dry land" (Haggai 2:6).

Similarly, in the distant past, there was a worldwide cataclysm at the time of the great Flood, and similar scenes took place then. David's experiences thus became also a retrospective type of those experienced by Noah, as he was saved through the trauma of a world covered with the deep waters of judgment. Both Noah and David, in fact, were types of the incarnate Creator, testifying both to "the sufferings of Christ, and the glory that should follow" (I Peter 1:11).

In this remarkable passage, therefore, one can see not only David's deliverances, but also those of Noah in the distant past, Christ at the cross, and all the saints in the climactic time of judgment in the future. The earth once shook terribly at the time of the Flood, then again when its Creator died on the cross. But one greater still is yet to come—"so mighty an earthquake, and so great"—that "every island [will flee] away, and the mountains [will not be] found" (Revelation 16:18, 20).

The Essence of Sin

Now the serpent was more subtil than any beast of the field which the LORD *God had made. And he said unto the woman, Yea, hath God said, Ye shall not eat of every tree of the garden?* (Genesis 3:1).

The first entrance of sin into the world was Satan's subtle suggestion to Eve that God's Word might not be true and authoritative after all. Then came Satan's blatant "Ye shall not surely die" (Genesis 3:4), openly charging the Creator with falsehood. Ever since that time, the basic root of every sin has been unbelief—the implicit denial of the Creator's Word.

Therefore, God's judgment on human sin will be in relation to His Word. Jesus said: "There is one that accuseth you, even Moses, in whom ye trust. For had ye believed Moses, ye would have believed Me" (John 5:45, 46). He also said: "He that rejecteth Me, and receiveth not My words, hath One that judgeth him: the word that I have spoken, the same shall judge him in the last day" (John 12:48). In principle, the Lord Jesus tells us that both Old Testament ("the law of Moses") and New Testament ("the law of Christ") will be witnesses against us at God's judgment throne.

In fact, at the final judgment, the "books" are specifically said to be the basis of God's condemnation of the unsaved: "And I saw the dead, small and great, stand before God; and the books were opened: . . . and the dead were judged out of those things which were written in the books, according to their works" (Revelation 20:12). These books surely include the books of the Bible, wherein are written the laws of God, against which men and women are to be judged. Since even one transgression makes one guilty (James 2:10), none could ever stand at the Judgment by his own works. But since unbelief is the essence of sin, faith in God's Word, and in the person and work of the Savior revealed in God's Word, brings forgiveness, and salvation, and righteousness.

Jesus Christ: Past, Present, Future

For of Him, and through Him, and to Him, are all things: to whom be glory for ever. Amen (Romans 11:36).

Modern Christians, being mostly self-centered rather than God-centered in their thinking, usually emphasize only the blessings of the Christian life. While it is surely true that all good things come through Christ, it is just as true and just as important that all things were created by Him and for Him. The beautiful doxology in our text thus presents, in outline form, the tremendous scope of His work. "Of Him" speaks of His past work—creating all things. "Through Him" speaks of His present work—preserving all things and mediating to us our great salvation. "To Him" speaks of His future work—consummating all things in His own eternal reign.

The threefold aspect of the person and work of Jesus Christ is also presented in the magnificent testimony of Colossians 1:16–20): Past work: "By Him were all things created" (Colossians 1:16); Present work: "By Him all things consist" (Colossians 1:17); Future work: "By Him to reconcile all things unto Himself" (Colossians 1:20). That all of this is comprehended within the "gospel" is evident, in that Colossians 1:5, introducing this passage and its claims, speaks of "the word of the truth of the gospel," and Colossians 1:23, following it, calls it all "the hope of the gospel."

This tremendous panorama is also stressed in Hebrews: "His Son . . . made the worlds . . . upholding all things by the word of His power, . . . He . . . by Himself purged our sins. . . . Whom He hath appointed heir of all things" (Hebrews 1:2, 3).

Finally, there is the witness of the Apostle Peter, in his last chapter: "By the word of God the heavens were of old, and the earth . . . " (II Peter 3:5). Then, " . . . the heavens and the earth, which are now, by the same word are kept in store" (II Peter 3:7). Finally, . . . " we, according to His promise, look for new heavens and a new earth" (II Peter 3:13).

Too Hard or Too Small

Ah Lord *God! behold, Thou hast made the heaven and the earth, by Thy great power and stretched out arm, and there is nothing too hard for Thee* (Jeremiah 32:17).

This mighty declaration of faith in the Creator of heaven and earth was given by Jeremiah in respect to what may have seemed a mundane sort of need—the need of assurance that his real estate investment would be safe, even if he were forced to be away from it for many years. There is nothing too small for the Lord, just as there is nothing too hard for Him, and He delights to "show Himself strong in the behalf of them whose heart is perfect toward Him" (II Chronicles 16:9).

Since God created all things, He certainly can control all things. If a person really believes the very first verse of the Bible—the simple declaration that the entire space/mass/time universe had been called into existence by our omnipotent and eternal God—then he or she will never find it difficult to believe any of the other declarations or promises of His inspired Word.

In response to Jeremiah's great statement of faith, God gave him the assurance he sought: "Behold, I am the Lord, the God of all flesh: Is there any thing too hard for Me?" (v. 27). God, who made the sea, could roll back its waters to enable His people to pass through its very midst unharmed (Exodus 14:29). He who made the earth could cause the earth to cease its rotation, to give His people victory (Joshua 10:12–14). There is nothing too hard for the God of creation!

We can be confident that 20th-century problems are no more difficult for God than those of 600 B.C. May our mighty Creator grant us trusting and obedient hearts, in both the great problems and the small problems of life. In this verse, the Hebrew word for "hard" is the same as for "wonderful" (Psalm 107:8). God delights in transforming the hard things of life into the wonderful works of God!

MAY 17

The Honest Use of Scripture

Making the word of God of none effect through your tradition, which ye have delivered: and many such like things do ye (Mark 7:13).

Jesus uttered these sharp words of rebuke to the scribes and Pharisees, who had encumbered the plain teachings of Scripture with numerous "interpretations" which enabled them to ignore whatever teachings they found inconvenient. The Lord Jesus Himself always took the Scriptures literally and as of divine authority, and so should we.

Furthermore, He taught that every word was true and authoritative: "For verily I say unto You, Till heaven and earth pass, one jot or one tittle shall in no wise pass from the law, till all be fulfilled" (Matthew 5:18). He also said that "the scripture cannot be broken" (John 10:35).

Skeptics may pose certain difficulties in the Bible, evolutionists may ridicule its account of creation, and sinners in general may try to wriggle away from its moral constraints, but the Scripture cannot be broken! Jesus said: "He that rejecteth me, and receiveth not my words, hath one that judgeth him: the word that I have spoken, the same shall judge him in the last day" (John 12:48). He Himself is the living word of God, and we dare not tamper with the written word inspired by the Holy Spirit. Christ, of course, could and did in some cases extend and apply the Old Testament Scriptures, because He Himself was their author, but He never questioned their factuality or literal accuracy, and neither should we.

Nevertheless, many modern "Christian" intellectuals and cultists are following in the example of the Pharisees, rather than that of Christ, "wresting" the Scriptures for their good but "unto their own destruction" (II Peter 3:16). God has spoken plainly in His word. It is our responsibility to believe and do what He says.

A Very Present Help

God is our refuge and strength, a very present help in trouble. Therefore will not we fear, though the earth be removed, and though the mountains be carried into the midst of the sea; Though the waters thereof roar and be troubled, though the mountains shake with the swelling thereof. Selah (Psalm 46:1–3).

The modifier "very," in this verse, is a strong word. God is an intensively present helper in time of trouble, "Let not your heart be troubled, neither let it be afraid" (John 14:27). Those who hold a deistic philosophy argue that God is far away, leaving the earth and its inhabitants to work out their own evolutionary salvation after He first started it going billions of years ago. But they are wrong, for God is right here, right now! "The LORD of hosts is with us" (Psalm 46:11).

There had, indeed, been a time when the earth was removed (literally, "the ground was changed"), and even the mountains had been eroded away and washed into the oceans. The waters swelled higher and the mountains quaked until finally, in the words of the Apostle Peter, "the world that then was, being overflowed with water, perished" (II Peter 3:6).

This was the great Flood in the days of Noah—the greatest "trouble" in the world's history. Even then, God had provided a refuge for His people—the Ark which He instructed Noah to build. When the Flood came, "the LORD shut him in," and throughout the height of the cataclysm, "God remembered Noah, and every living thing" (Genesis 7:16; 8:1).

There are great judgments coming on the earth in future days as well (Psalm 46:6–9), when the earth itself will be melted (literally "dissolved"—see II Peter 3:10).

Again, the Lord's people in that day can still say: "The LORD of hosts is with us; the God of Jacob is our refuge" (Psalm 46:7). From the beginning of creation to the end of the age, God is a very present help to His people.

MAY 19

The Finished Works of God

Thus the heavens and the earth were finished, and all the host of them. And on the seventh day God ended His work which He had made; and He rested on the seventh day from all His work which He had made (Genesis 2:1, 2).

At the end of the six work days of creation week, God rested on the seventh day, blessing and sanctifying it. "In six days the LORD made heaven and earth, the sea, and all that in them is, and rested the seventh day" (Exodus 20:11).

This testimony of a finished creation, with nothing further to be created, completely repudiates the humanistic philosophy of evolution, according to which, the supposed laws of nature are still "creating" new kinds of organisms, as well as new stars and new planets.

But there is also another vital work of God—the work of redemption. As soon as man sinned, God began the long process of preparing the world for the coming of the Savior to pay the price for man's redemption. "When the fulness of the time was come" (Galatians 4:4), God entered the realm of human life, becoming a Man, in order to die for the sins of all men. Finally, as He hung on the cross, having fulfilled every prophecy and endured the full wrath of God against human sin, He shouted the great shout of victory: "It is finished" (John 19:30). As He had once finished the great work of creation, He now had finished the greater work of redemption. The Lord Jesus Christ is both Creator and Redeemer.

What, then, is there left for us to do? Nothing! He has already paid the full price. Just as there is nothing God's finished creation can do to evolve itself higher, so there is nothing God's redeemed creation can do to finish paying the price for its salvation. Both are completed works of God alone.

The only thing we can do is to receive what He has done, with gratitude. We can believe in Him as Creator and Savior. Then, we can love Him and live for Him, forever.

Four Cosmologies

Nevertheless we, according to His promise, look for new heavens and a new earth, wherein dwelleth righteousness (II Peter 3:13).

The *cosmos* consists of "all things"—every system, every structure, every organism, every process, *everything*—in heaven and in Earth. Cosmology is the system and study of the whole cosmos. In his final epistle, the Apostle Peter outlines four different cosmologies. One is false, the other three are each true, but at different times in history.

The false cosmology is that of *evolutionary uniformitarianism,* the doctrine taught by latter-day intellectuals, who will scoff: "Where is the promise of His coming? . . . all things continue as they were from the beginning of the creation" (II Peter 3:3, 4). But this is altogether wrong! The first cosmos—the heavens and the earth which were "of old"—"the world that then was, being overflowed with water, perished" (II Peter 3:6). The primeval cosmos, in which "every thing that He had made . . . was very good" (Genesis 1:31), was destroyed in the waters of the great Flood.

The present cosmos, "the heavens and the earth, which are now . . . are . . . reserved unto fire against the day of judgment and perdition of ungodly men" (II Peter 3:7). This "present evil world" (Galatians 1:4) was to last many a long year, but "the day of the Lord will come . . . in the which the heavens shall pass away with a great noise . . . the earth also and the works that are therein shall be burned up" (II Peter 3:10).

But then, out of the ashes of the old corrupt world, so to speak, God will make a new and incorruptible world. "We, according to His promise, look for new heavens and a new earth, wherein dwelleth righteousness" (II Peter 3:13).

That cosmos will continue forever! "The new heavens and the new earth, which I will make, shall remain before Me, saith the Lord" (Isaiah 66:22).

MAY 21

Creation Evangelism

And many other signs truly did Jesus in the presence of His disciples, which are not written in this book. But these are written, that ye might believe that Jesus is the Christ, the Son of God; and that believing ye might have life through His Name (John 20:30, 31).

According to John's testimony, his purpose in writing his Gospel was that of evangelism, hoping to win those who would read it to saving faith in Jesus Christ as the Son of God. It is thus appropriate that Christians, through the years, have used the Gospel of John, more than any other book of the Bible, in seeking to win people to Christ.

Since John was also inspired by the Holy Spirit in what he wrote, we would be well advised to follow his initial approach in witnessing. With that in mind, note that he began his soul-winning message with *creation!* "In the beginning was the Word, and the Word was with God, and the Word was God. The same was in the beginning with God. All things were made by Him; and without Him was not any thing made that was made" (John 1:1–3).

He then noted that we are in rebellion against Him. "He was in the world, and the world was made by Him, and the world knew Him not. He came unto His own, and His own received Him not" (John 1:10, 11). Next, John stressed the miracle of His incarnation. "And the Word was made flesh, and dwelt among us (and we beheld His glory, the glory as of the only begotten of the Father), full of grace and truth" (John 1:14).

He proceeded then to His substitutionary atonement, "Behold the Lamb of God, which taketh away the sin of the world" (John 1:29). John's inspired approach would surely imply that true faith in Christ must first be based on recognition of Him as Creator and ourselves as sinful rebels against Him, then of His true but perfect humanity, and finally, His work as our sin-bearing personal Savior.

To Every Creature Under Heaven

If ye continue in the faith grounded and settled, and be not moved away from the hope of the gospel, which ye have heard, and which was preached to every creature which is under heaven; whereof I Paul am made a minister (Colossians 1:23).

Before the Lord ascended back to heaven, He commanded His disciples to "preach the Gospel to every creature" (Mark 16:15), and one might receive the impression from the words of our text that this had already been accomplished, just 30 years after the command was given.

Yet, it is hardly plausible to infer from this that Christian missionaries had already reached the entire globe. The problem may be our far-too-limited appreciation of God's witness in the creation. The phrase, "to every creature," in our text, could better be read "in everything created." That is, the Gospel which was now being brought in explicit terms to the Colossians, was consistent with what they already should have known from God's great witness in the very structure and behavior of everything He had created.

This is the testimony of such familiar verses as Psalm 19:1 ("the heavens declare. . . ."), Romans 1:20 ("the invisible things of Him from the creation of the world are clearly seen. . . ."), Acts 14:17 ("He left not Himself without witness"), and Acts 17:28 ("in Him we live, and move, and have our being"). In the verses just preceding our text (Colossians 1:16–22), Paul had defined this universal Gospel as embracing the creation, salvation, and consummation of "*all things*" by Christ (vv. 16, 17, 20). The essence of this truth can be seen (if one's eyes are willing to see it) in "all the world" (v. 6) in the beauty, complexity, unity in diversity, purposefulness, continuance of energy, and process, as found in "every creature which is under heaven." Every aspect of God's creation has been designed to reveal Christ as Maker and Savior.

MAY 23

Process Creation

By the word of the Lord were the heavens made; and all the host of them by the breath of His mouth. . . . For He spake, and it was done; He commanded, and it stood fast (Psalm 33:6, 9).

These striking verses (along with many others in the Scriptures) make it emphatically clear that God's work of creation was not accomplished by "process," but by *fiat!* No time was involved at all, since His Word is of infinite power. "He spake, and it was done."

The great heresy of modern scientism is to try to reduce God to a being of finite abilities, insisting that He must take long ages to accomplish His work, using the slow processes of "Nature" to get it done. In effect, God eventually becomes nothing but Nature, and all systems must then be explained by "natural" processes. This attempt is not science (which means "knowledge" or "truth") but *scientism* (the search for non-supernatural explanations of all things, along with the insistence that one can never find absolute knowledge about anything).

Scientism is so patently false (if God exists at all), that one can only be amazed at the eager readiness of Christian "intellectuals" to compromise with it. Such compromise is especially dangerous when we recognize that the Biblical truth of special, fiat creation is foundational to all the rest of Scripture and the Christian world view.

But creation was not a natural process; it was a supernatural miracle! Were it not so, God Himself becomes redundant, and all such compromises inevitably lead eventually to atheistic or pantheistic apostasy. It did not take months for the water to evolve into wine when Christ spoke His creative Word (John 2:1–11). Neither did it take billions of years for God to bring the mighty universe into being. His Word is a word of omnipotence and order, not randomness and confusion.

Wondrous Things

Open thou mine eyes, that I may behold wondrous things out of Thy law (Psalm 119:18).

Wondrous, indeed, is the marvelous universe God has created. "Hearken unto this," we are challenged, "stand still, and consider the wondrous works of God" (Job 37:14). And as we "consider thy heavens, the work of thy fingers, the moon and the stars, which thou hast ordained" (Psalm 8:3), we can only "stand still" in awe at God's infinite power.

We are even more amazed as we study the intricate complexity of living creatures—especially human beings. "I will praise thee; for I am fearfully and wonderfully made: marvelous are thy works" (Psalm 139:14). God's omniscience is more wondrous than even His omnipotence.

Then there is His miraculous ordering of history for the accomplishment of His purposes. "We will not hide them from their children, shewing to the generation to come the praises of the LORD, and His strength, and His wonderful works that He hath done" (Psalm 78:4).

But even greater than the wondrous world He created or His wondrous works in history are the wonders of God's written Word, for "thou hast magnified thy Word above all Thy Name" (Psalm 138:2).

Note the testimony of the familiar 19th Psalm. "The heavens declare the glory of God; and the firmament sheweth His handiwork." But then: "The law of the LORD is perfect converting the soul" (Psalm 19:1, 7). As far as God's works in history are concerned, God's Word was completed before history began, and will endure after the present world is gone. "For ever, O LORD, thy Word is settled in heaven" (Psalm 119:89). "Heaven and earth shall pass away, but my words shall not pass away" (Matthew 24:35).

There are "wondrous things" without end in "thy law," and we will continue discovering them forever.

MAY 25

The Trinity in Creation

> *In the beginning God created the heaven and the earth. And the earth was without form, and void; and darkness was upon the face of the deep. And the Spirit of God moved upon the face of the waters. And God said, Let there be light: and there was light* (Genesis 1:1–3).

These incomparable words open God's written revelation to man, telling us how our time/space/matter universe came to exist. No other religious writings, ancient or modern, do this. All others begin with the assumption of an eternal, self-existing universe. The truth is, however, that the eternal, self-existing, transcendent, omnipotent Triune *God* simply *called* the universe into being by His Word. "By the Word of the LORD were the heavens made. . . . For He spake, and it was done" (Psalm 33:6, 9).

The Hebrew for "God" is the uni-plural *Elohim,* a plural noun (as noted by the "im" ending), yet normally represented by a singular pronoun "He." This is the first foreshadowing of the marvelous doctrine of the Trinity—only one Creator God, yet functioning as three divine Persons. It is significant that His created universe is actually a tri-universe, with each of its distinct components ("beginning" = time; "heaven" = space; "earth" = matter) comprising and pervading the whole universe. Just as the Father is the source and background of all being, so space is the background of all that happens in the physical universe. Just as the Son manifests and speaks for the Father, so matter manifests and functions in space. Just as the Spirit interprets and energizes the Son and the Father in human experience, so space and matter are interpreted and experienced in phenomena operating in time.

The Father planned the work of creation, the Son did the work ("all things were made by Him"—John 1:3), and the Spirit energized it ("the Spirit of God moved"). The Triune God created and now sustains our tri-universe!

The Days of Yore

For ask now of the days that are past, which were before thee, since the day that God created man upon the earth, and ask from the one side of heaven unto the other, whether there hath been any such thing as this great thing is, or hath been heard like it? (Deuteronomy 4:32).

This challenge was given by Moses to the children of Israel as they were preparing to enter the promised land. It was vital that they cease all complaining, and begin to behave in a manner appropriate to their stature as God's chosen people.

For this they needed to regain a sense of historical perspective, and Moses urged them to study the history of the world since the beginning. Presumably, this would be possible only through studying the book of Genesis, "since the day that God created Adam (same word as 'man') upon the earth."

It is significant that "the days that are past" were implied by Moses to have begun essentially at creation, with no hint of any long geological ages before that. The 25 or more centuries from Adam to Moses had provided enough history to instruct that particular generation about God's plans for the world, and to prepare them for their own key role in their accomplishment, and to appreciate the real meaning of their own lives as they awaited the promised Redeemer who was to come someday with salvation.

Now if the Israelites needed a true historical perspective, we need one today far more. In addition to what they had, we now also have the history of Israel, the first coming of Christ, God's completed revelation, and the Christian dispensation, from which to learn and profit. Our understanding of God and His purposes *should* be far greater than theirs, so we have much greater responsibility. May God help us to study and believe and understand all that has gone before, as recorded in His Word, so that we also can be prepared to fulfill our own role in God's great plan of the ages for eternity.

MAY 27

A Call to Remembrance

> *I have considered the days of old, the years of ancient times. I call to remembrance my song in the night: I commune with mine own heart: and my spirit made diligent search* (Psalm 77:5, 6).

It is so easy to forget. The burdens and pressures of these present times easily drown out the voices of the past.

God, however, remembers. It is good also for us to consider the olden days, not simply in sad nostalgia, but for our guidance in the present. With reference, particularly to those instances which the Lord selected to be recorded in Scripture, "they are written for our admonition" (I Corinthians 10:11). Not only were they written as warnings, but also for comfort. "For whatsoever things were written aforetime were written for our learning, that we through patience and comfort of the scriptures might have hope" (Romans 15:4).

To the Christian, an annual Memorial Day should have still an additional special meaning. Not only do we desire to honor those who died for their country (and many of us do, indeed, recall with deep love and respect close friends and family members in this honored company), but also to remember those who lived for the Lord, and whose lives and ministries have helped guide us to the light for our own difficult pathways today. Parents and teachers, authors and preachers, counselors and friends—many of whom have already gone to be with the Lord—deserve to be remembered and honored, for it will make that great future Homecoming Day all the more blessed when we are all together, with the Lord, when He returns (I Thessalonians 4:17).

Most importantly of all, of course, we must remember the Lord, not annually, but always. "I will remember the works of the LORD: surely I will remember thy wonders of old. I will meditate also of all thy work, and talk of thy doings" (Psalm 77:11, 12).

The Christian Rest

There remaineth therefore a rest to the people of God. For he that is entered into his rest, he also hath ceased from his own works, as God did from His (Hebrews 4:9, 10).

This is an important New Testament affirmation that God's work of creation was "finished from the foundation of the world" (Hebrews 4:3). The reference is to Genesis 2:1–3, where the writer has told us that God had "rested from all His work which God created and made," thus completely denying the contention of theistic evolutionists that the processes of "creation" (that is, evolution) are still going on.

In addition, it makes a significant comparison between the believer's rest and God's rest. The word "rest" here is not the usual word for "rest," and is used only this once in the New Testament. It means, literally, "sabbath rest," or "keeping of the Sabbath." In the context of Chapters 2 and 3 of Hebrews, the concept of rest is being expounded with several meanings. The original warning was in Psalm 95:11, where it referred both to the Israelites entering into the promised land under Joshua and to God's own rest after His work of creation. Psalm 95 is repeatedly quoted in Hebrews, where other meanings are also implied: the keeping of a weekly Sabbath in commemoration of God's rest after creation, the promised future rest to the world and its believing inhabitants—possibly in the millennium but certainly in the new earth, and the believer's present spiritual rest after he puts his faith in Christ, no longer trusting in his works for salvation.

With such a rich investiture of meaning in the fact of God's past rest and the promise of our future rest, it is appropriate that there should be a perpetual weekly commemoration and expression of faith in that rest in every generation, until its ultimate fulfillment in the eternal rest in the New Jerusalem.

In the meantime, we are urged to "*labor*" to "enter into that rest" (Hebrews 4:11).

MAY 29

Good Courage

Be strong and of a good courage: for unto the people shalt thou divide for an inheritance the land, which I sware unto their fathers to give them (Joshua 1:6).

This admonition to be strong and of "good courage" (Hebrew *amats*) is given some ten times in the Old Testament, plus another nine times using a different word (*chasaq*).

The first occurrence of *amats* is in Deuteronomy 3:28 where it is translated "strengthen": "But charge Joshua, and encourage him, and strengthen him: for he shall go over before his people, and he shall cause them to inherit the land which thou shalt see."

Christians today surely need good courage to face a dangerous world, with all its temptations and intimidations, but nothing today could compare to the challenge facing Joshua. Trying to lead a nondescript multitude of "stiffnecked" desert nomads into a land of giants and walled cities would surely require courage beyond anything we could imagine today.

But Joshua had access to invincible resources, and so do we. "Be strong and of a good courage," God told him: "Be not afraid, neither be thou dismayed: for the Lord thy God is with thee whithersoever thou goest" (Joshua 1:9).

Giants and walled cities are no match for the children of God when He goes with them, for "if God be for us, who can be against us?" (Romans 8:31).

God *did* go with Joshua, and the Israelites defeated the giants, destroyed the walled cities, and took the land. And we have the same promise today, for "He hath said, I will never leave thee, nor forsake thee. So that we may boldly say, The Lord is my helper, and I will not fear what man shall do unto me" (Hebrews 13:5, 6). Courage is really another name for faith, and what God "hath promised, He is able also to perform" (Romans 4:21).

Pilgrims on the Earth

These all died in faith, not having received the promises, but having seen them afar off, and were persuaded of them, and embraced them, and confessed that they were strangers and pilgrims on the earth. For they that say such things declare plainly that they seek a country (Hebrews 11:13, 14).

This is the heart-touching testimony of the great "heroes of faith" of Hebrews 11. The experiences of all these godly men and women of the past are outlined as an example for us, as we pass through the years of our own "pilgrimage" on the earth. "Wherefore seeing we also are compassed about with so great a cloud of witnesses, let us . . . run with patience the race that is set before us" (Hebrews 12:1).

There is another group who also gave their own lives, and the testimony of our text seems appropriate for them as well. Once a year, on Memorial Day, we remember, in a special way, those who died in defense of our own country. They had seen its promises and embraced them, and were willing to die for them. Many of those were also Christians, and they loved their country, especially because of its unique Christian heritage and its freedom to practice and propagate their faith.

One of these was this writer's younger brother, who died in the jungles of Burma, as a young pilot flying the famous "Hump" into China during World War II. Before his death, he had given a faithful Christian witness to many of his buddies, as he ran his own race with patience. Many readers of these lines no doubt remember their own friends and loved ones, who likewise offered up their lives for God and country.

As we remember them, we surely must remember, with even greater love and appreciation, the one who made the greatest sacrifice of all, "looking unto Jesus the author and finisher of our faith; who for the joy that was set before Him endured the cross, despising the shame, and is set down at the right hand of the throne of God" (Hebrews 12:2).

Good, Very Good, and Not Good

And God saw every thing that He had made, and, behold, it was very good (Genesis 1:31).

Six times during creation week, God saw His handiwork and pronounced it "good" (Genesis 1:4, 10, 12, 18, 21, 25). Finally, when it was all finished, He surveyed all He had just completed, and judged it all to be *very* good!

That is the way with God. And if He can make a flawless universe, we can be confident He knows what He is doing with us. "For we are His workmanship, created in Christ Jesus unto good works, which God hath before ordained, that we should walk in them" (Ephesians 2:10). What God does must be, by definition, *good!* We can affirm, therefore, with confidence (even though it must often be by faith rather than sight) that "all things work together for good to them that love God, to them who are the called according to His purpose" (Romans 8:28).

There is, of course, an important scientific principle also established by this verse: Whenever we see anything in the world which is *not* good (e.g., sin, suffering, death), we can know that such things constitute an intrusion into God's perfect creation. They were not "created" as a part of the primeval creation, nor will God allow them to continue their intrusion forever. They all eventually must be eliminated when God makes His "new earth." In the meantime, this principle tells us that the great sedimentary rocks of the earth's crust, containing as they do the fossilized remains of billions of dead animals, plants, and people, must have all been formed sometime *after* the end of creation week. At least most of them must therefore have been formed at the time of the great Flood (Genesis 6–9) when "the world that then was, being overflowed with water, perished" (II Peter 3:6).

Because of sin, the *present* world is groaning in pain (Romans 8:22), but the *first* world was all "very good."

Judgment

For, lo, He that formeth the mountains, and createth the wind, and declareth unto man what is His thought, that maketh the morning darkness, and treadeth upon the high places of the earth, The Lord, the God of hosts, is His name (Amos 4:13).

This awesome ascription of judgmental power to God is in the midst of a dire prophecy by Amos to the ten-tribe northern kingdom of Israel. He had reminded them of earlier judgments, including even that of Sodom and Gomorrah, concluding with the fearsome warning: "prepare to meet thy God, O Israel" (Amos 4:12).

Then, in our text verse, He seems to carry them still further back in time, to remind them of an even greater destruction. The great winds of the earth, like its rains, first blew over its surfaces at the time of the mighty Deluge (Genesis 8:1), and the present mountains of the earth likewise rose out of the churning waters of the Flood (Psalm 104:6–9). It was at the time of the Flood that dark clouds first obscured the sunlight, which before had perpetually shown through the pre-Flood "waters which were above the firmament" (Genesis 1:7), which had then condensed and fallen to the earth in great torrents from "the windows of heaven" (Genesis 7:11).

This awful judgment had come because the antediluvians, like the Israelites, had rejected their Creator and gone after other gods (Genesis 6:5). As if to confirm that he was, indeed, referring to the great Deluge, Amos, a few verses later, exhorted the Israelites to "Seek Him . . . that calleth for the waters of the sea, and poureth them out upon the face of the earth" (Amos 5:8).

It is dangerous and foolish for any nation or any person to question the true God of creation. He made all things, He knows all things, and He judges all things. "The Lord, the God of Hosts, is His name."

Conformed to His Image

And as we have borne the image of the earthy, we shall also bear the image of the heavenly (I Corinthians 15:49).

One of the most amazing promises of the Word of God is that those who "love God" and are "the called according to His purpose" are those whom "He also did predestinate to be conformed to the image of His Son" (Romans 8:28, 29).

Adam and Eve were created in His image physically in the beginning. "So God created man in His own image . . . male and female created He them" (Genesis 1:27). Presumably this means they were created in the physical form that God knew He would assume when, in the fulness of time, He would become man Himself, in the person of His Son, Jesus Christ.

That image was marred when Adam (and, in Adam, all men) sinned. Nevertheless, it can be restored spiritually when we receive Christ and "have put on the new man, which is renewed in knowledge after the image of Him that created him" (Colossians 3:10).

But this is not all. As our text reveals, we who have been made in God's earthly image (both physically and spiritually) will also, in due time, receive His heavenly image. This will take place when Christ returns. At that time, "We shall all be changed, In a moment, in the twinkling of an eye . . . and the dead shall be raised incorruptible, and we shall be changed" (I Corinthians 15:51, 52).

In what way shall we be changed? The Lord Jesus Himself "shall change our vile body, that it may be fashioned like unto His glorious body" (Philippians 3:21). His body, after His resurrection, was still His physical body, but it was no longer subject to pain or death, and was able to pass through walls and to speed rapidly from earth to heaven. That is "the image of the heavenly" to which we shall be conformed some day soon! For "we know that, when He shall appear, we shall be like Him; for we shall see Him as He is" (I John 3:2).

The Arm of the Lord

The L*ORD hath made bare His holy arm in the eyes of all the nations; and all the ends of the earth shall see the salvation of our God* (Isaiah 52:10).

The human arm is often used in the Bible to symbolize spiritual strength or power. The word is first used in Jacob's dying prophecy concerning His beloved son Joseph: "But his bow abode in strength, and the arms of his hands were made strong by the hands of the mighty God of Jacob" (Genesis 49:24).

The source of all true strength is in the mighty God, so it is not surprising to find at least 40 Biblical references to the Lord's powerful "arm" or "arms." One of the most striking is our text, promising that when God "bares His arm" for His great work of delivering the lost world from its bondage to Satan and sin and death, then the whole world will see His salvation (literally, His "Jesus").

In a real sense, therefore, "the arm of the LORD" is none other than Jesus Christ. When He came into His world, however, the world refused Him. Just a few verses later, introducing the incomparable 53rd chapter of Isaiah, appears this tragic question: "Who hath believed our report? and to whom is the arm of the LORD revealed?" (Isaiah 53:1).

Nevertheless, some believed, and the first was His own mother. In her "Magnificat," spoken in faith before Jesus was born, Mary said: "God my Saviour . . . hath showed strength with His arm" (Luke 1:47, 51). This confession of faith is the first use of "arm" in the New Testament and again refers to the saving arm of God, the Lord Jesus Christ.

Finally, His arm is not only mighty to save, but also secure to hold: "His arm shall rule for Him . . . He shall feed His flock like a shepherd: He shall gather the lambs with His arm, and carry them in His bosom" (Isaiah 40:10, 11).

JUNE 4

Creator of Wind and Calm

But the men marvelled, saying, What manner of man is this, that even the winds and the sea obey Him! (Matthew 8:27).

Waves large enough to cover a ship on a small lake in a short time could only have been generated by a tremendously powerful wind, and such a wind would require a mighty complex of forces in the atmosphere, triggered by the sun itself. Furthermore, even when the wind dies down, the waves will continue for a time. But suddenly both ceased at once, and "there was a great calm" (v. 26). No known natural force could have produced such a phenomenon, yet there it was.

A man had simply spoken a word: "Peace, be still" (Mark 4:39). How could He control the sea? "The sea is His, and He made it" (Psalm 95:5)—that is how! And what about the stormy wind? God Himself "bringeth the wind out of His treasuries" (Psalm 135:7), even when need be, the "stormy wind fulfilling His Word" (Psalm 148:8).

God can use the storms of life to cause us to call on Him for deliverance. "For He commandeth, and raiseth the stormy wind, which lifteth up the waves thereof. . . . Then they cry unto the LORD in their trouble, and He bringeth them out of their distresses. He maketh the storm a calm, so that the waves thereof are still (Psalm 107:25, 28, 29).

What manner of man can do such things? Only the God/Man, Jesus Christ. He is the omnipotent, living Word, the "Creator of the ends of the earth" (Isaiah 40:28). It is He by whom "were all things created," and it therefore follows that "by Him all things consist" (Colossians 1:16, 17). "For in Him we live, and move, and have our being" (Acts 17:28).

If this eternal Word (who was "made flesh" and was now sleeping in a small boat on the Sea of Galilee) could speak the mighty cosmos into being, it is no great thing for Him to speak peace to a stormy sea or to bring rest to His loved ones in their times of turmoil and fear.

Joshua's Long Day

And there was no day like that before it or after it, that the Lord *hearkened unto the voice of a man: For the* Lord *fought for Israel* (Joshua 10:14).

One of the most amazing events of history occurred when "the Lord fought for Israel" as He had promised long before, to enable them to conquer and occupy the promised land. God helped Israel even to the extent that, on one occasion, "the sun stood still in the midst of heaven, and hasted not to go down about a whole day" (Joshua 10:13).

Some quibble about the language employed, suggesting that Joshua thought the sun "moves" instead of the earth. The fact is, the motion of any heavenly body must be given in terms of *relative motion* (since all objects in the universe are moving in some way). Scientists normally *assume* the fixed point of zero motion to be the one which makes their equations most convenient to use, and this usually is the earth's surface at the location of the observer. Joshua's language was quite scientific!

Furthermore, many scholars have documented numerous traditions of a "long day" (or "long night," in the western hemisphere), about the time of Joshua. The Biblical story is well supported as a real fact of history. There *was* a long day!

Such an event required the direct intervention of the Creator Himself. He who had started the earth rotating in the first place, when He separated day and night (Genesis 1:3–5), now slowed it down again until it stopped, and the daylight continued until Joshua could rout the Amorites.

God may not usually answer prayers and fulfill promises by such a mighty miracle as this, but He *does* answer prayer and keep His Word, and this unique event shows He is willing and able to do whatever is needed to accomplish His will. "The sun and moon stood still in their habitation: At the light of Thine arrows they went, . . . Thou wentest forth for the salvation of Thy people" (Habakkuk 3:11, 13).

JUNE 6

Those Who Destroy the Earth

And the nations were angry, and thy wrath is come, and the time of the dead, that they should be judged, and that thou shouldest give reward unto thy servants the prophets, and to the saints, and them that fear thy name, small and great; and shouldest destroy them which destroy the earth (Revelation 11:18).

In the coming day of God's wrath, one group singled out for destruction is "them which destroy the earth." When God finished creating, Adam and his descendants were told to "replenish the earth, and subdue it: and have dominion over . . . every living thing that moveth upon the earth" (Genesis 1:28). But "dominion" did not mean "destruction," and "subduing the earth" did not mean spoiling it.

In these days, however, men are indeed in the process of destroying the earth and its inhabitants. Note the following partial list of global problems, all of which have resulted from human rebellion against the will of God: (1) global water pollution; (2) global air pollution; (3) global spread of AIDS and other deadly pestilences; (4) global spread of nuclear and other sophisticated weapons of mass slaughter; (5) global erosion of essential layers of topsoil; (6) destruction of vital rain forests and other important ecological communities; (7) global spread of addictive drugs; (8) legalization of abortion and homosexuality; (9) chemical pollution of lands and food chains with toxic wastes, nuclear wastes, insecticides, and other noxious substances; and, (10) animal and plant extinctions, averaging over one per day throughout recorded history.

Any one of these, left unrestrained, could eventually destroy all life on earth, and God has warned of coming judgment. At the same time, however, the promise is that "the kingdoms of this world are become the kingdoms of our Lord, and of His Christ; and He shall reign for ever and ever" (Revelation 11:15).

A Time to Die

Be not over much wicked, neither be thou foolish: why shouldest thou die before thy time? (Ecclesiastes 7:17).

In the mysteries of God's eternal counsels, He has apparently established a set span of human life on earth for each soul created by Him. There is "a time to be born, and a time to die" (Ecclesiastes 3:2). Why some die in infancy, or even before birth, and some die in old age is not for us to understand now (I Corinthians 13:12).

It is wonderful to know that our times are in His hand, from conception, to death, and into eternity. The first mention of "time" in the Bible is when God promised to send Isaac to Abraham and Sarah, even before he was conceived: "I will certainly return unto thee according to the time of life; and, lo, Sarah thy wife shall have a son. . . . At the time appointed I will return unto thee, according to the time of life, and Sarah shall have a son" (Genesis 18:10, 14). Then, later, "Sarah conceived, and bare Abraham a son in his old age, at the set time of which God had spoken to him" (Genesis 21:2). The "time of life" was *God's* "set time," not Abraham's.

And so it is with the time of death. As long as sin is in the world, death must be in the world, for all have sinned (Romans 5:12). Nevertheless, to a Christian, the time of death is only an entrance to a better life: "For to me to live is Christ, and to die is gain" (Philippians 1:21). "We are confident . . . willing rather to be absent from the body, and to be present with the Lord" (II Corinthians 5:8). "A good name is better than precious ointment; and the day of death than the day of one's birth" (Ecclesiastes 7:1).

However, the "time to die," like the time of life, is in God's hands, not ours. Life is a precious gift of God, to be carefully nourished and preserved, insofar as we can do so within His revealed will. But when His time for death does arrive, that also—in His hand—is good.

JUNE 8

God in the Garden

And the LORD God planted a garden eastward in Eden; and there He put the man whom He had formed (Genesis 2:8).

This was the world's first garden, and it must have been a beautiful garden, for God had planted it Himself. Every tree was "pleasant to the sight"; there was a lovely river "to water the garden" (Genesis 2:9, 10), and God was there.

Then one day God was "walking in the garden," only to find that "Adam and his wife hid themselves from the presence of the LORD God amongst the trees of the garden" (Genesis 3:8). Sin had entered, and Adam and Eve had to be cast out, leaving God alone in the garden (Genesis 3:23).

Many years later, God entered another garden with his loved ones. "He went forth with His disciples over the brook Cedron, where was a garden, into the which He entered, and His disciples" (John 18:1). There in the garden of Gethsemane, the disciples soon fell asleep, once again leaving Him alone in the garden, "withdrawn from them about a stone's cast" (Luke 22:41). There He "offered up prayers and supplications with strong crying and tears" (Hebrews 5:7) as He faced the death that He had pronounced on His very first loved ones long before in that first garden.

There was yet another garden where He must be alone. "In the place where He was crucified there was a garden: and in the garden a new sepulchre, wherein was never man yet laid. There laid they Jesus . . . " (John 19:41, 42).

God had walked alone in the first garden, seeking His own. He knelt alone in the second garden, praying for His own. He was buried alone in the third garden, dying for His own. Therefore, in the new "Paradise of God," where the pure river flows and the tree of life grows, eternally, "His servants shall serve Him" and reign with Him "for ever and ever" (Revelation 2:7; 22:1–3, 5).

Praise from the Creation

Let the heaven and earth praise Him, the seas, and every thing that moveth therein (Psalm 69:34).

We may not yet understand the full purpose of God in creation, but at least one aspect of that purpose is that all things created should somehow praise their Creator. This theme occurs often in Scripture, especially in the psalms. For example, in addition to the exhortation in our text:

"The heavens declare the glory of God; and the firmament sheweth His handywork" (Psalm 19:1).

"Let the heavens rejoice, and let the earth be glad; let the sea roar, and the fullness thereof. Let the field be joyful, and all that is therein: then shall all the trees of the wood rejoice before the LORD: for He cometh . . . " (Psalm 96:11–13).

"All thy works shall praise thee, O LORD; and thy saints shall bless thee" (Psalm 145:10).

"Praise ye Him, sun and moon: praise Him, all ye stars of light. Praise Him, ye heavens of heavens, and ye waters that be above the heavens. . . . Praise the LORD from the earth, ye dragons, and all deeps: Fire and hail; snow, and vapors; stormy wind fulfilling His Word: Mountains, and all hills; fruitful trees, and all cedars: Beasts, and all cattle; creeping things, and flying fowl" (Psalm 148:3, 4, 7–10).

The Lord Jesus said that if men should refuse to praise Him and "should hold their peace, the stones would immediately cry out" (Luke 19:40). Yet, even though the whole creation—in its beauty, complexity, and providential orderliness—gives continual praise to its Creator, men perversely have "worshipped and served the creature [or better, the creation] more than the Creator, who is blessed for ever" (Romans 1:25).

How poignant, therefore, is the final verse of the book of Psalms: "Let every thing that hath breath praise the LORD. Praise ye the Lord" (Psalm 150:6).

JUNE 10

My King of Old

The day is Thine, the night also is Thine: Thou hast prepared the light and the sun. Thou hast set all the borders of the earth: Thou hast made summer and winter (Psalm 74:16, 17).

The 74th Psalm is a sad lamentation over the apparent triumph of the enemies of God, but its central verse is a beautiful statement of faith: "For God is my King of old, working salvation in the midst of the earth" (Psalm 74:12). Then, in support of his faith, the psalmist remembers the mighty creative acts of God in ancient times, giving assurance that He could indeed work salvation in these present times.

Those who believe that man is the measure of all things, sufficient unto himself, ignore how dependent all people are on God's provisions. The very rotation of the earth, with its cycle of day and night, has set the basic rhythm of biological life, and it was God—not man—who "divided the light from the darkness" (Genesis 1:4).

There is even the testimony in Genesis that God "prepared the light" before He prepared the sun (Genesis 1:3, 14), thus rebuking all those who later would worship the sun as the source of the earth and life.

God also "set all the borders [or 'boundaries'] of the earth." This refers both to the emergence of the continental land masses after the Flood, and then also to the enforced scattering of the peoples from Babel into all the world, when He "determined the times before appointed, and the bounds of their habitation" (Acts 17:26).

He has even made "summer and winter, and day and night [that] shall not cease" (Genesis 8:22).

God did all this—not man! Evolutionary humanism is futile foolishness, and one day soon God will answer the cry of the psalmist: "Arise, O God, plead thine own cause: remember how the foolish man reproacheth thee daily" (Psalm 74:22).

Established Forever

Who laid the foundations of the earth, that it should not be removed for ever (Psalm 104:5).

Secular astronomers and geologists have become increasingly concerned that the earth might be shattered some day by collision with a swarm of asteroids, or even with a star. Apart from this, they say, the sun is going to burn out (or maybe explode!), and this would also terminate the earth. Possibly some future nuclear war will set off a chain reaction which will disintegrate the earth.

We can allay their fears. God has assured us that both the heavens and the earth will abide forever. He is the Creator, and, being omniscient, He does not make mistakes.

Note a few of the verses which verify this, in addition to our text: "Thy faithfulness is unto all generations: thou hast established the earth, and it abideth" (Psalm 119:90).

"Praise ye Him, sun and moon: . . . all ye stars of light. . . . For He commanded, and they were created. He hath also stablished them for ever and ever" (Psalm 148:3, 5, 6).

"[David's] seed shall endure for ever, and his throne as the sun before me. It shall be established for ever as the moon, and as a faithful witness in heaven" (Psalm 89:36, 37).

"They that be wise shall shine as the brightness of the firmament; and they that turn many to righteousness as the stars for ever and ever" (Daniel 12:3).

The earth will *not* last for ever in its present form, of course, for it is under God's curse because of man's sin. In their present form, the earth and the heavens are "passing away," Jesus said (Matthew 24:35), and one day the very "elements shall melt" and the earth "shall be burned up" (II Peter 3:10). But then, "according to His promise," God will create "new heavens and a new earth, wherein dwelleth righteousness" (II Peter 3:13), and then it "shall remain before me, saith the LORD" (Isaiah 66:22).

JUNE 12

Instant Creation

Mine hand also hath laid the foundation of the earth, and my right hand hath spanned the heavens: when I call unto them, they stand up together (Isaiah 48:13).

This is one of many passages in Scripture which not only tells us that God is Creator of both heaven and earth, but also that He created them instantaneously. Creation is not a "process," but a miraculous event! With a wave of the hand, so to speak, God simply called them into being.

This is also the testimony of the incomparable account of creation in Genesis. "In the beginning God created the heaven and the earth," (Genesis 1:1). This primeval testimony does not say: "From the beginning, God has been creating heaven and earth" as theistic evolutionists would say. Creation of all things was an event completed in the past.

The divinely inspired psalmist agrees: "By the Word of the LORD were the heavens made; and all the host of them by the breath of His mouth. . . . For He spake, and it was done; He commanded, and it stood fast" (Psalm 33:6, 9). "For He commanded, and they were created. He hath also stablished them for ever and ever" (Psalm 148:5, 6).

Furthermore, according to our text, when God spoke into existence the heavens and the earth, they both proceeded to "stand up together!" He did not create the heavens 15 billion years ago, then the earth only five billion years ago, as some creationists allege. They stood up together! "In six days the LORD made heaven and earth, the sea, and all that in them is" (Exodus 20:11).

It is important to recognize the recent creation of all things, not only because God said so, but also because the multi-billion-year framework of cosmic evolution, pushing God as far away and long ago as possible, is merely the modern pseudo-scientific way of getting rid of Him altogether! Christians should not compromise with such a system!

Since the World Began

As He spake by the mouth of His holy prophets, which have been since the world began (Luke 1:70).

According to the theory of evolution, as taught in most schools and colleges today, the world began about 18 billion years ago in a "big bang," when the cosmos evolved into existence out of nothing. The sun and planets evolved out of cosmic dust about five billion years ago, life evolved from chemicals about four billion years ago, and human life, perhaps a million years ago.

But this is not what God's Word says! According to the priest Zacharias, as in our text, God has been speaking through His prophets ever since the world began—not beginning 18 billion years *after* it began.

Similarly, Peter, in his temple sermon, preached that God had promised someday to restore all things, "which God hath spoken by the mouth of all His holy prophets since the world began" (Acts 3:21). The restoration of all things obviously was meant to refer to conditions in Eden, not to the primeval cosmic dust cloud of the evolutionists.

The Lord Jesus Christ also taught that man has been here since the world began. Referring to the creation of Adam and Eve, and quoting Genesis 1:27, He said: "But from the beginning of the creation God made them male and female" (Mark 10:6).

Adam and Eve were not created 18 billion years after the beginning of the creation, but just six days after the beginning in a "very good" world.

It is dangerously close to mocking God for modern Christian teachers to urge people to accept the Big Bang theory of cosmic evolution and the geologic ages' framework of organic evolution. Men and women were given dominion over the earth when the world first began, and God has been promising His coming Redeemer through His prophets ever since, just as the Bible says.

JUNE 14

The Christian Banner

He brought me to the banqueting house, and His banner over me was love (Song of Solomon 2:4).

Americans honor their nation's flag (or at least many do!), especially on Flag Day, for the "red, white, and blue" has symbolized the dedication of our nation to liberty and justice for all—especially religious liberty and true legal justice. These concepts are being undermined today, but our nation still has the fullest measure of freedom and equity of any nation on earth. God has been gracious to us, largely because of the faith of our founding fathers.

There is another flag that we also honor. The Christian banner, unfurled in our hearts instead of on a flagpole, symbolizes the love of Christ which accompanies God's perfect justice and gift of freedom. In the beautiful imagery of Solomon's Song, the heavenly bridegroom shares His banquet of blessing with those who constitute His bride, all united together under His banner (Hebrew, *degel*) of love.

Yet how can this be—that God's justice, demanding judgment on our sins, can be sublimated by His love into forgiveness and freedom? There is another word commonly translated "banner" (Hebrew, *nee*), meaning essentially the same. However, in its first use (and, therefore, definitive occurrence), it is translated "pole." And the LORD said unto Moses, Make thee a fiery serpent, and set it upon a pole: and it shall come to pass, that every one that is bitten, when he looketh upon it, shall live" (Numbers 21:8). The flag, in this case, is the pole with the impaled serpent, symbolizing sin judged by death. And here is how love overcomes sin, satisfies justice, and brings liberty! Jesus said: "As Moses lifted up the serpent in the wilderness, even so must the Son of man be lifted up. . . . For God so loved the world, that He gave His only begotten Son, that whosoever believeth in Him should not perish, but have everlasting life" (John 3:14, 16).

The Patriarchs

And He gave him the covenant of circumcision: and so Abraham begat Isaac, and circumcised him the eighth day; and Isaac begat Jacob; and Jacob begat the twelve patriarchs (Acts 7:8).

The word "patriarch" comes directly from the Greek and means "first father." Thus the patriarchs begotten by Jacob were the first fathers of the twelve tribes of Israel.

The Genesis patriarchs are types of all fathers. Adam was *the* patriarch of the human family. Through his sin, death came into the world, and death was first mentioned when God warned Adam he would die (Genesis 2:17).

But if Adam is the *dying father,* Noah can be called the *righteous father*. The word "just" (or "righteous") is first used where it says "Noah found grace in the eyes of the LORD" (first mention of "grace"), and then "Noah was a just man" (Genesis 6:8, 9).

Abraham is the *believing father,* for "he believed in the LORD; and He counted it to him for righteousness" (Genesis 15:6). This is the first mention of "believe." Abraham is thus a type of all who are justified by faith. The first mention of sowing (symbolic of witnessing) is with Isaac, the *sowing father*. "Isaac sowed in that land, and received in the same year an hundredfold: and the LORD blessed him" (Genesis 26:12; compare with Matthew 13:23).

Jacob was named Israel because "as a prince hast thou power with God and with men, and hast prevailed" (Genesis 32:28). A single Hebrew word, only used here, is translated "power as a prince." Jacob, able to prevail in prayer with the angel of the Lord, is the *powerful father*.

These are the honored patriarchs "of whom as concerning the flesh Christ came" (Romans 9:5). May all who are fathers today, like they, be believing, righteous, sowing fathers, powerful with God and men.

Many Books

And further, by these, my son, be admonished: of making many books there is no end; and much study is a weariness of the flesh (Ecclesiastes 12:12).

It seems amazing, at first, that we should be reading a complaint from almost 3,000 years ago that too many books were already being published!

The greatest book, of course, is the collection of 66 books known as the Bible—that is, the Book (which is the meaning of "Bible"). This Book has been "for ever . . . settled in heaven" and "endureth for ever" (Psalm 119:89, 160).

The first mention of "book" in the Bible is found in Genesis 5:1, "This is the book of the generations of Adam." Similarly, the first mention of "book" in the New Testament is Matthew 1:1, "The book of the generation of Jesus Christ." These "books" are now incorporated into the Book and, in a striking way, emphasize the continuity of Old and New Testaments: the one dealing with the first Adam; the other with the last Adam.

The final mentions of "book" also are very important, again dealing not with books that are temporal, but with books that are eternal. In the Old Testament, we have the beautiful promise of Malachi 3:16: "Then they that feared the LORD spake often one to another: and the LORD hearkened, and heard it, and a book of remembrance was written before Him for them that feared the LORD, and that thought upon His name."

The final mention of "book" in the Bible, on the other hand, is a sober warning not to tamper with the Book. "If any man shall take away from the words of the book of this prophecy, God shall take away his part out of the book of life, and out of the holy city, and from the things which are written in this book" (Revelation 22:19). Let us honor it, guard it, believe it, and follow it.

The Peace of Thy Children

And all thy children shall be taught of the LORD*; and great shall be the peace of thy children* (Isaiah 54:13).

This prophetic verse has its primary fulfillment still in the future. Nevertheless, it states a basic principle which is always valid, and which is especially relevant on Father's Day. The greatest honor that children can bestow on a father is a solid Christian character of their own, but that must first be his own gift to them. Before sons and daughters can experience real peace of soul, they must first be taught of the Lord themselves, and the heavenly Father has delegated this responsibility first of all to human fathers.

The classic example is Abraham, "the father of all them that believe" (Romans 4:11). God's testimony concerning Abraham was this: "For I know him, that he will command his children and his household after him, and they shall keep the way of the LORD, to do justice and judgment" (Genesis 18:19). This is the first reference in Scripture to the training of children and it is significant that it stresses paternal instruction in the things of God. Furthermore, the instruction should be diligent and continual: "When thou sittest in thine house, and when thou walkest by the way, and when thou liest down, and when thou risest up" (Deuteronomy 6:7).

The classic New Testament teaching on child training has the same message: "Ye fathers, provoke not your children to wrath: but bring them up in the nurture and admonition of the Lord" (Ephesians 6:4).

Not wrath, but peace, as our text suggests. Great shall be the peace of our children, when they know the Lord and keep His ways. Great, also, is the joy of a godly father when he can see the blessing of the Lord on his children, and then on his grandchildren. "Children's children are the crown of old men; and the glory of children are their fathers" (Proverbs 17:6).

JUNE 18

The Unperfect Substance

Thine eyes did see my substance, yet being unperfect; and in thy book all my members were written, which in continuance were fashioned, when as yet there was none of them (Psalm 139:16).

This is an amazing verse, testifying as it does to the omniscient foreplanning of our Creator for each human being. Each person has been separately planned by God before he or she was ever conceived; His eyes oversaw our "unperfect (not imperfect, but unfinished) substance"—that is, literally, our embryo—throughout its entire development. Not only all its "members," but also all its "days" (the literal implication of "in continuance") had been "written" in God's book long ago.

While modern evolutionists argue that a "fetus" is not yet a real person, and so may be casually aborted if the mother so chooses, both the Bible and science show that a growing child in the womb is a true human being. Instruments called fetoscopes have been able to trace every stage of embryonic development, showing that each is distinctively human, never passing through any non-human evolutionary stages, such as the evolutionists' theory of "recapitulation" would imply.

Not much is known about how a baby receives its soul, but the baby is surely an eternal human being from the moment of conception, with all its future days already well known in the mind of God, "when as yet there was none of them," as our text points out.

But that is not all. All those who are saved (or, like the innocents who die before birth, "safe" in Christ) and whose names, therefore, are "written in the book of life of the Lamb slain from the foundation of the world" (Revelation 13:8), are also predestined "to be conformed to the image of His Son" in the ages to come (Romans 8:29).

Children in Heaven

And [David] said, While the child was yet alive, I fasted and wept: for I said, Who can tell whether God will be gracious to me, that the child may live? But now he is dead, wherefore should I fast? Can I bring him back again? I shall go to him, but he shall not return to me (II Samuel 12:22, 23).

The death of a loved one is always a time of great sorrow, but the death of a beloved child is perhaps the keenest sorrow of all. Nevertheless, for the Christian believer, we "sorrow not, even as others which have no hope" (I Thessalonians 4:13).

Our text verse makes it clear that, when a child dies (even one born of a sinful relationship such as this child of David and Bathsheba), that child goes to be with the Lord in heaven. Jesus said: "Suffer little children, and forbid them not, to come unto me: for of such is the kingdom of heaven" (Matthew 19:14).

Heaven is thus a place where there are many "little children." Their inherited sin-nature never yet has generated acts of willful sin, and their maker is Himself "the Lamb of God, which taketh away the sin of the world" (John 1:29), so they are safe in Him. Although there are few specific Scriptures on this subject, what we do know, both from the love of God and the Word of God, suggests that the souls of all little children are with the Lord in heaven, not only those from loving Christian homes, but also those who died in early childhood (and even before birth) from every time and place since the world began. There they, along with all those who were saved by personal faith in Christ and are now awaiting the resurrection, will receive new bodies when Christ returns to Earth. The old and lame will be young and strong again, and the children will grow to perfect maturity, for all will become "like Him" (I John 3:2). "God shall wipe away all tears" (Revelation 21:4), and all will say: "As for God, His way is perfect" (Psalm 18:30).

JUNE 20

Creation in Praise of God

For ye shall go out with joy, and be led forth with peace: the mountains and the hills shall break forth before you into singing, and all the trees of the field shall clap their hands (Isaiah 55:12).

Every now and again, the Biblical writers were so lifted up in spirit as they contemplated the glory of God and His great works of creation and redemption that they could sense the very creation itself singing out in happy praises. For example, note the following verses, among many others. "The heavens declare the glory of God" (Psalm 19:1) is one of the most familiar of these divinely inspired figures of speech, but there are many others. "Make a joyful noise unto the LORD, all the earth: . . . Let the sea roar, and the fulness thereof. . . . Let the floods clap their hands: let the hills be joyful together before the LORD; for He cometh to judge the earth" (Psalm 98:4, 7–9).

Often, these praises are in contemplation of God's final return to complete and fulfill all His primeval purposes in creation, as in the above passage. This is also true in our text, which looks forward to a time when "instead of the thorn shall come up the fir tree, and instead of the brier shall come up the myrtle tree: And it shall be to the Lord for a name, for an everlasting sign that shall not be cut off" (Isaiah 55:13).

And this all points ahead to the eventual removal of the great curse which now dominates creation because of man's sin (Genesis 3:14–19). For the present, "the whole creation groaneth and travaileth in pain together until now" (Romans 8:22). One day, however, the groaning creation "shall be delivered from the bondage of corruption" (Romans 8:21). Therefore, "let the heavens rejoice, and let the earth be glad; . . . Let the field be joyful, and all that is therein: then shall all the trees of the wood rejoice" (Psalm 96:11, 12).

Fathers and Sons

I have written unto you, fathers, because you have known Him that is from the beginning. I have written unto you, young men, because ye are strong, and the Word of God abideth in you, and ye have overcome the wicked one (I John 2:14).

This is the final reference in the Bible both to fathers and to young men. The Greek word for the latter refers to grown young men under about age 40, but still under the guidance of their fathers. The aged Apostle John had been a teacher of both, and was thankful for their response to his pastoral leadership.

The fathers had "known Him that is from the beginning," recognizing the Lord Jesus Christ as the Creator who "was in the beginning with God. All things were made by Him" (John 1:2, 3). To them the Apostle had then shown "that eternal life, which was with the Father, and was manifested unto us" (I John 1:2), and they had entered into eternal "fellowship with the Father, and with His Son, Jesus Christ" (I John 1:3).

Then their own sons—soon to become fathers also—proceeded to follow their fathers' lead. As they also received that "Word of Life" (v. 1), so that the "Word of God" began to "abide in" them, they were enabled to triumph over youthful lusts, becoming "strong" and able to "overcome the wicked one" (I John 2:13).

What a testimony, even today, for Christian fathers and Christian sons! The key to having such a testimony, by implication at least, is that if the fathers truly honor the Heavenly Father as their Creator and Savior, living in the light of that fellowship, then the sons also will come to know His Son, Jesus Christ. They will be able to overcome the wicked one, manifesting in their strong young lives the abiding Word of God. May the fathers and sons in our own fellowship today have the same testimony!

JUNE 22

Our Ministry to Angels

To the intent that now unto the principalities and powers in heavenly places might be known by the church the manifold wisdom of God (Ephesians 3:10).

There is "an innumerable company of angels" in heaven (Hebrews 12:22) who serve as "ministering spirits, sent forth to minister for them who shall be heirs of salvation" (Hebrews 1:14).

At the same time, it is instructive to realize we also have a ministry to the angels. Despite their great power and knowledge, angels are not the "heirs of salvation" themselves, and so will never personally experience that peculiar type of love and fellowship which we share with our Lord and Savior. Nevertheless, as personal beings with the free will to reject their role as God's servants if they choose, they are intensely interested in our salvation. "Which things the angels desire to look into" (I Peter 1:12).

In addition to serving for the protection and guidance of individual believers, apparently certain angels are also assigned by God to serve Christian congregations functioning corporately, especially in true local churches. Paul mentions the observing presence of angels in the Corinthian church (I Corinthians 11:10), for example. In His letters to the seven representative churches, Christ addressed the individual angels of each church (Revelation 2:1, etc.). That these are heavenly angels (not human pastors) is evident from the fact that the word "angel" is used 65 other times in Revelation, and always refers to real angels.

Finally, the words of our text for the day give a special incentive for our lives, for there we are reminded that it is through God's dealings with "the church" that His holy angels are able to learn for themselves "the manifold wisdom of God."

Creation and the Constellations

Which alone spreadeth out the heavens, and treadeth upon the waves of the sea. Which maketh Arcturus, Orion, and Pleiades, and the chambers of the south (Job 9:8, 9).

The book of Job is the oldest book in the Bible. It is not surprising, therefore, that it contains a number of references to creation and the flood, for these great events were still relatively fresh in the thinking of Job and his contemporaries. The first of these creation references in Job is our text above, and it is remarkable that it centers especially on the stars and their constellations. Still another constellation is mentioned in Job 26:13: "By His Spirit He hath garnished the heavens; His hand hath formed the crooked serpent." Finally: "Canst thou bind the sweet influences of Pleiades, or loose the bands of Orion? Canst thou bring forth Mazzaroth in his season? or canst thou guide Arcturus with his sons? Knowest thou the ordinances of heaven? canst thou set the dominion thereof in the earth?" (Job 38:31–33). The term "Mazzaroth" actually means the twelve constellations of the Zodiac.

Thus God not only created the stars but arranged them in star groupings that could be used for "signs and for seasons" (Genesis 1:14). Since God does nothing without a holy purpose, we can be sure that these sidereal signs were not to be used as astrological signs. God's Word, in fact, forbids the practice of astrology (e.g., Isaiah 47:12–14). The constellations must all in some way have testified of the coming Savior. "For God, who commanded the light to shine out of darkness, hath shined in our hearts, to give the light of the knowledge of the glory of God in the face of Jesus Christ" (II Corinthians 4:6). Before the Scriptures were given, the testimony of God's primeval promises had somehow been written indelibly in the heavens, for those in Earth's earliest ages who had eyes and hearts to see.

JUNE 24

The Battle is the Lord's

And all this assembly shall know that the L*ORD saveth not with sword and spear: for the battle is the* L*ORD's, and He will give you into our hands* (I Samuel 17:47).

These were the ringing words of faith uttered by young David as he faced the Philistine giant, Goliath. Without armor, or spear, or shield, and with only a sling and five smooth stones, David confronted the nine-foot champion of the pagan army in the name of the true God, and soon the giant lay dead with his face to the ground.

The battle must always be the Lord's, "for we wrestle not against flesh and blood, but against . . . the rulers of the darkness of this world, against spiritual wickedness in high places" (Ephesians 6:12). Spiritual battles are not won by bullets, nor by ballots, nor by any human means. "Some trust in chariots, and some in horses: but we will remember the name of the LORD our God" (Psalm 20:7). "There is no king saved by the multitude of an host: a mighty man is not delivered by much strength. . . . Behold, the eye of the LORD is upon them that fear Him, upon them that hope in His mercy" (Psalm 33:16, 18).

We even have a mandate to attack the enemy in His stronghold. Christ taught: "Upon this rock [of faith in Christ as divine Savior] I will build my church; and the gates of hell shall not prevail against it" (Matthew 16:18).

It is easy, in trying to do a work for God, to rely on human abilities and devices, but these will fail, for the battle is the Lord's. When the battle is going well, we must not boast, for the battle is the Lord's. When the battle is going hard, we must not despair, for the battle is the Lord's.

He is our strength. "For though we walk in the flesh, we do not war after the flesh: [For the weapons of our warfare are not carnal, but mighty through God to the pulling down of strong holds]" (II Corinthians 10:3, 4).

Allegories in Scripture

Which things are an allegory: for these are the two covenants; the one from the Mount Sinai, which gendereth to bondage, which is Agar (Galatians 4:24).

This verse is often used as a justifying proof text for allegorizing Biblical narratives. Here Paul is saying that the ancient conflict between Abraham's wives, Hagar and Sarah, the mothers of Ishmael and Isaac, respectively, was a spiritual allegory, depicting the conflict between law and grace.

Many of the early church fathers indulged in such an allegorical approach to Scripture, attempting to harmonize Christianity with Greek philosophy. Modern theological liberals often do the same thing whenever modern scientific philosophy seems to conflict with a Biblical narrative. The most important example is the story of creation in the very first chapter of the Bible. The allegorical interpretation of this record denies its historicity, but tries to retain its supposed "spiritual" message by finding a devotional application in its narratives. Similarly, the record of the fall of Adam and Eve in Genesis 3 is explained away as an allegory of the yielding of "every man" to temptation.

However, the only narrative actually called an allegory in Scripture is the one mentioned in our text. In fact, this is the only time the word for "allegory" (Greek *allegoreo*) is used in the Bible at all. It is significant that Paul's use of the word does not suggest in any way that the story of Hagar and Sarah was not real history. There are numerous other references to Abraham, and at least three to Sarah, in the New Testament, and all clearly treat them as real persons.

This Biblical example, therefore, tells us that, if we draw allegorical applications from its historical records, it can only be on the basis that the events themselves really happened.

The Uttermost Parts of the Earth

Ask of me, and I shall give thee the heathen for thine inheritance, and the uttermost parts of the earth for thy possession (Psalm 2:8).

This colorful and comprehensive phrase, usually translated "ends of the earth," occurs no less than thirty times in the Old Testament and five in the New. The verse in our text is God's promise to His Son (v. 7), and it appears again and again. For example: "He shall have dominion also from sea to sea, and from the river unto the ends of the earth" (Psalm 72:8). "Now shall He be great unto the ends of the earth" (Micah 5:4); "All the ends of the world shall remember and turn unto the LORD" (Psalm 22:27).

This divine Son, whose future dominion will extend to the uttermost parts of the earth, is also the Creator of the ends of the earth. "Who hath ascended up into heaven, or descended? Who hath gathered the wind in His fists? Who hath bound the waters in a garment? Who hath established all the ends of the earth? What is His name, and what is His Son's name, if thou canst tell?" (Proverbs 30:4). He who both created and will ultimately regain all the ends of the earth will also be their judge. "The LORD shall judge the ends of the earth; and He shall give strength unto His King, and exalt the horn of His anointed" (literally, *Messiah;* I Samuel 2:10).

For the present, however, He is still "despised and rejected of men" (Isaiah 53:3), both as Creator and as coming King, by all the nations of the world. Nevertheless, He has provided "salvation unto the ends of the earth" for all who will receive Him (Acts 13:47), and He has both commanded and prophesied that His followers must be "witnesses unto me . . . unto the uttermost part of the earth" (Acts 1:8). The great message we carry from Him is: "Look unto me, and be ye saved, all the ends of the earth" (Isaiah 45:22).

One God

Hear, O Israel: The L*ORD our God is one* L*ORD* (Deuteronomy 6:4).

This great verse has been recited countless times by Israelites down through the centuries, setting forth their distinctive belief in one great Creator God. The Jews had retained their original belief in creation, handed down from Noah, while the other nations had all allowed their original monotheistic creationism to degenerate into a wide variety of religions, all basically equivalent to the polytheistic evolutionism of the early Sumerians at Babel.

But along with its strong assertion of monotheism, there is also a very real suggestion that this declaration, with its thrice-named subject, is also setting forth the Triune God. The name, "LORD," of course, is Yahweh, or Jehovah, the self-existing One who reveals Himself, while "God" is Elohim, the powerful Creator/Ruler. "Jehovah our Elohim is one Jehovah" is the proclamation. A number of respected Jewish commentators have acknowledged that the verse spoke of a "unified oneness," rather than an "absolute oneness." The revered book called the Zohar, for example, even said that the first mention was of the Father; the second one the Messiah; and the third, the Holy Spirit.

The key word "one" (Hebrew *achad*) is often used to denote unity in diversity. For example, when Eve was united to Adam in marriage, they were said to be "one flesh" (Genesis 2:24). Similarly, on the third day of creation, the waters were "gathered together unto one place," yet this gathering together was called "Seas" (i.e., more than one sea; Genesis 1:9, 10).

Thus, Israel's great declaration should really be understood as saying in effect: "The eternally omnipresent Father, also Creator and Sustainer of all things, is our unified self-revealing Lord."

JUNE 28

Seven Mountains

His foundation is in the holy mountains (Psalm 87:1).

It is fascinating to study God's selection of several key mountains to mark key events in human history. Mount Ararat was the first great mountain of Scripture, where God's Ark of safety would rest (Genesis 8:4). Then, when the first nations failed and God had to form a new nation, it was on Mount Moriah that Abraham passed the great test with his son, Isaac, and became "the father of all them that believe," testifying that "in the mount of the LORD it shall be seen" (Romans 4:11; Genesis 22:14). When the time came for God's Law to be revealed, "the Lord came down upon Mount Sinai," and gave Moses "upon Mount Sinai, two tables of testimony, tables of stone, written with the finger of God" (Exodus 19:20; 31:18).

"Beautiful for situation, the joy of the whole earth, is Mount Zion," where the holy city was built and where Christ will reign in the great age to come. For God has promised concerning Christ: "Yet have I set my King upon my holy hill of Zion" (Psalm 48:2; 2:6).

Insignificant in size, but preeminent in importance, is the small hill outside Jerusalem that has come to be called Mount Calvary. There a "stone was cut out of the mountain" which "became a great mountain, and filled the whole earth" (Daniel 2:45, 35) when Christ died there and conquered death. He arose from the grave and then ascended into heaven from the Mount of Olives, to which, one day, He shall "so come in like manner as ye have seen Him go into heaven" (Acts 1:11).

Finally, in the new earth, "every mountain and hill shall be made low" (Isaiah 40:4), and the only mountain will be "a great and high mountain," the beautiful city of God, towering "twelve thousand furlongs" (Revelation 21:10, 16) over the fruitful plains of the eternally new earth below.

Living in the Real World

For, behold, I create new heavens and a new earth: and the former shall not be remembered, nor come into mind (Isaiah 65:17).

People often think they are being practical when they place material values ahead of spiritual, emphasizing that we have to "live in the real world." The fact is, however, that we are not living in the real world at all, but in a world that is dying and will soon be gone. "The world passeth away, and the lust thereof: but he that doeth the will of God abideth for ever" (I John 2:17).

This is not even the world that God created, for that world was "very good" (Genesis 1:31). Because "sin entered into the world, and death by sin" (Romans 5:12), therefore, "the whole creation groaneth and travaileth in pain together until now" (Romans 8:22). In fact, this world is not even as it was soon after God's curse, for "the world that then was, being overflowed with water, perished" (II Peter 3:6).

The present, post-Flood world is now under the dominion of Satan, who is "the prince of this world" (John 12:31) and of "all the kingdoms of the world" (Matthew 4:8). The Lord Jesus Christ came to "deliver us from this present evil world" (Galatians 1:4). As our text says, this world shall not even "be remembered, nor come into mind." It "shall be delivered from the bondage of corruption into the glorious liberty of the sons of God" (Romans 8:21).

Therefore, we must "be not conformed to this world" (Romans 12:2). We must "live soberly, righteously, and godly, in this present world; Looking for that blessed hope, and the glorious appearing of the great God and our Saviour Jesus Christ" (Titus 2:12, 13). In the meantime, our true citizenship, if we have been born again in Christ, is in the real world to come, and we are His ambassadors to an alien land (II Corinthians 5:20).

God with Us

And Adam knew Eve his wife; and she conceived, and bare Cain, and said, I have gotten a man from the L*ORD* (Genesis 4:1).

Here is Eve's testimony concerning the first child born to the human race. To understand it, we need to recall God's first promise: "I will put enmity between thee and the woman, and between thy seed and her seed: [He] shall bruise thy head, and thou shalt bruise His heel" (Genesis 3:15). These words, addressed to Satan, promised that the woman's "seed" would destroy Satan. Thus, that seed would have to be a man, but the only one capable of destroying Satan is God Himself. Eve mistakenly thought that Cain would fulfill this promise, and when he was born, she testified: "I have gotten a man—even the LORD" (literal rendering).

Over three millennia later, essentially the same promise was renewed to the "house of David," when the Lord said: "Behold, [the] virgin shall conceive, and bear a Son, and shall call His name Immanuel" (Isaiah 7:13, 14). The definite article reflects the primeval promise that the divine/human Savior, when He comes, would be born uniquely as the woman's seed, not of the father's seed like all other men. His very name, Immanuel, means "God with us" (Matthew 1:23). He is "the Word . . . made flesh" (John 1:14).

While questions have been raised about the precise meaning of *almah* (Hebrew word translated "virgin"), there is no question in the New Testament: "Behold, a virgin [Greek *parthenos,* meaning 'virgin,' and nothing else] shall be with child" (Matthew 1:23). "When the fulness of the time was come, God sent forth His Son, made of a woman" (Galatians 4:4). "Forasmuch then as the children are partakers of flesh and blood, He also Himself likewise took part of the same; that through death He might destroy him that had the power of death, that is, the devil" (Hebrews 2:14).

The Price of Sparrows

Are not two sparrows sold for a farthing? and one of them shall not fall on the ground without your Father (Matthew 10:29).

This fascinating bit of first-century pricing information, seemingly so trivial, provides a marvelous glimpse into the heart of the Creator. Of all the birds used for food by the people of those days, sparrows were the cheapest on the market, costing only a farthing for a pair of them. In fact, they cost even less in a larger quantity, for, on another occasion, Jesus said: "Are not five sparrows sold for two farthings, and not one of them is forgotten before God?" (Luke 12:6). The "farthing" was a tiny copper coin of very small value, so that a sparrow was all but worthless in human terms.

And yet the Lord Jesus said that God knows and cares about every single sparrow! God had a reason for everything He created; each kind of animal has its own unique design for its own intended purpose. Modern biologists continue to waste time and talent developing imaginary tales about how all these multitudes of different kinds of creatures might have evolved from some common ancestor, but they would really be better scientists if they would seek to understand the creative purpose of each creature, rather than speculating on its imaginary evolution.

The better we comprehend the amazing complexity and purposive design of each creature, the better we realize the infinite wisdom and power of their Creator. Then, all the more wonderful it is to learn that their Creator is our Father! He has placed them all under our dominion, and we need to learn to see them through His eyes, if we would be good stewards of the world He has committed to us. We can also thank our heavenly Father that we "are of more value than many sparrows" (Matthew 10:31).

Be Sure

But if ye will not do so, behold, ye have sinned against the L*ORD*: *and be sure your sin will find you out* (Numbers 32:23).

Most things in this life are uncertain; nevertheless, there are some things about which we can be absolutely sure. Just as God warned Adam that if he disobeyed His Word, he would "surely die" (Genesis 2:17), so He warns us that we can be sure our sins will ultimately be exposed. "The foundation of God standeth sure" (II Timothy 2:19).

On the other side of the coin, we can also be sure of God's mercy and faithfulness, and we can be sure of the truth of His Word. "We have also a more sure word of prophecy; whereunto ye do well that ye take heed, as unto a light that shineth in a dark place" (II Peter 1:19). We also can be sure of His promised salvation. "Which hope we have as an anchor of the soul, both sure and stedfast" (Hebrews 6:19). Thus we can, through faith and patience, show "the same diligence to the full assurance of hope unto the end" (Hebrews 6:11).

Finally, we can be sure that our Lord Jesus, who came once to die for our sins, will come back again to complete His work of redemption and reconciliation. The very last promise of the Bible consists of His gracious words: "Surely I come quickly" (Revelation 22:20).

However, each of us must first make sure that we believe His sure word and have appropriated this sure hope. "Wherefore the rather, brethren, give diligence to make your calling and election sure: for if ye do these things, ye shall never fall: For so an entrance shall be ministered unto you abundantly into the everlasting kingdom of our Lord and Saviour Jesus Christ" (II Peter 1:10, 11). We can be sure that our sins must be judged, but we also can be sure of His forgiveness, if we believe His sure promises and receive His sure salvation.

Glorious Liberty

Because the creature itself also shall be delivered from the bondage of corruption into the glorious liberty of the children of God (Romans 8:21).

This verse contains the first of eleven occurrences of the Greek word *eleutheria,* "liberty," and defines the basic spiritual message of this splendid word. Because of sin, God has subjected the whole creation to "the bondage of corruption."

That is, everything is governed by a law of decay—a law of such universal scope that it is recognized as a basic law of science—the law of entropy, stipulating that *everything* tends to disintegrate and die.

Christ died for sin, however, and defeated death, so that He will someday deliver the whole groaning creation from its bondage into the glorious freedom from decay and death that will also be enjoyed by all who have received eternal life through faith in Christ.

This ultimate, perfect liberty can even now be appropriated in type and principle through looking into "the perfect law of liberty" (James 1:25), the Holy Scriptures.

When we become children of God, the Holy Spirit henceforth indwells our bodies, and "where the Spirit of the Lord is, there is liberty" (II Corinthians 3:17).

Sometimes, however, Christians may abuse this new freedom from the law of sin and death, turning it into license, and this becomes a tragic perversion of Christian liberty. "For, brethren, ye have been called unto liberty; only use not liberty for an occasion to the flesh, but by love serve one another" (Galatians 5:13).

While not abusing our freedom in Christ, we must nevertheless "stand fast therefore in the liberty wherewith Christ hath made us free" (Galatians 5:1), and look forward to the glorious liberty of the ages to come.

JULY 4

One Nation, Under God

Blessed is the nation whose God is the LORD:*And the people whom He hath chosen for His own inheritance* (Psalm 33:12).

The primary thought of the psalmist as he wrote these words, no doubt, was in reference to Israel, which did, indeed, have a godly heritage (same word in the Hebrew as "inheritance." Nevertheless, the promise is broad enough to apply to any nation whose God is the God of Israel, and our own nation has surely experienced great blessing in accordance with this promise.

It is significant that this promise follows one of the strongest statements of absolute creation to be found in the Bible. "By the Word of the LORD were the heavens made; and all the host of them by the breath of His mouth. . . . For He spake, and it was done; He commanded, and it stood fast" (Psalm 33:6, 9).

It is no coincidence that America's long-standing recognition of the God of the Bible was founded on the belief of its people in the literal creation record of Genesis. Evolutionary speculations were permeating Europe at that time, but they did not begin to influence American thought until much later.

But just as God will bless any nation whose God is the true God of creation—the God of ancient Israel and the Father of our Lord and Savior Jesus Christ—so He will curse any nation that turns away from Him. "The wicked shall be turned into hell, and all the nations that forget God" (Psalm 9:17).

America, with its great Christian heritage of the past, has been blessed by "the God of our fathers." But its rapidly growing apostasy from the true God and His Word are now placing it in deadly peril of God's judgment. We should pray, especially on Independence Day, that God will forgive our wicked, forgetting nation, and bring us back to the faith of our fathers.

The Potter and the Clay

What shall we say then? Is there unrighteousness with God? God forbid (Romans 9:14).

Every believer goes through difficult experiences from time to time—loss of a job, a painful injury, failure of some plan, death of a needed loved one, even facing a terminal illness of his own—and the natural tendency is to cry out: "Why, O God?"

God surely understands our longing for an answer, because He made us—"He knoweth our frame; He remembereth that we are dust" (Psalm 103:14). But He would have us merely to trust Him. Job, who surely suffered more than any of us, could say: "Though He slay me, yet will I trust in Him" (Job 13:15).

Job did indeed plead for an understanding of His undeserved sufferings, but God answered merely by reminding him of His great creation and His providential care for all living things (Job 38–41). As our great Potter, He has the right to make His vessels for both honor and dishonor (Romans 9:21). "For we are His workmanship" (Ephesians 2:10).

We who have been redeemed by His mercy should be grateful that He chose us even before the world began (Ephesians 1:3, 4; II Timothy 1:9), confident that He—by whatever means He chooses—is preparing His "vessels of mercy" to receive the full manifestation of His glory in the ages to come (Romans 9:23; Ephesians 2:7). The fact that our finite minds cannot fully comprehend right now what He is doing in our lives merely gives us an opportunity to trust Him more.

"We know that all things work together for good" (Romans 8:28) in those who are His. Therefore He would say: "Let them that suffer according to the will of God commit the keeping of their souls to Him in well doing, as unto a faithful Creator" (I Peter 4:19).

JULY 6

Preaching the Resurrection

And with great power gave the apostles witness of the resurrection of the Lord Jesus: and great grace was upon them all (Acts 4:33).

There are multitudes today who believe that Christ's resurrection was a "spiritual" resurrection, insisting that the idea of a dead body returning to life after three days in the grave is completely unscientific and impossible.

This was not what the apostles preached with great grace and great power, however. They would hardly have been excited about any kind of spiritual resurrection, since everyone—both Jews and the pagan Gentiles—believed in life after death. If that was their message, no one would have doubted, and no one would have cared. Even when the disciples saw the resurrected Christ, they first "supposed that they had seen a spirit" (Luke 24:37). Christ even had to urge them to "handle me, and see; for a spirit hath not flesh and bones, as ye see me have" (Luke 24:39).

When the disciples finally became convinced of His bodily resurrection, they were quickly transformed into courageous evangelists, willing even to die in support of their glorious message of salvation. The resurrection was, indeed, contrary to scientific law and all human experience, and this very fact proved to them that their Lord was Himself the divine Lawgiver and Author of all human experience. All other founders and leaders of human religions, ancient or modern, are themselves subject to death, but He alone has triumphed over death. Only the Creator of life can conquer death, and the resurrection proves that Jesus Christ is Creator, as well as Savior.

Therefore, when we today, like the apostles of old, proclaim the resurrection of Christ, we know that His name is above every name, and this enables us also to witness with great power, in great grace.

Cities of Refuge

Ye shall give three cities on this side of the Jordan, and three cities shall ye give in the land of Canaan, which shall be cities of refuge. (Numbers 35:14).

When the Israelites entered the promised land, God told Joshua to provide six "cities of refuge" into which those who had slain someone could flee for refuge until a trial could ascertain the facts and render a proper verdict. As such, these cities are a type of Christ through whom "we might have a strong consolation, who have fled for refuge to lay hold upon the hope set before us" (Hebrews 6:18).

The names of the six cities are given in Joshua 20:7, 8 as Kedesh, Shechem, Hebron, Bezer, Ramoth, and Golan. The meanings of these names seem planned especially to foreshadow this spiritual application.

Kedesh means "holy place," and Christ in the New Jerusalem is the ultimate refuge, for "the Lamb [is] the temple of it" (Revelation 21:22). *Shechem* means "strong shoulder" which answers to the "strong consolation" we have in Christ when we flee to Him for refuge.

Hebron means "fellowship," and we who have come to Christ have been "called unto the fellowship of His Son Jesus Christ our Lord" (I Corinthians 1:9). *Bezer* means "strong hiding place." The Scripture assures the believer that "your life is hid with Christ in God" (Colossians 3:3).

Ramoth means "high place," and when we are hidden in Christ, God also has "made us sit together in heavenly places in Christ Jesus" (Ephesians 2:6). Finally, *Golan* apparently means "enclosure for captives," and this would speak of our being set free from sin and death to become captive to Christ. "When He ascended up on high, He led captivity captive" (Ephesians 4:8). Thus the cities are appropriately named, both for their immediate purpose, and as a picture of Christ as the Savior of sinners.

Christ the King

Which in His times He shall shew, who is the blessed and only Potentate, the King of kings, and Lord of lords (I Timothy 6:15).

Of the many descriptive titles of the Lord Jesus Christ, perhaps the most significant is that of King, because this speaks of His universal dominion. The day is coming when "every knee should bow, of things in heaven, and things in earth, and things under the earth" (Philippians 2:10).

First of all, since He created all things, He is the King of Creation. "For the LORD is a great God, and a great King above all gods. In His hand are the deep places of the earth: the strength of the hills is His also. The sea is His, and He made it: and His hands formed the dry land" (Psalm 95:3–5).

In a special sense, of course, He is the King of the Jews. "He shall reign over the house of Jacob for ever, and of His kingdom there shall be no end" (Luke 1:33).

He is also our King of redemption, having set us free from the kingdom of the wicked one. He "hath delivered us from the power of darkness, and hath translated us into the kingdom of His dear Son: In whom we have redemption through His blood, even the forgiveness of sins" (Colossians 1:13,14).

There is a day coming in which all the kings of the earth shall unite against Him. "These shall make war with the Lamb, and the Lamb shall overcome them: for He is Lord of lords, and King of kings: and they that are with Him are called, and chosen, and faithful" (Revelation 17:14). "And out of His mouth goeth a sharp sword, that with it He should smite the nations: and He shall rule them with a rod of iron: . . . And He hath on His vesture and on His thigh a name written, KING OF KINGS, AND LORD OF LORDS" (Revelation 19:15, 16). Until then, let us serve Him as King, and submit to Him as Lord.

Atonement

Make thee an ark of gopher wood; rooms shalt thou make in the ark, and shalt pitch it within and without with pitch (Genesis 6:14).

It may be surprising to learn that God's instructions to Noah concerning the ark's design contain the first reference in the Bible to the great doctrine of atonement. The Hebrew word used here for pitch (*kaphar*) is the same word translated "atonement" in many other places in the Old Testament.

While the New Testament word "atonement" implies reconciliation, the Old Testament "atonement" was merely a covering (with many applications). As the pitch was to make the ark watertight, keeping the judgment waters of the Flood from reaching those inside, so, on the sacrificial altar, "it is the blood that maketh an atonement for the soul" (Leviticus 17:11), keeping the fires of God's wrath away from the sinner for whom the sacrifice was substituted and slain. The pitch was a covering for the ark, and the blood was a covering for the soul: the first assuring physical deliverance; the second, spiritual salvation.

However, not even the shed blood on the altar could really produce salvation. A sacrifice could assure salvation through faith in God's promises on the part of the sinner who offered it, but "the blood of bulls and of goats" could never "take away sins" (Hebrews 10:4). Both the covering pitch and animal blood were mere symbols of the substituting death of Jesus Christ, "whom God hath set forth to be a propitiation through faith in His blood, to declare His righteousness for the remission of sins that are past, through the forbearance of God" (Romans 3:25). Through faith in Christ, our sins are "covered" under the blood, forgiven by God, and replaced by His own perfect righteousness, by all of which we become finally and fully reconciled to God.

JULY 10

The Father of Spirits

Furthermore we have had fathers of our flesh which corrected us, and we gave them reverence: shall we not much rather be in subjection unto the Father of spirits, and live? (Hebrews 12:9).

Human parents transmit physical characteristics to their offspring, but our spiritual attributes come from God, for He is "the Father of spirits." Paul recognized that all men are "the offspring of God" (Acts 17:29), and that each man is still "the image and glory of God" (I Corinthians 11:7).

Thus our spirit/soul nature, as distinct from our body of physical/mental flesh, has come from God who created it and united it with our body, evidently at the moment of physical conception in the womb. It is obvious that the "image of God," man's spirit/soul nature, could not be transmitted genetically via the "genetic code" and the DNA molecules, for these are simply complex chemicals programed to transmit only the physical and mental attributes of the ancestors to the children. Nevertheless, the spirit/soul attributes of each person also seem to be associated inseparably with the body from conception onwards, continuing so until separated again at death, when the spirit goes "to be absent from the body, and to be present with the Lord" (II Corinthians 5:8).

In the meantime, however, the "image of God" in man is marred by its incorporation in man's "sinful flesh," for "the body is dead because of sin" (Romans 8:3, 10). By this union of flesh and spirit, man inherits Adam's fallen nature as well as his mortal body, and both are in need of salvation. Christ "gave Himself for us, that He might redeem us from all iniquity" (Titus 2:14). Therefore, we, like Paul, can pray that our "whole spirit and soul and body be preserved blameless unto the coming of our Lord Jesus Christ" (I Thessalonians 5:23).

Job and Adam

If I covered my transgressions as Adam, by hiding mine iniquity in my bosom:. . . (Job 31:33).

The patriarch Job lived long before Moses and the writing of the Pentateuch, yet he knew about Adam and his fall and likewise about God's curse on the world because of Adam's sin.

Note the following references in the book of Job to death and the curse: "Man that is born of woman is of few days, and full of trouble" (Job 14:1; compare Genesis 3:16). "All flesh shall perish together, and man shall turn again unto dust" (Job 34:15; note Genesis 3:19).

Evidently Job still had access to the records of primeval history, either by verbal tradition from his ancestors or perhaps through actual written records of the ancient patriarchs handed down from Adam to Moses.

There are also a number of references in Job to man's original creation. After speaking first of the beasts, the fowls of the air, and the fishes of the sea, Job asks: "Who knoweth not in all these that the hand of the LORD hath wrought this? In whose hand is the soul of every living thing, and the breath of all mankind" (Job 12:9, 10). Note also Elihu's testimony: "The Spirit of God hath made me, and the breath of the Almighty hath given me life" (Job 33:4).

The book of Job was almost certainly the first written of all the books of the Bible, and it testifies abundantly that the knowledge of the true God and His creation was still the common heritage of mankind at that time. Job knew the Lord, and never tried to hide anything from Him, as Adam had done. His ancient testimony is still true today. Quoting what must have been an early revelation from God, he wrote: "And unto man He said, Behold, the fear of the LORD, that is wisdom; and to depart from evil is understanding" (Job 28:28).

JULY 12

After the Flood

Behold, He withholdeth the waters, and they dry up: also He sendeth them out, and they overturn the earth (Job 12:15).

The great Flood of the Bible was such a traumatic global cataclysm, practically all the people groups that developed from its survivors kept its memory alive in their traditions and legends. The Bible itself, of course, has the only completely accurate record (Genesis 6–9). In addition, the ancient book of Job, written only a few centuries after the Flood, reflects the still-fresh memories of the awful deluge.

Job knew, for example, that the Flood had literally "overturned the earth," eroding away the pre-flood mountains and depositing their debris to form new mountains after the Flood.

Job's friend, Eliphaz, said: "Hast thou marked the old way which wicked men have trodden? Which were cut down out of time, whose foundation was overflown with a flood" (Job 22:15, 16). Referring to God's promise after the Flood, Job said: "He hath compassed the waters with bounds, until the day and night come to an end" (Job 26:10).

In the climactic 38th chapter of Job, God Himself recalls this promise: "Who shut up the sea with doors, when it brake forth, as if it had issued out of the womb? . . . And said, Hitherto shalt thou come, but no further: and here shall thy proud waves be stayed?" (Job 38:8, 11).

The general atmosphere of the entire book of Job seems to reflect the conditions shortly after the Flood. Modern skeptics deny that such a flood ever occurred, but it was a real and terrible event to those whose immediate ancestors had gone through it! Today, its testimony is preserved not only in the Bible and ancient traditions, but also in the flood sediments themselves, now seen everywhere as the fossil-bearing rocks of the earth's crust.

Demonic Discouragement

Behold, He put no trust in His servants; and His angels He charged with folly: How much less in them that dwell in houses of clay, whose foundation is in the dust, which are crushed before the moth? (Job 4:18, 19).

This was the strange message delivered to Eliphaz, the first of the three friends who proved such "miserable comforters" to Job in his sufferings, by "a spirit" that "stood still, . . . an image . . . before mine eyes" (Job 4:15, 16). This "thing was secretly [literally 'stealthily'] brought to me," said Eliphaz (Job 4:12), and there is little doubt that its original source was Satan himself, in his efforts to discredit and destroy Job. The "spirit" who instructed Eliphaz was not sent from God, as he may have thought, but was one of those angelic servants who had been "charged with folly," when they followed Lucifer in his primeval rebellion.

Still smarting with wounded pride that God would make His angels mere "ministering spirits" (Hebrews 1:14) to Adam and his children, whose own bodies were mere "houses of clay," built out of the dust of the earth, these demonic rebels hate human beings—especially those who love and serve God—with great passion. If Satan could not destroy Job by tempting him into moral wickedness or rebellion against an "unjust" God, perhaps he could lead him into discouragement, using his self-righteous "friends" to cause him to lose faith in God's love and care.

But he failed! Job said: "Though He slay me, yet will I trust in Him," and "I know that my Redeemer liveth" (Job 13:15; 19:25).

Such defeatism is one of Satan's most effective weapons. When he strikes with it, we must, like Job, "resist steadfast in the faith" (I Peter 5:9), knowing "the end of the Lord; that the Lord is very pitiful, and of tender mercy" (James 5:11).

The Spiritual Senses

O taste and see that the LORD is good: blessed is the man that trusteth in Him (Psalm 34:8).

Frequently, Scripture uses our five physical senses (sight, hearing, touch, smell, taste) in a figurative way to help us comprehend our interaction with the heavenly realm of God's presence and power.

We can "see," for example, with spiritual eyes. Paul prayed thus for the believer: "The eyes of your understanding being enlightened; that ye may know what is the hope of His calling, and what the riches of the glory of His inheritance in the saints" (Ephesians 1:18).

Similarly, we are privileged to hear the voice of the Lord with spiritual ears. "My sheep hear my voice, and I know them, and they follow me" (John 10:27). "A stranger will they not follow, . . . for they know not the voice of strangers" (John 10:5).

The sense of touch is the sense of feeling, and God can both touch and be touched. We read, for example, of "a band of men, whose hearts God had touched" (I Samuel 10:26). Of Jesus Christ, it is said that He is not a remote deity "which cannot be touched with the feeling of our infirmities" (Hebrews 4:15). Even people who never knew Him can perhaps "feel after Him, and find Him" (Acts 17:27) if they truly desire His great salvation.

We can even become "unto God a sweet savor of Christ" (II Corinthians 2:15). To the world, the faithful Christian life and testimony can either be "the savor of death unto death" to those who refuse it, or "the savor of life unto life" (II Corinthians 2:16).

Finally, we are exhorted actually to taste the Lord, and see that He is good! His Word will be, according to our needs, either "sincere milk" (I Peter 2:2), "strong meat" (Hebrews 5:14), or "sweeter also than honey and the honeycomb" (Psalm 19:10).

The Firstborn of Every Creature

Who is the image of the invisible God, the firstborn of every creature (Colossians 1:15).

A widespread cultic heresy based on this verse claims that Jesus Christ was not eternal, but merely the first being created—perhaps an angel—before becoming a man. Note, however, that the verse does not say He was the "first created of every creature," but the "first born of every creature." In fact, the very next verse says that "by Him were all things created" (v. 16). He was never created, for He, Himself, is the Creator. "All things were made by Him; and without Him was not anything made that was made" (John 1:3).

He is "born" of God, not "made," the "only begotten Son" of God (John 3:16). "No man hath seen God at any time; the only begotten Son, which is in the bosom of the Father, He hath declared Him" (John 1:18). The eternal Father is omnipresent, and therefore invisible, inaudible, inaccessible to the physical senses. The eternally existing Son is the "image" of the invisible Father, the One who declares, reveals, embodies His essence. Although He is always "in the bosom of the Father," yet He is eternally also "the brightness of His glory, and the express image of His person" (Hebrews 1:3). He is the eternal, living Word, which was "in the beginning with God" (John 1:2), and which "was God" (John 1:1).

Thus the phrase, "firstborn of every creature" in our text, can be translated literally as "begotten before all creation." The eternal inter-relationship of the Persons of the Godhead is beyond human comprehension in its fullness, and the terms, "Son" and "begotten" are the best human language can do to describe it. Jesus Christ, the Word made flesh, is the only begotten, eternally generated, Son of the Father, forever shining forth as the image of the otherwise invisible God.

JULY 16

Graven in the Rock

Oh that my words were now written! oh that they were printed in a book! That they were graven with an iron pen and lead in the rock for ever! (Job 19:23, 24).

In the midst of terrible calamities and sufferings, righteous Job expressed a heartfelt longing to write down his experiences and meditations, that others might later understand. This longing no doubt later led him, when the Lord finally restored him to health and prosperity, to do just that.

Job apparently wrote his book, originally, not on some perishable material, but, as we see in our text, on tablets of stone with a pen of iron, so that his testimony might be permanently available to all future generations. Indeed, God in His providence has ordained exactly that, by incorporating it in the Bible.

And the essence of Job's testimony is surely one of the most wonderful statements of faith ever penned, all the more remarkable in view of Job's circumstances when he uttered it, and in light of the limited knowledge of God's plan of redemption available in his day.

Here it is: "For I know that my redeemer liveth, and that He shall stand at the latter day upon the earth" (Job 19:25). Even before the days of Moses, Job knew that God Himself would become, not just the world's Redeemer from its bondage under the great Curse, but his own personal Savior! He even sensed the necessity of God's bodily incarnation, for he said He would stand on the earth in the latter days. He knew that he himself would some day be resurrected from the dead, for he said that, even after worms had destroyed his body, "yet in my flesh shall I see God" (Job 19:26). In the many centuries since, multitudes of other believers have seen Job's testimony, written forever in the Book, and have made it their own, trusting their living Redeemer.

The Apple of the Eye

For thus saith the Lord *of hosts; After the glory hath He sent me unto the nations which spoiled you: for he that toucheth you toucheth the apple of His eye* (Zechariah 2:8).

This common phrase is often used to identify an object of one's special favor or affection. The apple of the eye, of course, is not a fruit, but the pupil of the eye, so essential for sight that it becomes a peculiarly apt symbol for a prized possession. It is used five times in the Bible as a translation of three different Hebrew nouns, none of which refer to the actual apple fruit. In each case, however, it speaks of something highly valuable to the owner.

Three of these (Deuteronomy 32:10; Lamentations 2:18; and our text above) are in reference to the chosen people, Israel, as the "apple of the eye" of God Himself. God has often punished Israel for her sins and has allowed other nations to be His rod of judgment, but woe to that nation that touches the apple of His eye in this way!

That individual believers can also be so regarded by the Lord is evident from one of David's prayers: "Show by thy marvelous lovingkindness. . . . Keep me as the apple of the eye, hide me under the shadow of thy wings" (Psalm 17:7, 8).

To be kept by God as He would keep the very apple of His own eye, requires an implicit trust in Him and His word. In fact, His word must become the apple of our eye! "My son, keep my words, and lay up my commandments with thee. Keep my commandments, and live; and my law as the apple of thine eye" (Proverbs 7:1, 2).

There are many beautiful and appropriate figures used for God's word ("light," "hammer," "sword," "milk," etc.), but none more personally meaningful than this. May the Holy Scriptures, the indispensable word of God, truly be the apple of the eye for each of us!

Magnify the Lord

Let all those that seek thee rejoice and be glad in thee: and let such as love thy salvation say continually, Let God be magnified (Psalm 70:4).

Here is a great verse to follow for those who love the Lord Jesus in sincerity. We live in a day when people tend to be hero worshipers on a vast scale. Multitudes magnify some charismatic political leader and follow him even to the death. Others magnify great athletes, or rock singers, or movie stars, almost to the point of worship.

It is appropriate to give honor and to express sincere appreciation where honor is due, of course. Nevertheless, it is dangerous to overly magnify any man or woman, for it is God who has given them their abilities and opportunities. These should all be used for Him, and He should receive the praise.

God has told us clearly what and whom we should magnify. The principle is that we should only magnify what He has magnified. For one thing, "He will magnify the law, and make it honorable" (Isaiah 42:21). There may be a temptation, in this age of grace, to play down the importance and validity of God's law, but He desires us, rather, to magnify it.

This, in fact, is true of the whole Bible: "For thou hast magnified thy word above all thy name" (Psalm 138:2). Some liberals have accused Bible-believing Christians of putting the Bible on too high a pedestal, but this is impossible! We could never magnify God's word as much as does God Himself. We, therefore, magnify the Lord when we magnify His word. It is noteworthy that the glorious exhortation of our text verse is repeated verbatim from Psalm 40:16, except that "Let God be magnified" is replaced by "The LORD be magnified." Therefore, says David: "O magnify the LORD with me, and let us exalt His name together" (Psalm 34:3).

The Judging Spirit of God

And the Lord *said, My spirit shall not always strive with man, for that he also is flesh: yet his days shall be an hundred and twenty years* (Genesis 6:3).

This is a difficult verse, but it is bound to be significant, for it contains the first reference in the Bible to God's judgment. The word for "strive" is almost always elsewhere rendered "judge," or "judgment." It is used in Deuteronomy 32:36 ("the Lord shall judge His people"). Thus our text seems to be telling us that, before the Flood, the Holy Spirit was directly dealing with people in judgment because of their increasing involvement with sin and rebellion against the Lord. God, through the Holy Spirit, was working earnestly in the antediluvians to enable them, before His written word was available, to discern right and wrong, but their insistent rebellion would soon lead to such depravity that God would leave them altogether, and send the destroying, cleansing Flood.

In this more enlightened age, with the complete Bible available and the saving work of God's Son now well known, the Holy Spirit has a new judging ministry: "When He is come," Jesus said, "He will reprove the world of sin, and of righteousness, and of judgment: Of sin, because they believe not on me; Of righteousness, because I go to my Father, and ye see me no more; Of judgment, because the prince of this world is judged" (John 16:8–11).

This time man has been given not 120 years, but almost 2000 years to respond to the convicting judgments of the Holy Spirit, yet "evil men and seducers . . . wax worse and worse" (II Timothy 3:13). Thus judgment is imminent once again, and to those who have "done despite unto the Spirit of grace" (Hebrews 10:29), the next time will not be merely a cleansing flood. "For our God is a consuming fire" (Hebrews 12:29).

Things to Beware

Beware of false prophets, which come to you in sheep's clothing, but inwardly they are ravening wolves (Matthew 7:15).

There are three Greek words translated "beware," all of which stress watchfulness and potential danger. In a world under the control of Satan, there are many of his devices which can deceive and undermine the faith and life of the unwary Christian.

Our text cautions against false prophets who *appear* to be true prophets (or teachers, or pastors), but whose apparently spiritual teachings are subversive of Biblical truth. John warns that "many false prophets are gone out into the world" (I John 4:1), and Jesus said they "shall deceive many" (Matthew 24:11).

Jesus also warned that His followers should "beware . . . of the doctrine of the Pharisees and of the Sadducees" (Matthew 16:12). These sects have their respective modern counterparts in the hypocrisy of legalists and the skepticism of liberals, both of which are destructive of true Biblical faith and life.

Very relevant to today's humanistic intellectualism is the warning of Colossians 2:8: "Beware lest any man spoil you through philosophy and vain deceit, after the tradition of men, after the rudiments of the world, and not after Christ." This is the Bible's only reference to philosophy, here equated evidently with "vain deceit."

Finally, the Apostle Peter says: "Beware lest ye also, being led away with the error of the wicked, fall from your own steadfastness" (II Peter 3:17). In context, Peter is referring to those Christian brethren who have distorted the Scriptures in order to seek an accommodation with the naturalistic world view of establishment intellectuals (II Peter 3:3–6, 16). Thus, Peter, John, and Christ Himself would urge constant wariness on our part.

The Meaning of Man

When I consider thy heavens, the work of thy fingers, the moon and the stars, which thou hast ordained; What is man, that thou art mindful of him? and the son of man, that thou visitest him? (Psalm 8:3, 4).

This question has been posed as a rhetorical question by many generations of skeptics, especially in our present generation when the tremendous size of the universe is often used to argue that God, if He exists, could not possibly be interested in such a small speck of dust as our own planet. But, essentially, the same argument was used against Job by one of his three "miserable comforters" (Job 16:2), over 3500 years ago. "How then can man be justified with God? . . . yea, the stars are not pure in His sight. How much less man, that is a worm? and the son of man, which is a worm?" (Job 25:4–6).

This dismal type of reasoning, however, is utterly fallacious. Significance is not a function of size, but of complexity, and the human brain is surely the most complex physical system in the entire known universe. Rather than being insignificant nonentities, men and women have been created in the very image of God and are the objects of His sacrificial, redeeming love.

The most wonderful measure of man's importance is the fact that God, Himself, became a man! "Christ Jesus . . . being in the form of God, . . . took upon Him the form of a servant, and was made in the likeness of men" (Philippians 2:5–7) to be able to take our death penalty upon Himself.

Furthermore, God's love for man is measured not only by His substitutionary death for our sins, but also by His eternal creative purpose for us. He has redeemed us so that "in the ages to come He might shew the exceeding riches of His grace in His kindness toward us through Christ Jesus" (Ephesians 2:7).

JULY 22

The Weight of the Wind

For He looketh to the ends of the earth, and seeth under the whole heaven; To make the weight for the winds; and He weigheth the waters by measure (Job 28:24, 25).

It was only discovered by scientists in modern times that the air actually has weight. This passage in Job, however, written thirty-five or more centuries ago, indicated that the two great terrestrial fluids of air and water forming Earth's atmosphere and hydrosphere are both "weighed" by God's careful "measure" to provide the right worldwide balance of forces for life on Earth.

Another remarkable "weighing" act of God is noted in Job 37:16. "Dost thou know the balancings of the clouds, the wondrous works of Him which is perfect in knowledge?" Clouds are composed of liquid drops of water, not water vapor, and water is heavier than air, so how are they "balanced" in the sky? "For He maketh small the drops of water: they pour down rain according to the vapor thereof: Which the clouds do drop and distill upon man abundantly" (Job 36:27, 28).

Meteorologists know that the weight of the small water droplets in the clouds is "balanced" by the "weight of the winds"—air rushing upward in response to temperature changes. Eventually, however, the droplets coalesce to form larger drops which overcome these updrafts and fall as rain. "By watering He wearieth the thick cloud" (Job 37:11). The coalescence is probably triggered electrically in the clouds themselves, "When He made a decree for the rain, and a way for the lightning of the thunder" (Job 28:26).

Although these verses are not couched in the jargon of modern science, they are thoroughly scientific and up to date. "Lo, these are parts of His ways: but how little a portion is heard of Him? but the thunder of His power who can understand?" (Job 26:14).

Modern Science in an Ancient Book

Who knoweth not in all these that the hand of the Lord *hath wrought this?* (Job 12:9).

The book of Job is one of the oldest books in the world, yet it contains numerous references to natural systems and phenomena, some involving facts of science not discovered by scientists until recent centuries, yet recorded in Job almost 4000 years ago.

A good example is in 26:7. "He stretcheth out the north over the empty place, and hangeth the earth upon nothing." While ancient mythologies may imagine the earth to be carried on the shoulders of Atlas or on the back of a giant turtle, Job correctly noted that it is suspended in space. The force of "gravity" is still not understood, and it is quite reasonable to believe that God Himself holds it in the assigned place in His creation.

There is a reference to the rotation of the earth in 38:14. "It is turned as clay to the seal." This speaks of the smooth turning of the globe to receive the sun's daily illumination.

"The springs of the sea" are mentioned in 38:16, even though it has only been discovered in recent decades that there are springs of water emerging from certain parts of the deep ocean floor. The fact that mountains have "roots," consisting of rocks of the same nature and density as the mountains themselves, is noted in 28:9.

The infinite extent of the stellar heavens, contradicting the ancient pagan notion of a vaulted sky with stars affixed to a sort of hemispherical dome, is suggested in 22:12. "Is not God in the height of heaven? and behold the height of the stars, how high they are" (see also Isaiah 55:9, etc.).

There are many other scientific insights in this remarkable book and no scientific errors. The logical conclusion, as our text says, is that "the hand of the Lord hath wrought this."

JULY 24

The New Creation

For in Christ Jesus neither circumcision availeth any thing, nor uncircumcision; but a new creature (Galatians 6:15).

In the original Greek text of the New Testament, the word translated "creature" is the same as "creation," so the Apostle Paul, in our text, is stressing the vital importance of being a "new creation" in Christ. The Lord Jesus Christ is nothing less than the mighty Creator of Heaven and Earth (Colossians 1:16), and the very same creative power which called the universe into existence must be exerted on each lost sinner to create in him a new nature, capable of having the eternal fellowship with God for which man and woman were created in the beginning.

This new creation is not only for the purpose of saving their souls, but also for transforming their lives. "Therefore if any man be in Christ, he is a new creature: old things are passed away; behold, all things are become new" (II Corinthians 5:17). Although good works can never bring salvation, salvation must inevitably bring good works, for we are thereby "created in Christ Jesus unto good works, which God hath before ordained that we should walk in them" (Ephesians 2:10). Paul exhorts us to continually "put on the new man, which after God is created in righteousness and true holiness" (Ephesians 4:24).

Adam and Eve were originally created "in the image of God" (Genesis 1:27), but that image has been grievously damaged by unbelief and overt sin. Although still resident in man—in fact, distinguishing him from the animals—this divine image must be renewed through saving faith in our Creator/Redeemer, Jesus Christ. Therefore, the Scripture reminds all true believers that they "have put off the old man with his deeds; And have put on the new man, which is renewed in knowledge after the image of Him that created him" (Colossians 3:9, 10).

The Cave Men

They were driven forth from among men, (they cried after them as after a thief;) To dwell in the cliffs of the valleys, in caves of the earth, and in the rocks (Job 30:5, 6).

To most people, the term "cave man" means a brutish ape-man, not yet fully evolved into a true human being. However, these people, given such names as Neanderthal and Cro-Magnon by evolutionary anthropologists, were evidently degenerate—not evolving—men. When God confused the languages of mankind at the Tower of Babel, the various family groups were forced to scatter and eventually to develop their own cultures and nations, competing with each other for the best locations and resources. The weakest groups among these rebels were forced out to the least desirable sites, and many such tribes eventually died out. These sad events were recalled only a few centuries later by Job: "He taketh away the heart of the chief of the people of the earth, and causeth them to wander in a wilderness where there is no way. They grope in the dark without light, and He maketh them to stagger like a drunken man" (Job 12:24, 25).

Certain of these degenerate cave dwellers were among those who dared to ridicule godly Job in his sufferings. In the verses following our text he noted: "Among the bushes they brayed; . . . They were children of fools, yea, children of base men: they were viler than the earth. And now am I become their song, yea, I am their byword" (Job 30:7–9).

In the last days, many will again be forced into caves. "And they shall go into the holes of the rocks, and into the caves of the earth, for fear of the LORD, and for the glory of His majesty, when He ariseth to shake terribly the earth" (Isaiah 2:19; see also Revelation 6:15). As in ancient times the enemies of the Lord will again flee from the light of His presence to seek the darkness of holes.

To the Animals

Go to the ant, thou sluggard; consider her ways, and be wise: Which having no guide, overseer, or ruler, Provideth her meat in the summer, and gathereth her food in the harvest (Proverbs 6:6–8).

Adam and Eve originally were given dominion over all the animal creation (Genesis 1:26), but sin came in and then, after the Flood, God placed the fear and dread of man "upon all that moveth upon the earth" (Genesis 9:2), and the primeval fellowship between man and his animal friends was broken.

More seriously, their fellowship with God was broken, and soon, in their autonomy, the source of true wisdom was largely forgotten. "Professing themselves to be wise, they became fools, And changed the glory of the incorruptible God into an image made like to corruptible man, and to birds, and fourfooted beasts, and creeping things" (Romans 1:22, 23).

Ironically, God now directs such foolish people to study the very animals they worship in order to find the wisdom they should have learned from God.

"Go to the ant," says the Lord, to learn industry and prudence. "There be four things which are little upon the earth," the Word says, "but they are exceeding wise: The ants . . . ; The conies . . . ; The locusts . . . ; The spider . . . " (Proverbs 30:24–28). "The ox knoweth his owner, and the ass his master's crib: but Israel doth not know, my people doth not consider" (Isaiah 1:3).

"But ask now the beasts, and they shall teach thee; and the fowls of the air, and they shall tell thee: Or speak to the earth, and it shall teach thee: and the fishes of the sea shall declare unto thee" (Job 12:7, 8).

If nothing else, the intricate design of even the lowest animal is eloquent testimony to the wisdom of its Creator and the madness of those who deny Him.

One Day As a Thousand Years

Beloved, be not ignorant of this one thing, that one day is with the Lord as a thousand years, and a thousand years as one day (II Peter 3:8).

It is sad that many Christians today are so eager to appear intellectual, they are willing to compromise God's clear revelation to do so. God has made it as clear as plain words could make it, that "in six days the LORD made heaven and earth, the sea, and all that in them is" (Exodus 20:11). Yet because evolutionary "science" has alleged that the earth is billions of years old, multitudes of evangelicals have fallen in line, rejecting God's plain statement of fact and then trying to find some interpretive loophole to hide behind.

Our text verse is perhaps the key verse of the so-called "progressive creationists" who try to correlate the days of creation in Genesis with the supposed 4.6—billion-year system of evolutionary geological ages, by citing Peter as agreeing that "one day is a thousand years."

No, Peter is saying that "one day is with the Lord *as* a thousand years!" That is, God can do in one day what might, by natural processes, take a thousand years. In context, the apostle is condemning the last-day uniformitarians (those who teach that "all things continue as they were from the beginning of the creation") as "willingly ignorant" of the tremendous significance of the historical facts of Creation and the Flood (II Peter 3:3–6). Real written records only go back a few thousand years, and to attempt to calculate any date before that requires use of a premise which, in context, the Scriptures have just condemned! God says the uniformitarians are willingly ignorant and then urges those who believe His word to "be not ignorant." The only way we can know the date and duration of creation is for God to tell us, and He says He did it all in six days, and not so long ago!

God the Owner

The earth is the Lord*'s, and the fulness thereof; the world, and they that dwell therein* (Psalm 24:1).

In communist countries, "the people" own the lands, while in capitalist countries, individuals may own "private property." Both are myths unless these are viewed as a stewardship from God. We don't really own anything, "for we brought nothing into this world, and it is certain we can carry nothing out" (I Timothy 6:7).

In the mineral kingdom, the most important substances are the precious metals upon which monetary standards are based, yet God makes it clear that all "the silver is mine, and the gold is mine" (Haggai 2:8). The greatest members of the plant kingdom are the mighty trees of the forest, and God reminds us that "the trees of the Lord are full of sap; the cedars of Lebanon, which He hath planted" (Psalm 104:16). All the birds and beasts are His also. "For every beast of the forest is mine, and the cattle upon a thousand hills" (Psalm 50:10).

Again and again God reminds us that "all the earth is mine" (Exodus 19:5) and even the infinite heavens. "Behold, the heaven and the heaven of heavens is the Lord's thy God, the earth also, with all that therein is" (Deuteronomy 10:14).

God has, indeed, given man "dominion . . . over all the earth" (Genesis 1:26), and Satan has, indeed, laid false claim to "all the kingdoms of the world" (Luke 4:5, 6), but the fact remains that "the most High ruleth in the kingdom of men, and giveth it to whomsoever He will" (Daniel 4:32).

Most of all, every Christian should understand that he and all he has belongs to God, by both creation and blood-bought redemption. "Ye are not your own. For ye are bought with a price: therefore glorify God in your body, and in your spirit, which are God's" (I Corinthians 6:19, 20).

The Joyful Sound

Blessed is the people that know the joyful sound: they shall walk, O Lord, in the light of thy countenance (Psalm 89:15).

Many have been the Christians who have joined in singing "We have heard the joyful sound: Jesus saves; Jesus saves!" Not all have known, however, that this beautiful phrase comes from a great psalm extolling God's marvelous works of creation and then His promises of redemption.

"The heavens are thine, the earth also is thine: as for the world and the fullness thereof, thou hast founded them. The north and the south thou hast created them" (Psalm 89:11, 12). Earlier verses note that "the heavens shall praise thy wonders, O Lord" (v. 5), speaking of the angels, "the sons of the mighty" (v. 6), literally, "the sons of God." It is exciting to realize that the very first "joyful sound" was heard when God "laid the foundations of the earth." Then it was that "the morning stars sang together, and all the sons of God shouted for joy" (Job 38:4, 7).

There was also a joyful sound when Christ was born, and the angel came bringing "good tidings of great joy, which shall be to all people. For unto you is born . . . a Savior, which is Christ the Lord. . . . And suddenly there was . . . the heavenly host praising God" (Luke 2:10, 11, 13).

Whenever a soul is saved, there is another joyful sound: "Joy shall be in heaven over one sinner that repenteth," said Jesus (Luke 15:7). Finally, there will be a most wonderful sound of joy on Earth when the Lord comes again. "And the ransomed of the Lord shall return, and come to Zion with songs and everlasting joy upon their heads: they shall obtain joy and gladness, and sorrow and sighing shall flee away" (Isaiah 35:10). Therefore, even now, "my soul shall be joyful in the Lord: it shall rejoice in His salvation" (Psalm 35:9).

JULY 30

The Swoon Fantasy

And there came also Nicodemus, which at the first came to Jesus by night, and brought a mixture of myrrh and aloes, about an hundred pound weight. Then took they the body of Jesus, and wound it in linen clothes with the spices, as the manner of the Jews is to bury (John 19:39, 40).

Skeptics refuse to believe in the bodily resurrection of Jesus Christ, but they have had an inordinately difficult time in trying to explain it away. One of the most widely advanced—yet most ridiculous—notions is that Jesus merely swooned, and later, in the cool air of the tomb, He regained consciousness, unwrapped His grave clothes, moved the great stone aside from the tomb's entrance, overpowered all the Roman soldiers stationed there, and returned triumphantly to His disciples, who then incorrectly reported that He had been raised from the dead.

This whole tale is an absurd fantasy for many reasons, born of desperation. In our text verses, for example, Nicodemus brought a great weight of burial spices and linen clothes in which to bury Jesus' body. John is careful to say that all these spices and clothes were "wound" together. When Lazarus had emerged alive from the tomb a few days earlier, he "came forth, bound [same word as 'wound'] hand and foot with grave clothes: and his face was bound about with a napkin," so that others had to "loose him, and let him go" (John 11:44).

The clothes about Jesus were thus tied together so firmly that He could not possibly have untied them by Himself, even if He had been strong and whole. He didn't have to untie them, of course, since His resurrected body simply passed through the clothes, leaving them lying there as though they still held Him in their folds (John 20:6, 7). The Lord Jesus assuredly did not swoon. He died for our sins, and rose again!

When the Rivers Run Dry

The beasts of the field cry also unto thee: for the rivers of waters are dried up, and the fire hath devoured the pastures of the wilderness (Joel 1:20).

After the Flood of Noah, God set a boundary for the waters, "that they turn not again to cover the earth" (Psalm 104:9). There is a time coming, however, when even such a mighty river as "the great river Euphrates" will run dry, and "the water thereof [will be] dried up" (Revelation 16:12). Instead of covering the earth, the life-giving waters will be withheld, as one of God's coming judgments on the rebellious world of the last days. His prophetic witnesses will be given power to "shut heaven, that it rain not in the days of their prophecy" (Revelation 11:6). Furthermore, the atmosphere will be so restrained that "the wind should not blow on the earth, nor on the sea, nor on any tree" (Revelation 7:1), yet the sun will burn so intensely that "men (will be) scorched with great heat" (Revelation 16:9).

All of this will generate great fires and famine around the world. The prophet Joel places all this in the context of the coming "day of the LORD . . . as a destruction from the Almighty" (Joel 1:15). The pastures will burn up, and the rivers will dry up, "for the day of the LORD is great and very terrible; and who can abide it?" (Joel 2:11). "Therefore hath the curse devoured the earth, and they that dwell therein are desolate: therefore the inhabitants of the earth are burned, and few men left" (Isaiah 24:6).

Yet there is also a time coming when the judgments are past and "the parched ground shall become a pool, and the thirsty land springs of water: . . . And the ransomed of the LORD shall return . . . : They shall obtain joy and gladness, and sorrow and sighing shall flee away" (Isaiah 35:7, 10). In that day—as in this—it is all-important to be among the ransomed.

AUGUST 1

The Face of Jesus Christ

For God, who commanded the light to shine out of darkness, hath shined in our hearts, to give the light of the knowledge of the glory of God in the face of Jesus Christ (II Corinthians 4:6).

The light that shines in the soul of a lost sinner when he first comes to know Jesus Christ can only be compared to the light that Christ called forth on Day One of Creation Week. We met this God of glory spiritually when we first beheld in our hearts the face of Jesus Christ.

But the face of Jesus Christ was not always deemed so glorious. We read of a time when ungodly men "did spit in His face" (Matthew 26:67), then took a blindfold "to cover His face" (Mark 14:65) and finally, with a rain of terrible blows "struck Him on the face" (Luke 22:64).

Once His "countenance [was] as Lebanon, excellent as the cedars" (Song of Solomon 5:15), but when they finished their assault, "His visage was so marred more than any man, and His form more than the sons of men" (Isaiah 52:14).

"The face of the Lord is against them that do evil" (I Peter 3:12), however, and the time is coming very soon when all those who have turned their faces from Him will call "to the mountains and rocks, Fall on us, and hide us from the face of Him that sitteth on the throne, and from the wrath of the Lamb" (Revelation 6:16). When finally they will have seen the glory of God in the face of Jesus Christ in all its consuming strength, not even the world itself could stand, "from whose face the earth and the heaven fled away" (Revelation 20:11).

For those who have looked on Him in faith, however, this will not be a time of judgment, but blessing, for "they shall see His face" (Revelation 22:4). The face of Jesus Christ, fierce as devouring fire to those He must judge, is glorious in beauty and love to those who believe.

Treasures of the Snow

Hast thou entered into the treasures of the snow? or hast thou seen the treasures of the hail? (Job 38:22).

It is interesting that this book, the oldest in the Bible, contains more references to snow, ice, and frost than any other book of the Bible. This is despite the fact that Job's homeland was in what is now essentially a desert region. Possibly the effects of the post-Flood Ice Age were still strong in Job's day.

In any case, the beautiful phrase, "treasures of the snow," is both appropriate and prophetic. Its crystal structure, though mostly in the form of delicate six-pointed "stars," is endlessly varied and always intricately symmetrical and incredibly beautiful.

The snow is a treasure in other ways as well. The winter's snow pack in the mountains is often called "white gold," because of its indispensable water storage capacity, released in the melting season each spring to provide life to teeming cities and irrigation in the desert for needed food supplies. The snow also aids in maintaining the planet's chemical cycles by returning various elements in the nuclei of its flakes back from the ocean to the lands from which they were leached and transported by rivers to the ocean. When the snowpack becomes a glacier, it can greatly assist in the breakup of rocks to form fertile soils.

In the Scriptures, its pure white color is often used to symbolize the cleansing of a sinful heart that trusts the Lord. "Wash me," said David, "and I shall be whiter than snow" (Psalm 51:7). "Though your sins be as scarlet, they shall be as white as snow" the Lord promises those who come to Him for salvation (Isaiah 1:18).

As the snow comes down from heaven, so comes the Word of God to ask the soul as in our text: "Hast thou entered into the treasures of the snow?" (Job 38:22).

Questioning God

Nay but, O man, who art thou that repliest against God? Shall the thing formed say to Him that formed it, Why hast thou made me thus? (Romans 9:20).

Whenever one begins a question with "Why?" he should realize that the answer must necessarily be theological, not scientific. Science can deal with the questions of "what" and "how," sometimes even with "where" and "when," but never with "why!" The "why" questions have to do with motives and purposes, even when dealing with natural phenomena ("Why does the earth rotate on its axis?" "Why do we have mosquitoes?"). Even though we can partially explain such things by secondary causes, we finally encounter a "first cause," and then the "why?" can be answered only by God.

The wise thing to do is simply to believe that He has good reasons for everything, whether we can discern them now or not. "Shall not the Judge of all the earth do right?" (Genesis 18:25). God the Creator "worketh all things after the counsel of His own will" (Ephesians 1:11), and it is our high privilege simply to trust Him, not to question Him.

On the other hand, He often asks us: "Why?" "Why are ye fearful, O ye of little faith?" Jesus asked His disciples when they thought they were in great peril (Matthew 8:26). "If I say the truth, why do ye not believe me?" (John 8:46) He would say to those who question His word.

Then to those who doubt His deity, the Apostle Paul speaking in His name, asks: "Why should it be thought a thing incredible with you, that God should raise the dead?" (Acts 26:8). As the popular chorus goes: "God specializes in things thought impossible!" Our God is omniscient, and knows what's best; He is omnipotent, so He can do it. He is all-loving, and will surely do what's best for those who trust Him.

Our Natural and Spiritual Bodies

It is sown in dishonor; it is raised in glory: it is sown in weakness; it is raised in power: It is sown a natural body; it is raised a spiritual body. There is a natural body, and there is a spiritual body (I Corinthians 15:43, 44).

In this portion of this great chapter on the resurrection—first that of Christ, then the future resurrection of the redeemed—death and resurrection are compared to seed-sowing and harvest. When a seed is planted in the ground, it is as though it had died and is buried. For a long time after its "death," the seed cannot be seen, but finally it rises again as a beautiful flowering plant, or sheaf of grain, or even a lovely tree.

Jesus made this same analogy. "Except a corn of wheat fall into the ground and die, it abideth alone: but if it die, it bringeth forth much fruit" (John 12:24; note also Mark 4:26–29). Our human bodies, because of sin and the curse, eventually die and are buried; but one day (like the planted seed) they will appear again, but now immortal and glorified, far greater than they were before—that is, of course, if their real inhabitants (their eternal created spirits) have been born again through faith in their already-resurrected Savior.

Our new spiritual bodies rising from the grave will be real physical bodies (like that of Jesus after He was raised), but will no longer be under bondage to gravitational and electro-magnetic forces, as at present, but only to spiritual forces, of which we have as yet very little knowledge. We do know, however, that our spiritual bodies will be "fashioned like unto His glorious body" (Philippians 3:21). Although "it doth not yet appear what we shall be: . . . when He shall appear, we shall be like Him" (I John 3:2). Then, in our glorious, powerful, spiritual bodies, we as "His servants shall serve Him" in love and joy forever (Revelation 22:3).

The Counting God

Doth not He see my ways, and count all my steps? (Job 31:4).

God is surely the Great Mathematician. All the intricacies of structure and process of His mighty cosmos are, at least in principle, capable of being described mathematically, and the goal of science is to do just that. This precise intelligibility of the universe clearly points to a marvelous intelligence as its Creator.

God even "telleth the number of the stars; He calleth them all by their names" (Psalm 147:4). Astronomers estimate that at least ten trillion trillion stars exist in the heavens, and God has counted and identified each one! And that is not all: "The very hairs of your head are all numbered," Jesus said (Matthew 10:30). From the most massive star to the tiniest hair, God has counted and controls each component of His creation.

Such countings are far beyond human capabilities, for "the host of heaven cannot be numbered, neither the sand of the sea measured" (Jeremiah 33:22). But God has also created "an innumerable company of angels" (Hebrews 12:22) and has promised that the redeemed will include "a great multitude, which no man could number" (Revelation 7:9).

No wonder that David exclaimed, "Many, O LORD my God, are thy wonderful works which thou hast done, and thy thoughts which are to us-ward: they cannot be reckoned up in order unto thee: if I would declare and speak of them, they are more than can be numbered" (Psalm 40:5).

Perhaps the most wonderful of all God's counting activities is that implied in Job's rhetorical question: "Doth not He see my ways, and count all my steps?" If He has numbered the hairs on our heads, we can be certain He numbers our steps along the way, and guides them all. "The steps of a good man are ordered by the LORD: and He delighteth in his way" (Psalm 37:23).

Signs of the Everlasting Covenants

And the bow shall be in the cloud; and I will look upon it, that I may remember the everlasting covenant between God and every living creature of all flesh that is upon the earth (Genesis 9:16).

The first mention of the key word, "covenant," is in Genesis 6:18 where God promised to establish a covenant with Noah after the Flood. This everlasting covenant was made with all the earth's future populations and is still in effect, symbolized continually by the beautiful rainbow after a rain.

God also made an everlasting covenant with Abraham and Isaac. "And I will establish my covenant between me and thee and thy seed after thee in their generations for an everlasting covenant, to be a God unto thee, and to thy seed after thee. And I will give unto thee, and to thy seed after thee, the land wherein thou art a stranger, all the land of Canaan, for an everlasting possession; and I will be their God" (Genesis 17:7, 8). This time, the symbol of God's everlasting covenant was that of circumcision, "a token of the covenant betwixt me and you" (Genesis 17:11).

There is still another everlasting covenant—this one with all the redeemed of all the ages. "I will make an everlasting covenant with them, that I will not turn away from them, to do them good; but I will put my fear in their hearts, that they shall not depart from me" (Jeremiah 32:40).

God has made this "new covenant" applicable to all the saved, and this time, the sign of the covenant is nothing less than the blood of Christ. "Now the God of peace, that brought again from the dead our Lord Jesus, that great shepherd of the sheep, through the blood of the everlasting covenant, Make you perfect in every good work to do His will" (Hebrews 13:20, 21).

The Marvel of Design

And they sat before him, the firstborn according to his birthright, and the youngest according to his youth: and the men marvelled one at another (Genesis 43:33).

When creationists calculate the extremely low probability of the chance origin of life, many evolutionists scoff at the calculation, alleging that any one arrangement of the components of a simple, living molecule is just as likely as any other arrangement. Therefore, they say, it is no great marvel that the components fell into this particular arrangement.

This is a puerile argument, of course, quite unworthy of the intelligent scientists who use it. There can be at best, only a few arrangements that will contain the organized information necessary for reproduction, compared to "zillions" of possible arrangements with no information at all.

This fact is beautifully illustrated in our text. Why should Joseph's brothers "marvel" when they were seated in chronological order of birth by a host who (presumably) was entirely unaware of that order? The reason why they marveled was because there are almost 40 million different ways (calculated by multiplying all the numbers, one through eleven, together) in which the eleven brothers could have been seated!

Maybe an evolutionist would not "marvel" that this unique seating arrangement happened by chance, since he somehow believes that far more intricately organized arrangements than this happened by chance to produce our universe and its array of complex systems. Anyone else, however, would immediately have realized this, and so the brothers of Joseph "marvelled one at another." So also, when we behold the wonders of design in the creation, should we "lift up [our] eyes on high, and behold who hath created these things" (Isaiah 40:26).

God's Care for Animals

I know all the fowls of the mountains: and the wild beasts of the field are mine (Psalm 50:11).

This verse occurs immediately following a verse widely quoted by those eulogizing the great riches of the Lord: "For every beast of the forest is mine, and the cattle upon a thousand hills" (Psalm 50:10). In context, however, God was not simply proclaiming His wealth, but rather the value of each individual animal in His creation.

His people had been offering their animal sacrifices as a mere ritual, without considering the intrinsic value of these animals to the God who had given them life. They were not merely items of property, the offering of which constituted monetary gifts to God by their owners. This "covenant with me by sacrifice" (Psalm 50:5) was a sacrifice of life, not of money!

The offering of the shed blood of an innocent animal on an altar was accepted by God as an atonement for the sins of a repentant sinner, but it was of no avail if offered carelessly or presumptuously. In fact, it only added still further to the guilt of the person presenting it. "For I desired mercy, and not sacrifice" (Hosea 6:6).

But if God was saddened by the careless slaying of animals for sacrifices, what must He think of their wanton slaughter for sport or for other purposes not intended and authorized by their Maker? He even notes when a sparrow dies (Matthew 10:29).

Even more seriously, what must be His feelings about those who trivialize or ignore the great sacrifice of His Son, as "the Lamb of God, which taketh away the sin of the world" (John 1:29)? "Of how much sorer punishment, suppose ye, shall he be thought worthy, who hath trodden under foot the Son of God, and hath counted the blood of the covenant, wherewith he was sanctified, an unholy thing?" (Hebrews 10:29).

The Folly of Humanism

The fool hath said in his heart, There is no God. They are corrupt, they have done abominable works, there is none that doeth good (Psalm 14:1).

Despite all their pretense of scientific intellectualism, those who deny the existence of a personal Creator God are, in God's judgment, nothing but fools. Psalm 14, psalm 53, Romans 3, etc., all describe the inner character of all such people—whether they call themselves atheists or humanists or pantheists or some other name. This repeated emphasis indicates how strongly God feels about those who dare to question His reality. It is bad enough to disobey His commandments and to spurn His love; it is utter folly to deny that He even exists!

The Bible describes the awful descent from true creationism into evolutionary pantheistic humanism. "When they knew God, they glorified Him not as God, neither were thankful; but became vain in their imaginations, and their foolish heart was darkened. Professing themselves to be wise, they became fools. . . . Who changed the truth of God into a lie, and worshipped and served the creature more than the Creator" (Romans 1:21, 22, 25).

Certain atheists/humanists claim to be moral people, though their criteria of morality are often quite different from those of the Bible. No matter how admirable their humane acts of "righteousness" may seem, however, they are guilty of the sin of unbelief, the greatest sin of all. "Without faith it is impossible to please Him: for he that cometh to God must believe that He is" (Hebrews 11:6). With all the innumerable evidences of God's reality as seen in the creation and throughout history, and then especially in the person and work of Jesus Christ, it is utter foolishness to plunge blindly into eternity to meet the God whom they deny.

The Brevity of Human Life

For a thousand years in thy sight are but as yesterday when it is past, and as a watch in the night (Psalm 90:4).

In this unique psalm, Moses is stressing the brevity of even the longest human life with the everlasting nature of God. In the pre-Flood world, men were able to live many hundreds of years, but no one ever lived as long as 1000 years.

By Moses' time, the typical life-span was 70 or 80 years (v. 10), much the same as today. Moses lived to age 120, but he was twice as old as most of his contemporaries when he finally died (note Numbers 14:29, 34; Deuteronomy 34:7).

Moses, therefore, was profoundly impressed with the ephemeral nature of a person's time on earth. Even if someone had lived a thousand years, this was only a little while in God's sight, and his life would soon "fly away" (v. 10) and be forgotten.

There is nothing in this passage, incidentally, or in II Peter 3:8 ("one day is with the Lord as a thousand years") to justify the misinterpretation that attributes billions of years to God's creation week. In context (and one must always be sensitive to the context if he wants to understand and properly apply any passage of Scripture) neither Moses nor Peter were referring to the creation week at all. Moses was stressing the brevity of human life, even that of the antediluvians, while Peter was rebuking the latter-day uniformitarians who would come denying the catastrophic effects of the great Flood. It is too bad that so many Christians are willing to distort Scripture like this in order to accommodate the imaginary ages of evolution.

The message we should really get from this Mosaic observation is the application He Himself makes. "So teach us to number our days, that we may apply our hearts unto wisdom" (Psalm 90:12)!

The Eternal Earth

And He built His sanctuary like high palaces, like the earth which He hath established for ever (Psalm 78:69).

There are a number of passages in the Bible which state unequivocally that the earth, in some form, is going to continue eternally. "One generation passeth away, and another generation cometh: but the earth abideth for ever" (Ecclesiastes 1:4).

However, this present earth and its atmospheric heavens must first be purged of all the age-long effects of sin and the curse, which now affect the very elements (or "dust of the earth"). Therefore, "the heavens shall pass away with a great noise, and the elements shall melt with fervent heat, the earth also and the works that are therein shall be burned up" (II Peter 3:10).

Evidently, this fiery cataclysm is not an annihilation of the earth and its atmosphere, but rather a great exchange of energies. The earth's very elements will probably be converted into sound and heat energies by mass-energy nuclear-conversion processes, in order to burn out the great fossil beds and all other relics of sin and the curse. Then, however, God will reverse the process, converting these and other energies back into matter, thus "renewing" the primeval earth, which originally had been "very good" (Genesis 1:31). "We, according to His promise, look for new heavens and a new earth, wherein dwelleth righteousness" (II Peter 3:13).

It is this new earth (that is, the earth made new) which will then continue forever. "For as the new heavens and the new earth, which I will make, shall remain before me, saith the LORD, so shall your seed and your name remain" (Isaiah 66:22). "Because the [creation] itself also shall be delivered from the bondage of corruption [that is, 'decay'] into the glorious liberty of the children of God" (Romans 8:21).

The Rest Is Yet to Come

There remaineth therefore a rest to the people of God (Hebrews 4:9).

This has long been a favorite verse of those who labor. Many employees may work a five or six day week, but mothers work seven days. Missionaries and people in special ministries are often heard to say that, while they never grow tired *of* the work, they do get weary *in* the work, for the needs seem so great that they dare not stop even for a day.

The Lord knew His people would need rest, of course, and so ordained a weekly day of rest. In fact, the only reason He took six days to do the work of creation was to set the pattern for man's six day work week (Exodus 20:8–11). Yet Jesus also indicated it is still "lawful to do well on the sabbath days" (Matthew 12:12), and the Scriptures command us to be always "redeeming the time, because the days are evil" (Ephesians 5:16), so it is often difficult for concerned Christians to find the time for needed rest, even on the "sabbath days," let alone an annual vacation.

Our text verse seems to have a threefold application. The word for "rest" is actually the special word for "sabbath rest," used only this one time in the New Testament, evidently indicating that the weekly rest day (like each of the other laws in the Ten Commandments) is still a divine principle in the Christian dispensation, and violating it is to our detriment. It also refers, in context, to the rest we find in Christ, "For he that is entered into His rest, he also hath ceased from his own works, as God did from His" (Hebrews 4:10).

There is surely also a most comforting application for our future life: "Blessed are the dead which die in the Lord from henceforth: . . . that they may rest from their labors; and their works do follow them" (Revelation 14:13).

AUGUST 13

From the Beginning

For this is the message that ye heard from the beginning, that we should love one another (I John 3:11).

The pungent phrase "from the beginning" occurs no less than nine times in the first three chapters of the little epistle of I John. Thus, while in one sense, Christ's command to love one another was a new commandment, in another sense it has been with us from the very beginning of the world. "Brethren, I write no new commandment unto you, but an old commandment which ye had from the beginning. The old commandment is the word which ye have heard from the beginning" (I John 2:7).

That this beginning is the same beginning as in Genesis 1:1 and John 1:1 is shown in the very first verses of John's epistle: "That which was from the beginning, . . . of the word of life, . . . that eternal life, which was with the Father, and was manifested unto us" (I John 1:1, 2). Note also I John 2:13: "I write unto you, fathers, because ye have known Him that is from the beginning" (see also I John 2:14).

"Let that therefore abide in you, which ye have heard from the beginning. If that which ye have heard from the beginning shall remain in you, ye also shall continue in the Son, and in the Father" (I John 2:24). This is an eternal commandment, for "God is love" (I John 4:16) and "love is of God" (I John 4:7). In the upper room, Jesus prayed to the Father: "Father . . . thou lovedst me before the foundation of the world. . . . and I have declared unto them thy name, . . . that the love wherewith thou hast loved me may be in them" (John 17:24, 26).

Love, therefore, has been at the center of God's plan from the beginning, but a new pattern and measure of that love was given us by Christ. "A new commandment I give unto you, That ye love one another; as I have loved you, that ye also love one another" (John 13:34).

Waters above the Mountains

Thou coverest it with the deep as with a garment: the waters stood above the mountains (Psalm 104:6).

Many Christian intellectuals have argued that the flood of Noah's day was only local, being unwilling to reject the current system of evolutionary geology. Modern geologists usually assume the earth's fossil-bearing sedimentary rocks represent billions of years of evolution rather than the deposits of the worldwide Flood, as the founding fathers of geology had all believed.

However, this idea is clearly refuted, not only in the actual record of the Flood (Genesis 7, 8), but also in later Biblical passages. Our text verse, for example, says that the waters of the "deep" once covered the earth like a garment covers the body. Furthermore, these waters stood above all the antediluvian mountains. This was no local flood!

These standing waters of the deep were finally caused to "haste away" (v. 7) by means of great movements of the earth's crust. "Mountains rose up and great basins opened up" (literal rendering of v. 8), and the vast flood waters rushed down off the newly elevated continents into the newly opened ocean basins, carving out great canyons and transporting great quantities of sediment into the ocean depths. In the process, as God has promised Noah (Genesis 9:11), He had "set a bound that they may not pass over; that they turn not again to cover the earth" (Psalm 104:9).

There have been many devastating local floods in all parts of the world ever since Noah, but God has kept His promise never again to send a flood which will cover the earth. The mountains of the present world were all uplifted towards the end of the flood period, but they still bear witness, in the form of marine sediments and marine fossils near their summits, of the time when the waters stood above the mountains.

AUGUST 15

The Living and True God

For they themselves shew of us what manner of entering in we had unto you, and how ye turned to God from idols to serve the living and true God (I Thessalonians 1:9).

There are "gods many, and lords many" (I Corinthians 8:5) in today's world, just as there were in the ancient pagan world. In fact, the worship of many of these ancient deities is being revived in various dark corners of the so-called "New Age" movement today. Idol worship can also involve adulation of men and women—such as rock stars (witness the annual memorial service to Elvis Presley), professional athletes, and movie idols, not to mention the humanistic worship of such political/religious leaders as Lenin, Mao, Hitler, Khomeini, and an increasing assortment of gurus and false prophets.

There is, however, only one true God, the God who created all things. "To us there is but one God, the Father, of whom are all things, and we in Him; and one Lord Jesus Christ, by whom are all things, and we by Him" (I Corinthians 8:6). The one thing all these false gods and false religions have in common is the denial of the true God and omnipotent Creator.

For such idolatry there is no legitimate excuse. "We know that an idol is nothing in the world, and that there is none other God but one" (I Corinthians 8:4). A dead idol obviously can be of no use. The infallible test as to just who this "true" God may be is that His identity is confirmed as the only living God; therefore, He is the only true God.

He died for our sins, yes, but now He lives forever as King of all His creation. We, like the Thessalonians, should turn from all our idols "to serve the living and true God; And to wait for His Son from heaven, whom He raised from the dead, even Jesus, which delivered us from the wrath to come" (I Thessalonians 1:9, 10).

Creation and the Finger of God

It is a sign between me and the children of Israel for ever: for in six days the LORD made heaven and earth, and on the seventh day He rested, and was refreshed. And He gave unto Moses, when He had made an end of communing with him upon Mount Sinai, two tables of testimony, tables of stone, written with the finger of God (Exodus 31:17, 18).

"All Scripture is given by inspiration of God" (II Timothy 3:16), but *this* portion of Scripture was given by direct *inscription* of God! Moses testified: "The LORD delivered unto me two tables of stone written with the finger of God; and on them was written according to all the words, which the LORD spake with you in the mount out of the midst of the fire in the day of the assembly" (Deuteronomy 9:10). "He wrote upon the tables the words of the covenant, the ten commandments" (Exodus 34:28). Thus, out of all the Holy Scriptures, God chose to write this section, not through one of His prophets, but with His own finger! It should, therefore, be taken literally and most seriously.

It is also significant that these commandments were structured around a weekly day of rest, "remembering" God's creation week—six days of creating and making everything in heaven and earth, followed by a sanctified day of rest and refreshment (note also Exodus 20:8–11 and Genesis 1:31–2:3). Ever since the creation, people have observed a weekly calendar. The seven day week (unlike the day, month, and year) has no astronomical basis at all. People keep time in weeks simply because God did! Even those who deny the six day week of creation must observe it, for their biological rhythms are constructed that way by God. "The Sabbath was made for man," said Jesus (Mark 2:27). Since God considered the truth of the literal creation week so important that He inscribed it Himself, we should believe *this* portion of His word first of all.

Shine on Us

The Lord make His face shine upon thee, and be gracious unto thee (Numbers 6:25).

This request is part of the well-known Mosaic benediction for the children of Israel (Numbers 6:24–27). The first occurrence in verb form of the word "shine" is in this verse, although in the noun form, translated as "light," it appears in the third verse of the Bible when God said, "Let there be light" (Genesis 1:3).

True light comes only from God, since "God is light" (I John 1:5). As the world depends on the sunshine for its physical life, so we continually must receive the Son's shining in our hearts to sustain our spiritual life. "In Him was life; and the life was the light of men" (John 1:4).

It is noteworthy that the prayer of our text occurs seven other times in the Scriptures. These are as follows:

"Make thy face to shine upon thy servant: Save me for thy mercies' sake" (Psalm 31:16); "God be merciful unto us, and bless us; and cause His face to shine upon us. Selah" (Psalm 67:1); "Turn us again, O Lord God of Hosts, cause thy face to shine; and we shall be saved" (Psalm 80:19; also vv. 3, 7); "Make thy face to shine upon thy servant; and teach me thy statutes" (Psalm 119:135); "O our God, hear the prayer of thy servant, and his supplications, and cause thy face to shine upon thy sanctuary that is desolate, for the Lord's sake" (Daniel 9:17).

Since God in His omnipotence dwells "in the light which no man can approach unto" (I Timothy 6:16), He shines on us for salvation, spiritual illumination, and daily guidance only through His Son, the word made flesh, for "in Him was life; and the life was the light of men" (John 1:4). "For God, who commanded the light to shine out of darkness, hath shined in our hearts, to give the light of the knowledge of the glory of God in the face of Jesus Christ" (II Corinthians 4:6).

To and Fro, Up and Down

And the LORD said unto Satan, Whence comest thou? Then Satan answered the LORD, and said, From going to and fro in the earth, and from walking up and down in it (Job 1:7).

This remarkable scene in heaven provides us a striking picture of Satanic activity. The devil, in his opposition to God and His program of salvation, evidently never rests. He is not omnipresent, like God, because he is a finite (though very powerful and brilliant) created being. To accomplish his goal, therefore, he is never at rest, but keeps going from place to place and working deception after deception, bringing everyone he can under his influence.

Therefore, God urgently warns us: "Be sober, be vigilant; because your adversary the devil, as a roaring lion, walketh about, seeking whom he may devour" (I Peter 5:8).

The same is true of the demonic spirits who have followed the devil in his rebellion against God. They never rest until they can take possession of some person's body and mind and then control that person's behavior. "When the unclean spirit is gone out of a man, he walketh through dry places, seeking rest, and findeth none. Then he saith, I will return into my house from whence I came out" (Matthew 12:43, 44).

This restlessness that characterizes the devil and his demons often also manifests itself in the unsaved, and this will be the ultimate state of those who yield to the pressures of these evil spirits. "They have no rest day nor night, who worship the beast and his image, and whosoever receiveth the mark of his name" (Revelation 14:11).

True rest of soul is found only in Christ, with His forgiveness and cleansing and guidance. "Come unto me, all ye that labor and are heavy laden," Jesus says, "and I will give you rest. Take my yoke upon you, and learn of me; for I am meek and lowly in heart: and ye shall find rest unto your souls" (Matthew 11:28, 29).

Books

This is the book of the generations of Adam. In the day that God created man, in the likeness of God made He him (Genesis 5:1).

The Bible (literally, "the book") contains over 200 references to books. This implies, among other things, God's approval of communication by books. Our text, containing the first mention of the word "book" in the Bible, indicates that the very first man wrote a book! "Give attendance to reading," Paul recommends (I Timothy 4:13), especially the Holy Scriptures (II Timothy 3:15–17).

The pattern of first and last mentions of "book" in the Bible is noteworthy, for all refer to divinely written or divinely inspired books. The first use in the New Testament is in the very first verse—"the book of the generations of Jesus Christ" (Matthew 1:1). The book of Adam's "generations" is in a special sense, the Old Testament, the book of the generation of Jesus Christ—the last Adam—is in a similar sense the New Testament.

The final mention of "book" in the Old Testament is in Malachi 3:16: "A book of remembrance was written before Him for them that feared the Lord, and that thought upon His name."

The third-from-last verse of the New Testament contains no less than three references to God's books: "If any man shall take away from the words of the book of this prophecy, God shall take away his part out of the book of life, . . . and from the things which are written in this book" (Revelation 22:19).

Note the significant modifiers attached to these six key references: "the book of the generations of Adam," "a book of remembrance," "the book of the generation of Jesus Christ," "the book of this prophecy," "the book of life," and finally, simply "this book!"

The Weary Dove

But the dove found no rest for the sole of her foot, and she returned unto him into the ark, for the waters were on the face of the whole earth: then he put forth his hand, and took her, and pulled her in unto him into the ark (Genesis 8:9).

Unlike the raven, which Noah had sent out first, the dove could not live on the carrion floating on the flood waters. After nine months cooped up in the ark, she had reveled in her freedom when Noah first released her from the window of the ark. Unaware of the outside perils while safe with Noah, she flew gaily off into the open spaces beyond, just like many a professing Christian, eager to cast off the constraints of his or her parental religion. "And I said, Oh that I had wings like a dove! for then would I fly away, and be at rest. Lo, then would I wander far off, and remain in the wilderness" (Psalm 55:6, 7).

But the dove could find no rest away from Noah, whose very name means "rest"! His father, Lamech, by prophetic inspiration, had called his name Noah, saying, "This same shall comfort us concerning our work and toil of our hands, because of the ground which the LORD hath cursed" (Genesis 5:29). So she finally returned, finding rest once again in Noah's outstretched hands.

Just so, the Lord Jesus, in His greater ark of secure salvation, is waiting at its open window, with arms outstretched, inviting all those weary of the doomed world outside to return to Him. "Come unto me, all ye that labor and are heavy laden, and I will give you rest. Take my yoke upon you, and learn of me; for I am meek and lowly in heart: and ye shall find rest unto your souls. For my yoke is easy, and my burden is light" (Matthew 11:28–30). Christ's message to the weary wanderer is: "I have blotted out, as a thick cloud, thy transgressions, . . . return unto me; for I have redeemed thee" (Isaiah 44:22).

AUGUST 21

The Way of Cain

Whoso boasteth himself of a false gift is like clouds and wind without rain (Proverbs 25:14).

Cain initially was a religious man, evidently proud of his achievements as a "tiller of the ground" which God had "cursed" (Genesis 4:2; 3:17). He assumed that God would be much impressed with the beautiful basket of his "fruit of the ground" which he presented as an "offering unto the LORD." Cain became bitterly angry when God "had not respect" to Cain and his offering (Genesis 4:3–5).

"By faith Abel offered unto God a more excellent sacrifice than Cain," shedding the blood of an innocent lamb in substitution for his own sin and guilt before God, "by which he obtained witness that he was righteous" (Hebrews 11:4). Since "faith cometh by hearing, and hearing by the word of God" (Romans 10:17), Abel was merely obeying God's word, but Cain, proud and self-righteous in attitude, was presuming to offer up his own merits in payment for the privilege of coming to God.

This was a "false gift," however, with no meritorious value at all before God, "like clouds and wind without rain." The Apostle Jude warns against any such presumption, especially now that we can freely come to God through His own perfect "Lamb of God, which taketh away the sin of the world" (John 1:29). "Woe unto them!" says Jude, "for they have gone in the way of Cain . . . clouds are they without water, carried about of winds, trees whose fruit withereth, without fruit, twice dead, plucked up by the roots" (Jude 11, 12). This severe indictment was lodged against all who, like Cain, are superficially religious, but who, by their self-righteous resentment against God, are "turning the grace of our God into lasciviousness, and denying the only Lord God, and our Lord Jesus Christ" (Jude 4). We must not boast of our gifts to God, but only of His gift to us.

Seeking Signs

An evil and adulterous generation seeketh after a sign; and there shall no sign be given to it, but the sign of the prophet Jonas: For as Jonas was three days and three nights in the whale's belly; so shall the Son of man be three days and three nights in the heart of the earth (Matthew 12:39, 40).

If there was ever "an evil and adulterous generation," it is surely this present one and, once again, there is a widespread seeking after signs (same word in the Greek as "miracles"). The almost explosive rise of the so-called New Age movement has produced an amazing interest in all forms of occultism and supernatural phenomena: astrology, channeling, ESP, near-death experiences, UFO's, meditation, and mysticism of many strange varieties.

Even in Christian circles, there is an unhealthy interest in new revelations and other supernatural signs. The Lord Jesus, however, rebuked those who wanted special signs before receiving Him. "Except ye see signs and wonders, ye will not believe" (John 4:48). He has already given us the greatest of all signs—His bodily resurrection from the dead, the best-evidenced fact of all history—and this should suffice, as He told the scribes and Pharisees in our text.

In fact, there is a real danger in seeking such signs and wonders, for many of these things—while perhaps supernatural—are not from God. "For there shall arise false Christs, and false prophets, and shall show great signs and wonders; insomuch that, if it were possible, they shall deceive the very elect" (Matthew 24:24).

We now have the complete written word of God, and it is sufficient for every need of the believer until Christ returns, "whereunto ye do well that ye take heed, as unto a light that shineth in a dark place, until the day dawn, and the day star arise in your hearts" (II Peter 1:19).

Uniformitarianism

Knowing this first, that there shall come in the last days scoffers, walking after their own lusts, And saying, Where is the promise of His coming? for since the fathers fell asleep all things continue as they were from the beginning of the creation (II Peter 3:3, 4).

Uniformitarianism is the modern name for the doctrine, prophesied long ago by Peter for those living in the last days, that "the present is the key to the past." That is, the study of present-day natural processes (biological recombination, geological sedimentation, etc.) operating in the past as they do at present, are sufficient to determine the origin and development of all things. To them, no supernatural cause (such as God!) is needed. Even "creation" is still going on by these natural processes, since "all things continue as they were from the beginning of the creation."

This ancient prophecy, of course, is being specifically fulfilled in our modern "scientific" age. Synonyms for uniformitarianism might include such philosophies as naturalism, materialism, and evolutionism.

These concepts dominate modern education, even among most professing "Christians": since there was no real supernatural *creation,* there will be no supernatural *consummation,* and all things continue as they were, so "Where is the promise of His coming?"

Peter, however, not only *predicts* this philosophy but also *condemns* it! "For this they willingly are ignorant of!" (v. 5). That is, people who believe in the unbroken continuity of all things are willful in their refusal to consider the overwhelming evidences of *dis*continuity, particularly at the times of the special creation of all things in the beginning and the cataclysmic destruction of all things at the great flood, when "the world that then was, being overflowed with water, perished" (v. 6).

The Godhead

For in Him dwelleth all the fulness of the Godhead bodily (Colossians 2:9).

The term "Godhead" occurs three times in the King James translation. Each time it translates a slightly different Greek noun, all being slight modifications of the Greek word for "God" (*theos,* from which we derive such English words as "theology"). It essentially means the nature, or "structure" of God, as He has revealed Himself in His word.

The first occurrence is in Acts 17:29: "We ought not to think that the Godhead is like unto gold or silver, or stone, graven by art and man's device." Men have been guilty throughout the ages of trying to "model" the Godhead, but this leads quickly to idolatry, whether that model is a graven image of stone or a philosophical construct of the mind.

What man cannot do, however, God has done, in the very structure of His creation. "The invisible things of Him from the creation of the world are clearly seen, being understood by the things that are made, even His eternal power and Godhead" (Romans 1:20). His tri-universe (space, matter, and time, with each component unique in definition and function, yet permeating and comprising the whole) perfectly "models" His tri-une nature (Father, Son, Holy Spirit—each distinct, yet each the whole).

This analogy can be carried much further, for this remarkable tri-unity pervades all reality. The tri-universe is not God (that would be pantheism), but it does clearly reflect and reveal the tri-une nature of His Godhead.

The last occurrence of the word is in our text. Although we cannot see the Godhead in its fullness, that fullness does dwell eternally in the Lord Jesus Christ. All that God is, is manifest in Him. "And ye are complete in Him" (Colossians 2:10).

AUGUST 25

The New Heavens and New Earth

For, behold, I create new heavens and a new earth: and the former shall not be remembered, nor come into mind (Isaiah 65:17).

There is a glorious future awaiting the redeemed. Although God's primeval creation of the heavens and the earth is eternal (note Psalm 148:6, etc.), these are now groaning in pain under the effects of sin and the curse. When the Lord returns, they will be "delivered from the bondage of corruption into . . . glorious liberty" (Romans 8:21), and God will make them all new again, with all the scars of sin and death burned away by His refining fires (II Peter 3:10).

There are four explicit references in the Bible to these "renewed" heavens and earth. In addition to our text, which assures us that they will be so wonderful that this present earth and its heavens will soon be altogether forgotten, there is the great promise of Isaiah 66:22: "For as the new heavens and the new earth, which I will make, shall remain before me, saith the LORD, so shall your seed and your name remain." Thus, *that* heavens and earth will remain eternally, and so will all who dwell there, with their true spiritual children. Note also that both God's "creating" and "making" powers will be applied to the new heavens and new earth, just as they were to the first (Genesis 2:3).

The third and fourth references are in the New Testament. "Nevertheless we, according to His promise, look for new heavens and a new earth, wherein dwelleth righteousness" (II Peter 3:13). Not only will no sin be present there, neither will the results of sin and the curse. "And I saw a new heaven and a new earth: for the first heaven and the first earth were passed away; . . . And God shall wipe away all tears from their eyes; and there shall be no more death, neither sorrow, nor crying, neither shall there be any more pain: for the former things are passed away" (Revelation 21:1, 4).

The Word of the King

Where the word of a king is, there is power: and who may say unto him, What doest thou? (Ecclesiastes 8:4).

Perhaps the arch-type of absolute monarchs was Babylonia's King Nebuchadnezzar, of whom the prophet Daniel could say: "Thou, O king, art a king of kings: for the God of heaven hath given thee a kingdom, power, and strength, and glory" (Daniel 2:37). The word of this and every true king was with power, the king being answerable to no man but himself, for his authority came from God. "For there is no power but of God" (Romans 13:1). Many kings have had to learn this truth the hard way, however, for they have found that God could remove them as quickly as He had ordained them when they abused that power.

But there is one King who will never fall; one "who is the blessed and only Potentate, the King of kings; . . . to whom be honor and power everlasting" (I Timothy 6:15, 16). The Lord Jesus Christ has asserted: "All power is given unto me in heaven and in earth" (Matthew 28:18), and one day all creatures in heaven and earth will acknowledge: "Thou art worthy, O Lord, to receive glory and honor and power: for thou hast created all things" (Revelation 4:11). In that day all "the kingdoms of this world [shall] become the kingdoms of our Lord, and of His Christ; and He shall reign for ever and ever" (Revelation 11:15).

This one, who is King of all kings, is also the one who is "called The Word of God" (Revelation 19:13). The word of *this* King is of such power that He could speak the mighty cosmos into existence. His word could calm a violent storm and call Lazarus back from death. "The word of God is quick, and powerful" (Hebrews 4:12), and "His word was with power" (Luke 4:32). Therefore, "all the promises of God in Him are yea, and in Him Amen" (II Corinthians 1:20).

Immortality

Who only hath immortality, dwelling in the light which no man can approach unto; whom no man hath seen, nor can see: to whom be honor and power everlasting. Amen (I Timothy 6:16).

In the Greek New Testament, there are two words translated "immortality." One is *athanasia* ("without death") which is used in our text to describe God in His eternal essence. The other is *aphtharsia* ("without corruption"), used in II Timothy 1:10: "[Christ] hath abolished death, and hath brought life and immortality to light through the gospel," and translated "incorruption" in I Corinthians 15:42: "So also is the resurrection of the dead. It is sown in corruption; it is raised in incorruption."

The doctrine of the "immortality of the soul" is a doctrine of both ancient paganism and modern "New Ageism." Such people all believe in some form of evolution, and reject the doctrine of resurrection, which uniquely accompanies creationist religions. These false religions believe that, at death, the body decays but the soul continues to exist, either in an eternally disembodied state or reincarnated in some other body. Atheists, of course, believe that both body and soul cease to exist at death.

But Christ, who "hath immortality" and who has died for the whole world and triumphed over death, promises a bodily resurrection to all who believe on Him, assuring *both* incorruption and immortality forever. "For this corruptible must put on incorruption, and this mortal must put on immortality" (I Corinthians 15:53). The law of entropy (involving decay, corruption, pain, sorrow, and disintegration) will be repealed when God's curse (Genesis 3:17) on the whole creation because of sin is removed (Romans 8:20–23; Revelation 22:3) and death will be abolished from His new creation forever.

The Vanishing Serpents

For they cast down every man his rod, and they became serpents: but Aaron's rod swallowed up their rods (Exodus 7:12).

Like the future image of the beast, which will seem to have life, these magician-induced serpents can only have been "lying wonders" (Revelation 13:15; II Thessalonians 2:9). Neither men nor demons can really create life; this is a prerogative of God alone, who "created every living creature" (Genesis 1:21). However, both human magicians and demons can generate hypnotic mental states and occult hallucinations, which ungodly people like Pharoah may be deceived into seeing as real physical entities. When their demonstration was over, however, there was nothing to show for it. Even their rods (not "serpents") were gone, for Aaron's genuine serpent had made a meal of them. In a true miracle of creation, Aaron's God had transmuted the dead atoms of a wooden stick (just as He later made it to produce blossoms and almonds, Numbers 17:8) into a living serpent, capable of consuming other sticks which only *appeared* to be serpents.

The deception of the magicians was revealed when they were unable later to imitate Moses' miracle of turning dust into lice throughout the land of Egypt (Exodus 8:18). Interestingly, many people believed for many centuries that similar phenomena—which they called "spontaneous generation"—occurred naturalistically, but this notion was scientifically demolished by Pasteur over a hundred years ago. Only the *living God* can create life!

The miracle of Aaron's rod is also a parable. Aaron's rod of life took on the nature of the serpent, just as Christ was made sin for us (II Corinthians 5:21). But then it swallowed up the other serpent-rods, and the sting of "that old serpent" was put away. Thus, "death is swallowed up in victory. O death, where is thy sting?" (I Corinthians 15:54, 55).

The Two Hosts of Heaven

"Therefore hear the word of the LORD; I saw the LORD sitting upon His throne, and all the host of heaven standing on His right hand and on His left" (II Chronicles 18:18).

This remarkable vision was granted to the prophet Micaiah, the only true prophet at the court of the evil King Ahab, of Israel. Other Scriptures confirm that there really is a great host of angels at God's throne in heaven (Job 1:6; Daniel 7:10; Revelation 5:11; etc.). These are mighty angels, and they go forth at God's command (Psalm 103:20, 21), especially in connection with their primary function as "ministering spirits, sent forth to minister for them who shall be heirs of salvation" (Hebrews 1:14).

In addition to the angels, there is another "host of heaven"—the stars, which "cannot be numbered" (Jeremiah 33:22). Like the stars, the angels also are said to be "innumerable" (Hebrews 12:22). Both "hosts" are mentioned in Nehemiah 9:6. Angels are often associated with stars in the Bible, and are even likened to stars on a number of occasions. However, a third of the angels "kept not their first estate" (Jude 6; Revelation 12:3–9). Although angels are not to be worshipped (Revelation 22:8–9), Satan, the "anointed cherub" (Ezekiel 28:14), desired to be "like the most high" (Isaiah 14:14), and led these now-fallen angels into a cosmic rebellion against their Creator, which continues to this day. They have, in fact, become associated with both the sky-images of astrology and the corresponding graven images of paganism. Paul warned that such idol worship was, in reality, demon worship (I Corinthians 10:20). It is this particular "host of heaven" which all devotees of false religions, ancient and modern, have really worshipped, when they reject the true God of creation and put their faith in some aspect of the cosmos itself. The faithful and obedient host of heaven worships God alone, and so should we.

Melting Elements

But the day of the Lord will come as a thief in the night; in the which the heavens shall pass away with a great noise, and the elements shall melt with fervent heat, the earth also and the works that are therein shall be burned up (II Peter 3:10).

When the atomic bomb burst over Hiroshima in 1945, the thoughts of Bible-believing Christians everywhere turned almost immediately to this verse. There was also widespread concern that man's newly discovered ability might get out of control and cause all "the elements to melt with fervent heat!" Seemingly, Peter had prophetically anticipated, 1900 years in advance, the modern discovery of nuclear fission.

In this verse, the word "elements" means fundamental parts, and could appropriately be applied to the basic elements of which matter is composed. The word for "melt" is usually translated "unloose," and this also is appropriate to describe atomic disintegration.

Now, over 50 years later, there is still widespread fear of a nuclear holocaust. The words of our text refer, however, not to something man will do, but to God's coming great purging of the very dust of the earth, and all the age-long effects of sin and the curse. At the very end of this present age, when the mighty Creator appears on His great white judgment throne, the ineffable glory of His countenance will cause the earth and its atmospheric heaven to flee away, "and there was found no place for them" (Revelation 20:11).

"Nevertheless, we, according to His promise, look for new heavens and a new earth, wherein dwelleth righteousness" (II Peter 3:13). God will make the earth new again, and the great Curse, which has permeated the "dust of the earth" (the "elements") ever since Adam (Genesis 3:17–20), will be "no more" (Revelation 22:3). This great hope is incentive enough to live now in the light of eternity.

AUGUST 31

They That Wait upon the Lord

But they that wait upon the LORD shall renew their strength; they shall mount up with wings as eagles; they shall run, and not be weary; and they shall walk, and not faint (Isaiah 40:31).

This is one of the best-loved promises of the Bible, for it is easy to grow weary and faint in our mortal bodies, even when doing the work of the Lord. The answer, we are told, is to "wait upon the LORD."

But what does this mean? The Hebrew word (*gavah*) does not mean "serve" (like a waitress), but rather, to wait for" or "look for." It is translated "waited for" the second time it is used in the Bible, when the dying patriarch, Jacob, cried out: "I have waited for thy salvation, O LORD" (Genesis 49:18).

The first time it is used, surprisingly, is in connection with the third day of creation, when God said: "Let the waters under the heaven be gathered together unto one place" (Genesis 1:9). That is, the all-pervasive waters of the original creation, divided on the second day of creation, now are told to wait patiently, as it were, while God formed the geosphere, the biosphere, and the astrosphere, before dealing again with the waters.

Perhaps the clearest insight into its meaning is its use in the picture of Christ forshadowed in the 40th Psalm. "I waited patiently for the LORD; and He inclined unto me, and heard my cry" (Psalm 40:1).

"The everlasting God, the LORD, the Creator of the ends of the earth, fainteth not, neither is weary" (Isaiah 40:28), and His gracious promise is that we can "renew our strength" (literally, "exchange our strength"—exchange our weakness for His strength!) by "waiting upon Him." We wait patiently for Him, we gather together unto Him, we look for Him, we cry unto Him, we trust Him, and He renews our strength!

Labor or Service?

Six days thou shalt labor, and do all thy work (Deuteronomy 5:13).

The term "labor" to many seems to connote drudgery or routine, repetitive, demeaning toil. As used here in the fourth of God's Ten Commandments, however, the Hebrew word *abad* means rather to "serve" and is so translated 214 times in the King James. Only one other time is it translated "labor," and that is in the first rendering of the commandments (Exodus 20:9). Thus, the command could well be read: "Six days shalt thou *serve*. . . ."

Furthermore, the word for "work" (Hebrew, *melakah*) does not denote servile labor, but "deputyship," or "stewardship." The one whom we are to serve or act as deputy for, of course, is God Himself, when we do our work.

In the ultimate and very real sense the Lord is our employer, and we serve Him, not man. Therefore, "whatsoever ye do, do it heartily, as to the Lord, and not unto men" (Colossians 3:23). Every honest occupation if carried out for the Lord's sake and to His glory is "divine service," and every Christian who holds this perspective on his or her work (be it preaching, or bookkeeping, or homemaking, or whatever) is in the Christian ministry—for "ministry" simply means "service."

Note also that God has ordained not a four-day or five-day work week: "Six days thou shalt labor, and do all thy work" He says, thus commemorating the six days in which He worked in the beginning, "for in six days the LORD made heaven and earth" (Exodus 31:17).

One day, Lord willing, we shall hear Him say: "Well done, thou good and faithful servant . . . enter thou into the joy of thy Lord" (Matthew 25:21). Then, throughout the ages to come, "His servants shall serve Him" (Revelation 22:3) with everlasting joy.

SEPTEMBER 2

Man and His Labor

Man goeth forth unto his work and to his labor until the evening (Psalm 104:23).

The 104th psalm is a beautiful psalm of Creation and the Flood, supplemented by God's providential care of His creatures in the post-Flood world. Our text makes man's activity seem almost incidental in the grand scope of God's activities on behalf of His whole creation.

Nevertheless, it reminds us of God's first great commission to mankind concerning that creation. "Have dominion . . . over all the earth . . . to dress it and to keep it" (Genesis 1:26; 2:15). This primeval mandate, though still in effect as man's stewardship responsibility for the earth and its creatures, has been seriously impacted by sin and the curse. "Cursed is the ground for thy sake," God told Adam; "in the sweat of thy face shalt thou eat bread" (Genesis 3:17, 19).

And so it is that men (women, too!) must work, and the work often is laborious, and stressful, and unappreciated. Yet the divine rule is "that ye study to be quiet and to do your own business, and to work with your own hands . . . that ye may walk honestly . . . and that ye may have lack of nothing" (I Thessalonians 4:11, 12). "For . . . if any would not work, neither should he eat" (II Thessalonians 3:10).

Thus labor is necessary, even for those who don't know the Lord. But it is far better if we work, not just to earn a living, but to please the Lord. "Whatsoever ye do, do it heartily, as to the Lord, and not unto men" (Colossians 3:23).

Whatever our job may be (assuming it is an honorable occupation), it can be regarded as serving Christ and as helping to fulfill His primeval dominion commandment, and even as helping to lead others to know Him. Therefore, whether the work is easy, or hard, we should be "always abounding in the work of the Lord, . . . your labor is not in vain in the Lord" (I Corinthians 15:58).

Remember the Day of Rest

Remember the sabbath day, to keep it holy. Six days shalt thou labor, and do all thy work: But the seventh day is the sabbath of the LORD thy God: in it thou shalt not do any work, thou, nor thy son, nor thy daughter, thy manservant, nor thy maidservant, nor thy cattle, nor thy stranger that is within thy gates (Exodus 20:8–10).

The Hebrew word for "remember" actually means to "mark," or "set aside." The Israelites didn't need to be told to "remember" the sabbath, because they, like other nations, had been keeping time in weeks ever since the first week (Genesis 2:1–3). Note the references to the sabbath in the sending of God's manna, prior to the giving of this commandment (Exodus 16:23–29). But they *did* need to be reminded to mark it as a holy day, or rest day, as God had done in that first week.

The Hebrew word for "sabbath" does not mean "Saturday" any more than it means "Sunday." It means, simply, "rest," or "intermission." The institution of the sabbath (that is, one day out of every seven days to be "set aside" as a day of rest, worship, and remembrance of the Creator) was "made for man" and his good, not as an arbitrary legalistic rule to be followed mindlessly (Mark 2:27). It was even of benefit to the animals used by man (note the mention of "cattle" in the commandment). It was not intended solely for Israel, since it had been a pattern observed since the completion of God's six days of creating and making all things at the very beginning of world history (note Genesis 2:1–3; Exodus 20:11).

It is still appropriate today, as well. "There remaineth therefore a rest [that is, 'a sabbath-keeping'] to the people of God" (Hebrews 4:9). All men have a deep need to remember their Creator and His *completed* work of creation at least once each week, as well as His completed work of salvation—especially in these days when both of these finished works are so widely denied or ignored.

SEPTEMBER 4

How Populations Can Grow

And the children of Israel were fruitful, and increased abundantly, and multiplied, and waxed exceeding mighty; and the land was filled with them (Exodus 1:7).

Populations can grow very rapidly. For example, one can calculate that the seventy who came into Egypt with Jacob (Genesis 46:27) could easily have multiplied to over five million in just ten generations, assuming only that the average family had six children who lived and reproduced, and that only two generations were living contemporaneously at any one time. This was less than half the number in Jacob's immediate family. The actual count of the grown Israelite men (not including the tribe of Levi) who left Egypt with Moses was "six hundred thousand and three thousand and five hundred and fifty" (Numbers 1:46). The total population was probably between two and three million at the time.

This illustrates how rapidly populations can grow when conditions are favorable. In fact, if a simple geometric growth rate is assumed (which was the assumption made by Charles Darwin in relation to his imagined "struggle for existence" in nature), it would only take about 1100 years—assuming 35 years per generation—to develop the present world population of about six billion people. Immediately after the Flood, with only eight people in that first generation, with the whole world before them, with long life spans still prevailing, and with every incentive to have large families, the population surely would have grown explosively. Yet the average annual growth rate since the Flood need only have been one-fourth the present growth rate to produce the world's present population in the 4000 years (minimum) since that time.

All of which indicates that the evolutionary scenario, which assumes that human populations have been on the earth for about a *million* years, is absurd. The whole universe could not hold all the people!

Three Arks

And when she could not longer hide him, she took for him an ark of bulrushes, and daubed it with slime and with pitch, and put the child therein; and she laid it in the flags by the river's brink (Exodus 2:3).

It is interesting to compare the three "arks" mentioned in Scripture. The Hebrew word means, simply, "box-like container." The first was the great ark of Noah, overlaid and inlaid with "pitch" (Genesis 6:14). This was not a petroleum-based pitch, for oil is a fossil fuel probably formed in the upheavals of the Flood. The word (Hebrew *kaphar*) simply means "covering," and is usually translated "atonement" (e.g., in Leviticus 17:11).

Moses' ark, on the other hand, was daubed with slime and pitch, and *this* pitch *was* a petroliferous material. Finally, God's "Ark of the Covenant," built for the holy place in the tabernacle, was overlaid "with pure gold" (Exodus 25:11). The first ark preserved the founders of the Gentile civilization; the second preserved the prophet of the Jewish dispensation; the third preserved the inscribed divine words for the saved of all generations (Exodus 31:17, 18; Deuteronomy 10:1–5).

Noah's ark, like the economy which he established, was built strong enough to endure throughout man's earthly existence, and its remains may still survive on Mount Ararat to this day. Moses' ark, like the economy which he founded, was enduring enough only for its immediate purpose.

God's Ark and its sacred contents, on the other hand, will last forever. When Nebuchadnezzar carried away all the treasures of the temple (II Chronicles 36:18, 19), no mention was made of this greatest of all treasures. John, in the last book of the Bible, reveals why. "And the temple of God was opened in heaven, and there was seen in His temple the Ark of His Testament" (Revelation 11:19), forever reminding the people of God and His eternal Word.

Preaching to Pagans

And saying, Sirs, why do ye these things? We also are men of like passions with you, and preach unto you that ye should turn from these vanities unto the living God, which made heaven, and earth, and the sea, and all things that are therein (Acts 14:15).

When Paul and Barnabas set out from Antioch on their first missionary journey, their first recorded preaching points were at Salamis and Paphos on the Isle of Cyprus, then Perga, Antioch of Pisidia, and Iconium, in what is now Turkey. At all of these, so far as the record goes, they began their witnessing in the local synagogues (Acts 13:5, 14; 14:1), where the people already knew and believed the Old Testament Scriptures, including the Genesis record of Creation. They could begin with this premise and proceed to show from Old Testament prophecy that Jesus was the Messiah, climaxing it with the evidence of His resurrection.

But when they came to nearby Lystra, their first audience was a street crowd of pagan worshipers of Roman gods. These had no knowledge of the Bible and only the vaguest knowledge, if any, of the long-forgotten true God of Creation. Paul, therefore, centered his message, first of all, around the latter, as indicated in our text. He later followed a similar procedure with the Athenian philosophers (Acts 17:22–31).

His pragmatic approach to soul-winning was the following: "I made myself servant unto all, that I might gain the more. . . . To them that are without [the] law, as without law. . . . I am made all things to all men, that I might by all means save some" (I Corinthians 9:19, 21, 22).

Christians today would do well to follow his example, stressing the message of creation to modern-day pagans, whether to those brought up in modern ethnic religions or to the Biblically illiterate pagans of our pseudo-intellectual American culture.

Infallible Proofs

To whom also He shewed Himself alive after His passion by many infallible proofs, being seen of them forty days, and speaking of the things pertaining to the kingdom of God (Acts 1:3).

To the first Christians, faith in the deity of Christ was not a blind leap into the dark. Only God could defeat death, and they knew—beyond all doubt—that Jesus Christ had risen bodily from the tomb. They had seen Him, touched Him, and eaten with Him, alone and in crowds, in closed rooms, and out in the open.

The term "infallible proofs" translates a Greek word used only this one time, meaning literally "many criteria of certainty," and it is significant that the inspired Word of God applies it *only* to the resurrection of Christ. It is not too much to say that Christ's resurrection is the most certain fact in all history, and many large volumes have been published setting forth the evidences thereof. No wonder the Apostle Peter could say: "We have not followed cunningly devised fables, when we made known unto you the power and coming of our Lord Jesus Christ, but were eyewitnesses of His majesty" (II Peter 1:16).

The Apostle John testified thus: "The life was manifested, and we have seen it, and bear witness, and shew unto you that eternal life, which was with the Father, and was manifested unto us" (I John 1:2). John not only saw Him in His resurrection body, but also in His glorified body, hearing Him say: "I am He that liveth, and was dead; and, behold, I am alive for evermore" (Revelation 1:18).

It is true that we, like the first Christians, must *believe* on Christ to receive salvation, but this faith is not a credulous faith, a leap into the dark. It is a reasonable faith, based on many infallible proofs, and we can, therefore, trust Him with our eternal souls.

SEPTEMBER 8

A House in the Land of Shinar

Then said I to the angel that talked with me, Whither do these bear the ephah? And he said unto me, To build it an house in the land of Shinar: And it shall be established, and set there upon her own base (Zechariah 5:10, 11).

This prophecy of the latter days shows a woman named "Wickedness" being translated rapidly in a great measuring basket (symbolizing commerce and finance "through all the earth," v. 6) to a base being built for it in the ancient land of Shinar (same as Sumeria). This was also the land of Nimrod, the leader of the post-Flood rebellion against God at Babel. "He began to be a mighty one in the earth. . . . And the beginning of his kingdom was Babel, . . . in the land of Shinar" (Genesis 10:8, 10).

From this first Babylon in the land of Shinar, the dispersed followers of Nimrod carried their anti-God, materialistic religion into every land, through every age. Its current form is mainly a pantheistic evolutionary humanism, promoting a "new world order," featuring a world government and (supposedly) universal prosperity, without God—a world order such as Nimrod tried to build at Babylon long ago.

In the final book of the Bible, this woman of Wickedness is called "MYSTERY BABYLON THE GREAT, THE MOTHER OF HARLOTS AND ABOMINATIONS OF THE EARTH"; she is said to be sitting upon "peoples, and multitudes, and nations, and tongues" (Revelation 17:5, 15). This monstrous system is evidently once again to have a house built for it in the land of Shinar.

It is interesting that Babylon (near Baghdad in Iraq) is already partially rebuilt. Being very near the geographical center of the earth's land masses, this site is the ideal location for a world government. In any case, the day will come when Babylon will fall forever, and there will be "a great voice of much people in heaven, saying, Alleluia" (Revelation 18:2; 19:1).

Emotional Decisions

And these are they likewise which are sown on stony ground; who, when they have heard the word, immediately receive it with gladness; And have no root in themselves, and so endure but for a time: afterward, when affliction or persecution ariseth for the word's sake, immediately they are offended (Mark 4:16, 17).

In Christ's parable of the sower, some of the seed (representing the word of God—Luke 8:11) fell on stony ground with little depth of earth. It sprang up immediately, but then quickly withered away. According to Christ's interpretation in our text, this represents the common situation in which a person makes an emotional decision to receive Christ without any real understanding of what it means. Such persons "have no root in themselves," and when they suddenly realize that being a Christian inevitably brings persecution "for the word's sake," then they "fall away" (Luke 8:13).

Modern evangelistic techniques too often generate such superficial conversions. Once such ephemeral converts fall away, they may well react so negatively to God's word as to be beyond reach the next time. "For if after they have escaped the pollutions of the world through the knowledge of the Lord and Saviour Jesus Christ, they are again entangled therein, and overcome, the latter end is worse with them than the beginning" (II Peter 2:20).

It is urgently important, therefore, that both evangelists and personal workers be thorough in their explanation of the gospel to potential converts, so that both mind and heart are willingly submitted to Christ. "As ye have therefore received Christ Jesus the Lord, so walk ye in Him: Rooted and built up in Him, and stablished in the faith; as ye have been taught, abounding therein with thanksgiving" (Colossians 2:6, 7).

SEPTEMBER 10

The Fear of the Lord

And unto man He said, Behold, the fear of the Lord, that is wisdom; and to depart from evil is understanding (Job 28:28).

This key phrase, "the fear of the LORD" ("Yahweh") occurs in a distinctive pattern in the Old Testament. There are 14 occurrences in the book of Proverbs and 7 in the other books, or a total of 3 x 7 altogether, both important Bible numbers .

As we see from the verses in Job preceding our text, when God first made man He told him that true wisdom is "the fear of the Lord" (*Adonai*—the only use of *Adonai* with this phrase). Unfortunately, Adam and Eve sought wisdom in the tree of knowledge instead (Genesis 3:6) and soon were hiding themselves in fear. The psalmist testifies: "the fear of the LORD is the beginning of wisdom" (Psalm 111:10). The final occurrence of the phrase is also in a wisdom context. "And wisdom and knowledge shall be the stability of thy times, and strength of salvation: the fear of the LORD is His treasure" (Isaiah 33:6).

There are numerous other references to fearing God, and a survey of all these would quickly show that the fear of the Lord is far more than mere "reverential trust," as some would define it. It means profound awe, intense awareness of God's absolute holiness and hatred of sin, as well as His omniscience and omnipresence, and living in light of the certainty of facing Him at His future judgment seat. It means unquestioning belief in God's word and in His unmerited gift of salvation.

But then it also means "the beginning of knowledge," "to hate evil," "prolonged days," "strong confidence," "a fountain of life," and a "satisfied life," as well as attaining true "riches and honor" (Proverbs 1:7; 8:13; 10:27; 14:26; 14:27; 19:23; 22:4). "The fear of the LORD is clean, enduring for ever" (Psalm 19:9), and those who truly fear the Lord have everlasting life.

Begin at the Beginning

And beginning at Moses and all the prophets, He expounded unto them in all the scriptures the things concerning Himself (Luke 24:27).

It is rather common for Christian counselors to suggest that new Christians or non-Christians begin reading the Bible at the Gospel of John or some other New Testament book. They feel it is most important to introduce them to what is revealed concerning Christ, leaving the histories and prophecies of the Old Testament for more mature Christians.

But this was not the way that Christ chose to teach. He began in Genesis! Perhaps we should follow His example, for the New Testament contains at least 200 quotations or clear allusions to Genesis, not to mention all the references to other Old Testament books. Since New Testament writers, inspired by the Holy Spirit, clearly expected their readers to understand these Old Testament allusions, it seems reasonable that people should be familiar with the Old Testament before tackling the New. One could even argue that the woeful Biblical illiteracy of modern Christians and their easy willingness to compromise on basic doctrinal issues is because of this cart-before-the-horse approach to Bible study. As Jesus Himself said: "Had ye believed Moses, ye would have believed Me: for he wrote of Me. But if ye believe not his writings, how shall ye believe My words?" (John 5:46, 47).

The person and work of Jesus Christ are clearly revealed in the Old Testament, of course, often more fully than in the New (e.g., Isaiah 53). It is especially vital that one know and believe the Book of Genesis, which is the foundation of all the rest of Scripture. Jesus Christ was our Creator before He became our Redeemer, and a person must comprehend something of the awful reality of sin and the curse, before he can comprehend his need for the atonement. Christ is in all the Scriptures, and one must begin at the beginning, to know His fulness.

Too Hard for God?

Is any thing too hard for the Lord*? At the time appointed I will return unto thee, according to the time of life, and Sarah shall have a son* (Genesis 18:14).

This rhetorical question posed to Abraham by the Lord was in response to Sarah's doubts concerning His promise that they would have a son. It would, indeed, require a biological miracle, for both were much too old for this to happen otherwise.

With God, however, all things are possible, and He can and will, fulfill every promise, even if a miracle is required.

This same rhetorical question was asked of the prophet Jeremiah. "Then came the word of the Lord unto Jeremiah, saying, Behold, I am the Lord, the God of all flesh: is there anything too hard for Me?" (Jeremiah 32:26, 27). The one who created all flesh, who raises up kings and puts them down, could surely fulfill His promise to restore Israel to its homeland when the set time is come.

But Jeremiah had already confessed his faith in God's omnipotence. "Ah Lord God! Behold, thou hast made the heaven and the earth by Thy great power and stretched out arm, and there is nothing too hard for Thee" (Jeremiah 32:17). The God who called the mighty universe into being would not find it too difficult to keep His promise and fulfill His will.

Actually, the word translated "hard" in these verses is more commonly rendered "wonderful," or "marvelous" or an equivalent adjective, referring usually to something miraculous that could only be accomplished by God. For example, "marvelous things did He . . . in the land of Egypt" (Psalm 78:12). "For Thou art great, and doest wondrous things. Thou art God alone" (Psalm 86:10).

The first occurrence of the word, however (Hebrew *pala*), is in our text for today. There is nothing—*nothing*—too hard for the Lord, and we should never doubt His Word.

Through Flood and Fire

When thou passest through the waters, I will be with thee; and through the rivers, they shall not overflow thee: when thou walkest through the fire, thou shalt not be burned; neither shall the flame kindle upon thee (Isaiah 43:2).

Although this tremendous promise is primarily to be understood in a spiritual sense (deliverance through overflowing sorrows and fiery trials), God has demonstrated His ability to fulfill the spiritual aspects of the promise by its miraculous literal fulfillment on special occasions. The crossing of the Red Sea by the children of Israel is an obvious example of safe passage through deep waters.

The amazing experience of Shadrach, Meshach and Abednego in Nebuchadnezzar's fiery furnace is the most spectacular example of deliverance from burning. As the three emerged unscathed from the "exceeding hot" flames, the king was astounded when he "saw these men, upon whose bodies the fire had no power, nor was an hair of their head singed, neither were their coats changed, nor the smell of fire had passed on them" (Daniel 3:22, 27).

The entire world once was caused to pass through the Flood, and one day must be destroyed by the Fire (II Peter 3:6, 10), but "eight souls were saved by water" (I Peter 3:20) as the Flood carried them safely away in Noah's Ark from the violent world of the antediluvians, and all those truly trusting in Christ will be "saved; yet so as by fire" (I Corinthians 3:15) when He comes again.

These great experiences of the past and promises of the future assure us that God is able to deliver us through the deep waters and burning trials of the present life. "That the trial of your faith . . . though it be tried with fire, might be found unto praise and honor and glory at the appearing of Jesus Christ" (I Peter 1:7). In flood or fire, in life or death, His grace is always sufficient.

SEPTEMBER 14

Death in the Pot

> *So they poured out for the men to eat. And it came to pass, as they were eating of the pottage, that they cried out, and said, O thou man of God, there is death in the pot. And they could not eat thereof* (II Kings 4:40).

The "sons of the prophets," studying under Elisha, became hungry, so Elisha told them to "see the pottage," evidently a soup primarily made of lentils. However, one of the young students proceeded to gather some wild gourds and grind them into the pottage, carelessly assuming that their attractive appearance and taste would spice up the otherwise dull meal. When the more mature students took the first sip, however, they realized the alien ingredient was poisonous, and cried out: "There is death in the pot!"

There is a parable in this experience. Modern Bible scholars often want to spice up the old truths of Scripture with some new and superficially attractive concoction from the outside world, but this almost always serves merely to adulterate "the sincere milk of the word" (I Peter 2:2) and insert "death in the pot." Like the woman in the New Testament parable who took leaven and secretly "hid [it] in three measures of meal, till the whole was leavened" (Matthew 13:33), Elisha's enterprising young student slipped in his attractive ingredient and it soon permeated the whole pot of soup with its poison. This is the way with false doctrine.

The remedy for the poison in the pottage was found when Elisha said, "Bring meal. And he cast it into the pot. . . . And there was no harm in the pot" (II Kings 4:41). The purifying "meal" was fine wheat flour, always in Scripture symbolizing the true Word of God. It is the Word which is the true bread by which man must live (Matthew 4:4), and the antidote to the poisonous doctrines of the world must always be the unadulterated Word of God.

God-Hardened Hearts

For it was of the LORD to harden their hearts, that they should come against Israel in battle, that He might destroy them utterly, and that they might have no favor, but that He might destroy them, as the LORD commanded Moses (Joshua 11:20.

One of the most bitter complaints of critics against the Bible is its portrayal of the severity of God, especially in His command to Moses to destroy all the Canaanites. "When the LORD thy God shall deliver them before thee; thou shalt smite them, and utterly destroy them" (Deuteronomy 7:2). This seems more severe than ever when we read in our text that God Himself hardened the hearts of the Canaanites so that Joshua could destroy them.

But the notion that God is merely a kindly grandfather figure is a self-serving figment of man's sinful imagination. The New Testament reminds us that "our God is a consuming fire," and "the wages of sin is death" (Hebrews 12:29; Romans 6:23), and God doesn't change. "The Lord Jesus shall be revealed from heaven with His mighty angels, In flaming fire taking vengeance on them that know not God, and that obey not the gospel of our Lord Jesus Christ" (II Thessalonians 1:7, 8).

As far as the Canaanites were concerned, God had given them 400 years to repent (Genesis 15:13–16), but each new generation had gone further away from God than the one before, and they were practicing (as archaeology has revealed) every form of debauchery known to man. It was an act of mercy by God toward all those who would come in contact with them in future generations to decree their destruction now. They had already irrevocably hardened their hearts toward God, so God now hardened their hearts against Israel. Thinking they could destroy God's people, they only hastened their well-deserved end.

SEPTEMBER 16

Waxing Old, Like a Garment

Of old hast thou laid the foundation of the earth: and the heavens are the work of thy hands. They shall perish, but thou shalt endure: yea, all of them shall wax old like a garment: as a vesture shalt thou change them, and they shall be changed. But thou art the same, and thy years shall have no end (Psalm 102:25–27).

This remarkable passage, quoted also in Hebrews 1:10–12, anticipates the famous second law of thermodynamics, or law of entropy, indicating that everything in the physical universe is growing old and wearing out. God created everything in the beginning, winding it up like a great clock, so to speak.

Because of sin and the curse, however, it has been running down and "perishing" ever since. Jesus also said: "Heaven and earth shall pass away" (literally, "are passing away"—Matthew 24:35).

This universal scientific law is also anticipated in Isaiah 51:6: " . . . the earth shall wax old like a garment, and they that dwell therein shall die in like manner." That is, the law of decay and death applies both to the earth and its inhabitants. The concept of universal evolution is clearly refuted both by Scripture and true science.

Note that our text also anticipates that, although the earth is growing old and seems about to die, it will suddenly be changed, like a garment. The old garment will be discarded and a new garment put on. Peter puts it this way: "The heavens being on fire shall be dissolved, and the elements shall melt with fervent heat? Nevertheless we, according to His promise, look for new heavens and a new earth, wherein dwelleth righteousness" (II Peter 3:12,13).

Now, although the universe is perishing and will one day be suddenly renewed, its Creator never changes. His years will never end, and His word will never pass away.

His Son's Name

Who hath ascended up into heaven, or descended? who hath gathered the wind in His fists? who hath bound the waters in a garment? who hath established all the ends of the earth? what is His name, and what is His Son's name, if thou canst tell? (Proverbs 30:4).

The obvious answer to these rhetorical questions must center in God, the Creator of all things. But the fascinating revelation in this Old Testament passage is that God has a Son and that both have names.

When Moses asked God His name, "God said unto Moses, I AM THAT I AM . . . This is my name for ever" (Exodus 3:14, 15). Later, Moses, in His song of deliverance said: "The LORD is a man of war: the LORD is His name" (Exodus 15:3). The name LORD (Hebrew *Jehovah,* or *Yahweh)* means essentially "I am, the self-existent one."

As far as His Son's name is concerned, He is revealed under many names. In the Old Testament prophecy, "His name shall be called Wonderful, Counselor, The mighty God, The everlasting Father, The Prince of Peace" (Isaiah 9:6). How remarkable that a "Son is given" who is also named the mighty God and everlasting Father!

In His incarnation, the angel commanded Joseph, "Thou shalt call His name JESUS" ("Jehovah saves"), but he also said: "They shall call His name Emmanuel, which being interpreted is, God with us" (Matthew 1:21, 23).

There are many other titles by which the Son of God is identified, but perhaps the most significant are noted in connection with His final return in triumph. "His name is called The Word of God" (Revelation 19:13), identifying Him as both eternal Creator and incarnate Savior (John 1:1–3, 14). As our eternal King, "He hath on His vesture and on His thigh a name written, KING OF KINGS, AND LORD OF LORDS" (Revelation 19:16).

My Necessary Food

Neither have I gone back from the commandment of His lips: I have esteemed the words of His mouth more than my necessary food (Job 23:12).

Very little of the word of God was available to Job, but what little he had was of more importance to him than food. On the other hand, the completed Scriptures are available today, yet most Christians barely spend five minutes a day in the word.

It is noteworthy how many passages compare the Scriptures to our physical food. David said they were "sweeter also than honey and the honeycomb" (Psalm 19:10). Jeremiah said: "Thy words were found, and I did eat them; and thy word was unto me the joy and rejoicing of my heart: for I am called by thy name, O Lord God of hosts" (Jeremiah 15:16).

The writer of Hebrews, in a very important passage, compared the Word both to milk for infants and meat for adults. "For when for the time ye ought to be teachers, ye have need that one teach you again which be the first principles of the oracles of God; and are become such as have need of milk, and not of strong meat. For every one that useth milk is unskilful in the word of righteousness: for he is a babe. But strong meat belongeth to them that are of full age, even those who by reason of use have their senses exercised to discern both good and evil" (Hebrews 5:12–14).

Moses said long ago: "Man doth not live by bread only, but by every word that proceedeth out of the mouth of the Lord doth man live" (Deuteronomy 8:3), and this truth was considered so vital that Christ Himself quoted it when contending with Satan (Matthew 4:4). Now, if great men like Job and Moses and Jeremiah and the Lord Jesus all believed the Bible to be our necessary food, then we surely need it even more.

Who Gets Weary?

Hast thou not known? hast thou not heard, that the everlasting God, the Lord, the Creator of the ends of the earth, fainteth not, neither is weary? there is no searching of His understanding (Isaiah 40:28).

Everyone gets weary, and everyone must rest. Even in Eden, before sin came into the world, there was a weekly day of rest, and each day of work in the Garden was followed by a night of rest in sleep. The Lord Jesus Christ, in the days of His sinless human flesh, occasionally became "wearied with His journey" (John 4:6) and had to rest.

On one occasion He was so weary that, during a violent storm on the Sea of Galilee, He was "asleep on a pillow" (Mark 4:38) while the disciples tried to keep their ship from destruction. He once advised these fretful and busy disciples to "come ye yourselves apart into a desert place, and rest a while" (Mark 6:31). We sometimes need to come apart before we fall apart!

In the New Jerusalem, with our new bodies, we perhaps will not need rest and sleep, for "there shall be no night there" (Revelation 22:5). In our present frail tents of clay, however, we *do* need rest, for God made us so. In one area of life, on the other hand, we are *twice* admonished to "be not weary in well doing" (Galatians 6:9; II Thessalonians 3:13).

And when we do get weary, and perhaps are not yet able to stop and rest, we can draw on God's strength, for He "fainteth not, neither is weary." "He that keepeth Israel shall neither slumber nor sleep" (Psalm 121:4). "Even the youths shall faint and be weary, and the young men shall utterly fall: But they that wait upon the LORD shall renew their strength; they shall mount up with wings as eagles: they shall run, and not be weary; and they shall walk, and not faint" (Isaiah 40:30, 31).

SEPTEMBER 20

Our Hiding Place

For in the time of trouble He shall hide me in His pavilion: in the secret of His tabernacle shall He hide me; He shall set me up upon a rock (Psalm 27:5).

There come times in the life of each believer when the trials become overwhelming and the whole world seems to be falling apart. Without the Lord, it would be impossible to escape, but with the Lord there can be safety and restoration, for He can be our precious hiding place until the storm is done.

There are many gracious promises to this effect in His word, and we need only to claim them to experience them. The "pavilion" in our text is best understood as the tent of the commander-in-chief, well-protected and away from the battlefront. Surely we are safe there. "Thou shalt hide them in the secret of thy presence from the pride of man; Thou shalt keep them secretly in a pavilion from the strife of tongues" (Psalm 31:20).

There is a wonderful Messianic promise in Isaiah 32.2: "And a man [that Man is Christ!] shall be as an hiding place from the wind, and a covert from the tempest; as rivers of water in a dry place, as the shadow of a great rock in a weary land."

There, sheltered from the storm, our gracious Lord gives comfort and sweet counsel, until we are able to face the tempest victoriously. "He that dwelleth in the secret place of the most High shall abide under the shadow of the Almighty. I will say of the LORD, He is my refuge and my fortress: my God; in Him will I trust" (Psalm 91:1, 2).

One of the most beautiful of these promises introduces David's great song of deliverance: "The Lord is my rock, and my fortress, and my deliverer; The God of my rock; in Him will I trust: He is my shield, and the horn of my salvation, my high tower, and my refuge, my savior; thou savest me from violence" (II Samuel 22:2, 3).

Judgment in the New Testament

In flaming fire taking vengeance on them that know not God, and that obey not the gospel of our Lord Jesus Christ: Who shall be punished with everlasting destruction from the presence of the Lord, and from the glory of His power (II Thessalonians 1:8, 9).

Many critics have decried what they contend is the Bible's inconsistency. The Old Testament is a harsh indictment of human sin and warning of coming divine judgment, they say, whereas the New Testament stresses God's grace and love.

The fact is, however, that the Old Testament contains numerous testimonies of the love and merciful loving-kindness of God (e.g., Psalm 103). Similarly, the most striking and fearsome warnings and prophecies of judgment to come are found in the New Testament. The above text for the day is an example with its revelation of the coming eternal separation from God of all who reject Christ and His saving gospel. The Lord Jesus Christ Himself uttered more warnings of future hell than anyone else recorded in either Testament. He said, for example, that those "on the left hand" will be commanded to "depart from me, ye cursed, into everlasting fire, prepared for the devil and his angels" (Matthew 25:41). Jude spoke of ungodly men "to whom is reserved the blackness of darkness for ever" (Jude 13).

And, of course, the very last book of the New Testament, written by John, the disciple who stressed God's love more than any other writer, focuses especially and in detail on the coming period of God's judgment on a rebellious world. The climax of these warnings is Revelation 20:15: "Whosoever was not found written in the book of life was cast into the lake of fire." God's grace and full forgiveness are free to all who receive Christ, but certain judgment will come to all who refuse.

SEPTEMBER 22

Shadows of the Almighty

And a man shall be as an hiding place from the wind, and a covert from the tempest; as rivers of water in a dry place, as the shadow of a great rock in a weary land (Isaiah 32:2).

In the context of this beautiful verse, the "man" is none other than the Lord Jesus Christ. To one who had been traveling in the heat of the desert, such as the Sinai wilderness, nothing was so welcome as the cool shadows behind a great rock, in which one could rest for a while from the hardships of the wearying land. The symbol of the shadow is often used in the Old Testament to illustrate the refreshing presence of the Lord.

"He that dwelleth in the secret place of the most High shall abide under the shadow of the Almighty" (Psalm 91:1). Wherever His loved ones go, He is there, and our dwelling place is there in His shadow.

There is safety there also. "Because Thou hast been my help, therefore in the shadow of Thy wings will I rejoice" (Psalm 63:7). "He shall cover thee with His feathers, and under His wings shalt thou trust" (Psalm 91:4). He is the great Eagle as well as the great Rock, and finally also the great Tree. "As the apple tree among the trees of the wood, so is my Beloved among the sons. I sat down under His shadow with great delight, and His fruit was sweet to my taste" (Song of Solomon 2:3).

The shadow of a great rock in a weary land, the shadow of the wings of a great eagle, the shadow of a delightful fruit tree—all of these speak beautifully of the refreshing, protecting, satisfying shadow of His presence. These are the shadows of the Almighty God, who made heaven and earth, and now holds us in His hand. "I have covered thee in the shadow of mine hand, that I may plant the heavens, and lay the foundations of the earth, and say unto Zion, Thou art my people" (Isaiah 51:16).

Chariots of Fire

And he answered, Fear not: for they that be with us are more than they that be with them (II Kings 6:16).

God has created "an innumerable company of angels" (Hebrews 12:22), mighty spirits who "excel in strength, that do His commandments, hearkening unto the voice of His word" (Psalm 103:20). They are "sent forth to minister for them who shall be heirs of salvation" (Hebrews 1:14).

Few have seen this invisible host, but one who did was the servant of Elisha. With the Syrian army surrounding them, the servant was in mortal fear, but the prophet assured him that God's host was far greater in number. "And Elisha prayed, and said, LORD I pray thee, open his eyes, that he may see. . . . and, behold, the mountain was full of horses and chariots of fire round about Elisha" (II Kings 6:17).

Some time later, this same Syrian army laid siege to Samaria, but the Lord "made the host of the Syrians to hear a noise of chariots, and a noise of horses, even the noise of a great host. . . . Wherefore they arose . . . and fled for their life" (II Kings 7:6, 7). The anti-God army *heard* the same chariots of fire the servant had *seen,* and the Syrians fled in terror. "The chariots of God are twenty thousand, even thousands of angels. The Lord is among them" (Psalm 68:17).

The psalmist testified: "He hath delivered my soul in peace from the battle that was against me: for there were many with me" (Psalm 55:18). Thus also could King Hezekiah assure his people, when the Assyrians besieged Jerusalem: "With him is an arm of flesh; but with us is the LORD our God to help us, and to fight our battles . . . For there be more with us than with him" (II Chronicles 32:8, 7).

God's fiery chariots are still available, and "greater is He that is in you, than he that is in the world" (I John 4:4). Therefore, "if God be for us, who can be against us?" (Romans 8:31).

Life in Christ

In Him was life, and the life was the light of men (John 1:4).

A host of biochemists and other scientists have tried for over a century to determine how life evolved from nonlife. Such a quest is absurdly impossible, for the simplest imaginary self-replicating system would be infinitely more complex than the most elaborate machine ever designed by man. Life can come only from life. The first human life, indeed the first living system of any kind, could only have come by special creation from the *living* God. "For I am fearfully and wonderfully made" (Psalm 139:14).

Thus, "in Him we live, and move, and have our being," and He is "not far from every one of us" (Acts 17:28, 27). The Lord Jesus Christ is the one "by whom also He made the worlds" and who now is "upholding all things by the word of His power" (Hebrews 1:2, 3). The beating of our hearts, the breathing of our lungs, the very atoms of our bodies, are continually sustained by Him. Were He to withdraw His power for a moment, life would cease and all light would become darkness. Even those who reject Him and blaspheme His name owe their very existence to His power and grace.

"As the Father hath life in Himself; so hath He given to the Son to have life in Himself" (John 5:26). Life is "in Him"; He alone can conquer death and raise the dead. "As the Father raiseth up the dead, and quickeneth them; even so the Son quickeneth whom He will" (John 5:21), for as "the first man Adam was made a living soul; the last Adam was made a quickening spirit" (I Corinthians 15:45).

Thus, "he that hath the Son hath life; and he that hath not the Son of God hath not life" (I John 5:12). Through faith in His sacrificial death and resurrection life, "ye are dead, and your life is hid with Christ in God." Henceforth is Christ Himself "our life" (Colossians 3:3, 4).

The Omniscience of God

Great is our Lord, and of great power: His understanding is infinite (Psalm 147:5).

Consider the great rhetorical question asked by the Apostle Paul: "For who hath known the mind of the Lord? or who hath been His counsellor?" (Romans 11:34). The most learned scholars of every age are mere infants in knowledge, but He is of infinite knowledge! He is the supreme Mathematician, the divine Architect, the wonderful Counselor, the master Teacher, the great Physician. "There is no searching of His understanding" (Isaiah 40:28).

Everyone who believes in God acknowledges that God, by definition, is omniscient. He created all things and upholds all things, and thus, understands all things. He even knows all the future, for He is "the high and lofty One that inhabiteth eternity" (Isaiah 57:15), and He created time itself.

Now, while every believer *acknowledges* this, few really live as if they believe it. Most of the time, we live and speak and choose just as though God neither knows nor cares what we do. But He *does* know! Not only does He know all the intricacies of mathematics and biochemistry, but He has also "searched me, and known me" (Psalm 139:1). "Thou knowest my downsitting and mine uprising, . . . and art acquainted with all my ways. For there is not a word in my tongue, but lo, O LORD, thou knowest it altogether" (Psalm 139:2–4).

Furthermore, He is "of great power." He has created all things and, because "He is strong in power; not one faileth" (Isaiah 40:26). Because He was omniscient, He knew *how* all things should be made and, because He is omnipotent, He made them that way. There would, obviously, be no thought whatever of a trial-and-error, random mutation, survival-of-the-fittest, extinction and redevelopment, sort of a creative process with such a God. Just as He made His creation "very good" (Genesis 1:31), so we also, as believers saved by His grace, are "created unto good works" (Ephesians 2:10).

The Light and the Sun

The day is thine, the night also is thine: thou hast prepared the light and the sun (Psalm 74:16).

One of the traditional "discrepancies" attributed by the skeptics to the Genesis account of creation is the fact that there was "light" (Hebrew *or*) on the first day of creation week, whereas God did not create the "lights" (Hebrew *ma-or*) to rule the day and the night until the fourth day.

However, it is interesting that modern evolutionary cosmologists find no problem in having light before the sun. According to their speculative reconstruction of cosmic history, light energy was produced in the imaginary "Big Bang" 15 billion years ago, whereas the sun "evolved" only five billion years ago. Thus, even in their attempts to destroy the divine revelation of Genesis, they inadvertently find it necessary to return to its concepts. Light energy somehow had to be "prepared" before the sun and other stars could ever be set up to serve as future generators of light energy. The fact that light is an entity independent of the sun and other heavenly bodies is one of the remarkable scientific insights of the Bible. As the basic form of energy (even intrinsic in the very nature of matter, as expressed in the famous Einstein equation), it is significant that the first recorded word spoken by the Creator was: "Let there be light" (Genesis 1:3).

In this chapter, the psalmist is entreating the Lord of light, the Creator of all things, to deliver His people from those who are seeking to destroy all genuine faith in the true God of heaven. "The tumult of those that rise up against thee increaseth continually" (v. 23). Nevertheless, "God is my King of old, working salvation in the midst of the earth" (v. 12). The mighty God of creation, who established and controls all the basic energies of the cosmos and their manifestation on the earth, is fully able to defeat His enemies and establish His people. We can be sure of that.

Threescore Years and Ten

The days of our years are threescore years and ten; and if by reason of strength they be fourscore years, yet is their strength labor and sorrow; for it is soon cut off, and we fly away (Psalm 90:10).

When Moses wrote these words, near the end of his life, he was 120 years old (Deuteronomy 34:7). All the rest of the people of Israel (except Caleb and Joshua), who had been over 20 at the beginning of the 40-year wilderness wanderings, had died there (Numbers 14:28–34), and so there were no others over 60 years old.

In former days, men had lived much longer. Adam died at 930 and Noah at 950, but then Shem only lived to 600, and Abraham died at 175 years of age. Thus, the normal life span by Moses' time was down to 70 or 80 years, and he prophesied that this would continue.

It is remarkable that, with all the increase in medical knowledge, this figure has stayed about the same, and there seems to be little the gerontologists can do to increase it.

Furthermore, the latter years are largely "labor and sorrow," just as God told Adam when his sin brought God's curse on the earth (Genesis 3:17–20). No matter how much we try to prolong our lives, we are "soon cut off."

But then, we "fly away!" The soul/spirit complex of the Christian believer, released from its weary body, flies away to be with the Lord. Those left behind may sorrow, but "to depart, and to be with Christ . . . is far better." The Christian may confidently say with Paul: "For to me to live is Christ, and to die is gain" (Philippians 1:23, 21). In the meantime, as our time grows shorter, it is more important than ever that we "walk in wisdom toward them that are without, redeeming the time" (Colossians 4:5). "So teach us to number our days," prayed Moses (and so should we), "that we may apply our hearts unto wisdom" (Psalm 90:12).

Who Shall Let It?

Yea, before the day was I am He; and there is none that can deliver out of my hand: I will work, and who shall let it? (Isaiah 43:13).

This is one of the classic "archaisms" of the King James Version, where the English word "let" does not mean "allow" (as we now use the word), but almost the exact opposite. This particular English word was originally written and pronounced "lat" and was from the same Teutonic root as the word "late." Thus, to our Old English ancestors, it meant essentially "make late," or "hinder." Note its similar use in the King James in Romans 1:13 and II Thessalonians 2:7.

However, the Hebrew word (*shub*) from which it is translated in the verse of our text is extremely flexible, being rendered no less than 115 different ways in the Old Testament, occurring about 1,150 times altogether, with the context controlling its meaning in any given case.

In this context, the great theme is that of God as omnipotent Creator and only Savior. The first occurrence of *shub*, however, is at the time of the primeval curse on the creation, implanted in the very dust of the earth because of Adam's sin. To Adam, God had said: "In the sweat of thy face shalt thou eat bread, till thou return unto the ground; for out of it wast thou taken: for dust thou art, and unto dust shalt thou return" (Genesis 3:19). Here, *shub* is twice rendered "return," and this is the way it is most often translated in its later occurrences.

God, therefore, challenges every man: "When I work, who can return anything (or anyone) to its (or his) prior condition?" Though none can deliver out of His hand, or "make late" His work, He has promised to be our Savior, "and will not remember thy sins" (Isaiah 43:11, 25). When it is time for God to do His work—whether of creation or judgment or salvation, there is no one in all His creation who can "make it late"!

The Flesh and the Spirit

This I say then, Walk in the Spirit, and ye shall not fulfill the lust of the flesh (Galatians 5:16).

The conflict between flesh and spirit is a frequent theme in Scripture, beginning way back in the antediluvian period: "And the LORD said, My spirit shall not always strive with man, for that he also is flesh" (Genesis 6:3). The "flesh," of course, refers to the physical body, with all its feelings and appetites, while man's "spirit" refers especially to his spiritual nature, with its ability to understand and communicate in terms of spiritual and moral values, along with its potential ability to have fellowship with God.

Because of sin, however, the natural man is spiritually "dead in trespasses and sins" (Ephesians 2:1), and "they that are in the flesh cannot please God" (Romans 8:8). When the flesh dominates, even the Apostle Paul would have to say, "I know that in me (that is, in my flesh) dwelleth no good thing" (Romans 7:18). This aspect of human nature became so dominant in the antediluvian world that "all flesh had corrupted his way upon the earth" (Genesis 6:12), and God had to wash the world clean with the Flood.

Now, however, the substitutionary death of Christ brings salvation and spiritual life to all who receive Him by the Holy Spirit. "If Christ be in you, the body is dead because of sin; but the Spirit is life because of righteousness. But if the Spirit of Him that raised up Jesus from the dead dwell in you, He that raised up Christ from the dead shall also quicken your mortal bodies by His Spirit that dwelleth in you" (Romans 8:10, 11). By the Lord Jesus Christ, the human spirit is made alive right now, through the indwelling Holy Spirit, and the body's resurrection is promised when Christ returns.

"They that are Christ's have crucified the flesh." The daily challenge to the believer is this: "If we live in the Spirit, let us also walk in the Spirit" (Galatians 5:24, 25).

Showers of Blessing

And I will make them and the places round about my hill a blessing; and I will cause the shower to come down in his season; there shall be showers of blessing (Ezekiel 34:26).

This verse provided the inspiration for the old gospel hymn, "Showers of Blessing." While it applies specifically to Israel, it states a divine principle which believers of all times have rightly appropriated to their own lives. The same word ("showers") is also frequently translated "rain," speaking of the rain which followed Elijah's contest with the prophets of Baal at the end of the three-year drought. "And Elijah said unto Ahab, Get thee up, eat and drink; for there is a sound of abundance of rain" (I Kings 18:41).

In general, the word is most commonly used to indicate very heavy rains. In fact, its first occurrence is in connection with the great Flood. "The rain was upon the earth forty days and forty nights" (Genesis 7:12). This rain had poured forth from the windows (literally, "sluiceways") of heaven, and it provides an impressive picture of the tremendous showers of blessing which God desires to pour down on His people.

In the context of our key verse, the promised showers follow the condition of the preceding verses: "And I the Lord will be their God, . . . And I will make with them a covenant of peace" (Ezekiel 34:24, 25). The greatest blessings of God, accordingly, must follow the knowledge of God and the peace of God, through the Lord Jesus Christ.

No doubt the greatest of all spiritual blessings, at least in this life, is the inspired Word of God, and the same word is so used: "For as the rain cometh down, and the snow from heaven, and returneth not thither, but watereth the earth, and maketh it bring forth and bud. . . . So shall my word be that goeth forth out of my mouth: it shall not return unto me void, but it shall accomplish that which I please, and it shall prosper in the thing whereto I sent it" (Isaiah 55:10, 11).

The Circle of the Earth

It is He that sitteth upon the circle of the earth, and the inhabitants thereof are as grasshoppers; that stretcheth out the heavens as a curtain, and spreadeth them out as a tent to dwell in (Isaiah 40:22).

The discovery that the world is round is considered one of man's greatest scientific achievements, often wrongly attributed to Christopher Columbus. Columbus was, indeed, a great and courageous thinker and explorer, as well as a Bible-believing Christian, but scholars have concluded that many people had already migrated to the New World, long before—the American Indians first of all.

As far as the sphericity of the earth is concerned, the "flat-earth" myth of the Middle Ages was not the belief of most scholars of antiquity. The Bible, in particular, never hints of a drop-off point at the earth's edge, or any such notion as that. Its few references to "the four corners" of the earth (e.g., Isaiah 11:12) literally mean "the four *quarters* of the earth"—that is, the four quadrants of the compass.

In our text for the day, the word for "circle" is translated "compass" in Proverbs 8:27: "[God] set a compass upon the face of the depth" (same as 'deep,' referring to the ocean). Other occurrences are in Job 26:10: "He hath compassed the waters with bounds, until the day and night come to an end," and Job 22:14: "[God] walketh in the circuit of heaven." All of these passages are best understood in terms of a spherical earth, with its basic shape at sea level determined by its ocean surface as controlled by gravity. The Hebrew word itself (*khug*) basically means a circle. Any vertical cross section through the earth's center is a "great circle," of course, with any "straight" line on the ocean surface actually representing an arc of such a circle.

This is only one of many "pre-scientific" insights of the Bible written by divine inspiration long before the rise of modern science.

The Mighty Word

Is not my word like as a fire? saith the Lord; and like a hammer that breaketh the rock in pieces? (Jeremiah 23:29).

The power resident in the Word of God—both His spoken Word and His written Word, the Holy Scriptures—is so great that the Biblical writers almost exhaust their resources of language in trying to describe it, using many and varied figures of speech to illustrate its wonders.

It is the Word which produces and maintains life. "Thy words were found, and I did eat them; and thy word was unto me the joy and rejoicing of mine heart" (Jeremiah 15:16). It is both "milk" for the babe and "strong meat" for the mature in Christ (Hebrews 5:12), and our daily bread. "Man shall not live by bread alone," said the Lord Jesus, "but by every word of God" (Luke 4:4). "How sweet are thy words unto my taste! yea, sweeter than honey to my mouth!" (Psalm 119:103).

The Word of God is also our daily light. "We have also a more sure word of prophecy; . . . a light that shineth in a dark place" (II Peter 1:19). "Thy word is a lamp unto my feet, and a light unto my path" (Psalm 119:105).

We also are admonished to take "the sword of the Spirit, which is the word of God" (Ephesians 6:17), for "the word of God is quick, and powerful, and sharper than any two-edged sword" (Hebrews 4:12). In our text, it is like a "hammer" that can break any resistance to God's will.

There are many other wonderful metaphors of the Word, for it so consumed Biblical writers that they could not help but write of its praises and powers. It was also Jeremiah who testified, after having decided no longer to preach the Word to those who disbelieved, "His word was in mine heart as a burning fire shut up in my bones, and I was weary with forbearing, and I could not stay [literally refrain]" (Jeremiah 20:9). The Word of God will not be silent. Let us pray for such a burning fire in our own souls.

The Powers of God

I am Alpha and Omega, the beginning and the ending, saith the Lord, which is, and which was, and which is to come, the Almighty (Revelation 1:8).

In these days of rampant humanism, blatant materialism, and effete religionism, the very concept of an all-powerful God who created, controls, and judges all things seems anachronistic, but God is still *there*, and is still the Almighty.

Three Greek words are translated "power" in Scripture—*exousia* ("authority"), *dunamis* ("ability"), and *kratos* ("strength"). Each is attributed, in unlimited extent, to God the Creator, as incarnate in Christ, the Redeemer. "All power ['authority'] is given unto me in heaven and in earth" (Matthew 28:18). "For thine is the kingdom, and the power ['ability'], and the glory, for ever" (Matthew 6:13). "That ye may know . . . the exceeding greatness of His power ['ability'] to us-ward who believe, according to the working of His mighty power ['strength'], Which He wrought in Christ, when He raised Him from the dead, and set Him at His own right hand in the heavenly places, Far above all principality, and power ['authority'], and might, and dominion" (Ephesians 1:18–21).

He is the "Almighty God" of Abraham (Genesis 17:1), "the everlasting God, the Lord, the Creator of the ends of the earth" (Isaiah 40:28). "Our God is in the heavens: He hath done whatsoever He hath pleased" (Psalm 115:3).

God can do whatever He pleases, except anything contrary to His nature. He "cannot lie" (Titus 1:2), for He is "the truth" (John 14:6). His inspired Word is inerrant—"the scripture of truth" (Daniel 10:21). We can be certain that He did not "create" the world by evolution, for that would be contradicted both by His infallible Word and by His omnipotence. Being all-powerful, God would surely not create by such a cruel, inefficient process as evolution.

OCTOBER 4

King at the Flood

The L*ORD* *sitteth upon the flood; yea, the* L*ORD* *sitteth King for ever. The* L*ORD* *will give strength unto His people; the* L*ORD* *will bless His people with peace* (Psalm 29:10, 11).

There are quite a few different Hebrew words which are translated "flood" in the Old Testament. The word in this passage (Hebrew *mabbul*), however, is unique in that it is only used elsewhere in the account of the Noahic Flood, thus indicating conclusively that the dramatic scenes described in this psalm occurred at the time of the great Flood.

There was never, in all history, such a time as this, when "the wickedness of man was great in the earth, and that every imagination of the thoughts of his heart was only evil continually" (Genesis 6:5). God, therefore, brought about "the end of all flesh" (v. 13)—no doubt millions, perhaps billions, of ungodly men and women—by the great *mabbul*.

In spite of the fact that nearly every culture, all around the globe (made up of descendants of the eight survivors of the Flood) remembers this terrible event in the form of "flood legends," the very concept of God's judgment on sin is so offensive to the natural mind that modern scholarship now even denies it as a fact of history.

Nevertheless, the epitaph of the antediluvian world is written in stone, in the sedimentary rocks and fossil beds, everywhere one looks, all over the world. The greatest rebellion ever mounted against the world's Creator by His creatures, both men and fallen angels, was put down by God simply by His voice! "The voice of the LORD is upon the waters: the God of glory thundereth: the LORD is upon many waters" (Psalm 29:3).

In all the great turmoil of the Flood, Noah and the righteous remnant in the ark were safe through it all. In every age, even in times of stress and danger, "the LORD will bless His people with peace."

Jesus Christ Our Creator

For by Him were all things created, that are in heaven, and that are in earth, visible and invisible, whether they be thrones, or dominions, or principalities, or powers: all things were created by Him, and for Him (Colossians 1:16).

Before one can really know Jesus Christ as Savior or Lord, he must acknowledge Him as offended and rejected Creator, because He was our Creator, first of all. This is such an important doctrine of the New Testament that it is remarkable how rarely it is emphasized in modern evangelicalism.

Creation by Jesus Christ is the doctrine with which John begins his great gospel of salvation: "In the beginning was the Word, . . . All things were made by Him; . . . and the world was made by Him, and the world knew Him not" (John 1:1, 3, 10). It is the foundational message of the Book of Hebrews: "God . . . Hath in these last days spoken unto us by His Son, whom He hath appointed heir of all things, by whom also He made the worlds" (Hebrews 1:1, 2).

The Apostle Paul said that he had been called specifically to preach "the unsearchable riches of Christ; And to make all men see what is the fellowship of the mystery, which from the beginning of the world hath been hid in God, who created all things by Jesus Christ" (Ephesians 3:8, 9). When a person becomes a believer in Christ, receiving His very life by the new birth, he is said to be "renewed in knowledge after the image of Him that created Him" (Colossians 3:10).

In the final book of the Bible, Jesus Christ is called "the Alpha, . . . the beginning . . . the Almighty" (Revelation 1:8), as well as "the beginning of the creation of God" (3:14).

But of all the Biblical passages identifying Jesus Christ as Creator, the most definitive of all is our text for today. Everything in heaven and earth was created by Him, and for Him! "For of Him, and through Him, and to Him, are all things: to whom be glory forever. Amen" (Romans 11:36).

The Living God

For who is there of all flesh, that hath heard the voice of the living God speaking out of the midst of the fire, as we have, and lived? (Deuteronomy 5:26).

This is the first time this wonderful description of God is used in the Bible. He is the *living* God! He is not the far-off god of the deist or theistic evolutionist, nor is He the impersonal force of the pantheist, but He is the God who lives and cares.

It is noteworthy that God is called "the living God" exactly 15 times in the Old Testament and 15 in the New. The two central occurrences—the last occurrence in the Old Testament and the first in the New—both speak of those who are "sons of the living God." In the first case, it is concerning those among God's chosen people who will receive His life as they turn to Christ when He comes again: "It shall come to pass, that in the place where it was said unto them, Ye are not my people, there it shall be said unto them, Ye are the sons of the living God" (Hosea 1:10). In the second, it is Peter's testimony concerning Christ, Himself: "Thou art the Christ, the Son of the living God" (Matthew 16:16).

The first occurrence of this great title, as recorded in our text for the day, refers to "the *voice* of the living God," speaking to His servants out of the awful fires on the holy mountain. The last occurrence, in Revelation 7:2, speaks of "the *seal* of the living God," protecting His servants through the awful persecutions of the great tribulation. "The Lord is the true God, He is the living God, and an everlasting king: at His wrath the earth shall tremble, and the nations shall not be able to abide His indignation" (Jeremiah 10:10). For the unbeliever, "It is a fearful thing to fall into the hands of the living God" (Hebrews 10:31), but for the Christian, it is a wonder and a comfort, when "we trust in the living God" (I Timothy 4:10) as our Savior and Lord.

All the People of the Earth

That all the people of the earth may know that the LORD is God, and that there is none else (I Kings 8:60).

This is the final, and climactic, petition in Solomon's great prayer at the dedication of the beautiful temple of God in Jerusalem (I Kings 8:22–61). The temple was not merely a place of worship for the people of Israel, but a testimony to all the people of the earth. "The LORD is God!" That is, *Jehovah* is *Elohim*, the God who created the heaven and the earth in the beginning (Genesis 1:1).

For this one time in history, the most magnificent building on earth had been erected by the greatest king of the earth as a testimony to all the people of the earth that Jehovah, the covenant God of Israel, was really the one God who had created all the earth. The testimony was thrilling while it lasted, but soon the great king fell into deep sin, the magnificent temple was eventually destroyed, and the chosen people were scattered through all the earth.

Still, "there is none else," for Israel's Lord is, indeed, the God of creation, whether or not He is accepted by either Jew or Gentile. It is still His purpose, as expressed by divine inspiration in this concluding petition of the prayer, "that all the people of the earth" may acknowledge Him as God and Creator (Revelation 4:11), and then as personal Redeemer (Revelation 5:9, 12). Since there can be only one Creator, it is only He who can be the Savior, and it *does* make a difference—an *eternal* difference—whether one accepts Him or not. "If ye believe not that I am" said Jesus (the "He" of the King James is not in the original), "ye shall die in your sins" (John 8:24). There is no other Creator and there is no other Savior than the Lord Jesus Christ, the eternal Word made flesh, who "tabernacled" among us (John 1:14), the One who was modeled in the great temple, and whom all people on the earth need to know.

OCTOBER 8

How to Save Your Life

Remember Lot's wife (Luke 17:32).

In this short verse, Jesus is commanding us to remember someone whose name we never knew! Nothing she ever said or did (with one exception) is recorded in Scripture, and yet the Lord wants us to remember her. When God tried to save Lot and his family from the fiery destruction of Sodom and Gomorrah, "his wife looked back from behind him, and she became a pillar of salt" (Genesis 19:26).

This strange miracle—whether it was an instantaneous chemical transmutation, or a sudden burial by erupting bodies of salt, or a gradual petrifaction process as her body was buried and later transformed in a fall of volcanic ash—really happened, and the Lord Jesus thus confirmed it, as He did the destruction of Sodom, itself (Luke 17:28, 29)! The reason why He commands us to remember it and profit by its lesson is given in the next verse: "Whosoever shall seek to save his life shall lose it; and whosoever shall lose his life shall preserve it" (Luke 17:33).

Therefore, one should "*remember Lot's wife,*" whenever he or she is tempted to hang on to a comfortable life style in a wicked world. Lot, himself, was a rather worldly-minded believer, but when he consented to flee the doomed city, his wife lagged "behind him," and kept "looking back," perhaps grieving over the imminent loss of her material comforts and high social position among her ungodly neighbors. Finally, the Lord's longsuffering patience was ended, and her carnal desire to save her old life caused her to lose her whole life. "For what is a man profited, if he shall gain the whole world, and lose his own soul [same Greek word as 'life']?" (Matthew 16:26).

The instruction for us is clear and pointed: "They which live should not henceforth live unto themselves, but unto Him which died for them, and rose again" (II Corinthians 5:15).

The Entropy of Unconcern

Awake to righteousness, and sin not; for some have not the knowledge of God: I speak this to your shame (I Corinthians 15:34).

In this verse, the Greek word translated "shame" is the fascinating word *entrope*, meaning, literally, "turning-in." It is used only one other time, in I Corinthians 6:5: "I speak to your shame. Is it so, that there is not a wise man among you? no, not one that shall be able to judge between his brethren?"

The scientist, Clausius, in 1865, selected this word ("entropy" in English) to describe the dissipation of energy, or state of disorder, in any functioning system. The famous Second Law of Thermodynamics, which he helped demonstrate to be a universal law of science, states that the entropy (i.e., the disorganization) of any system always *tends* to increase. That is, any system which "turns inward" to derive the energy or information to keep working will eventually run down and cease to function. It is this law which indicates that the very concept of evolution is essentially impossible. "Evolution" means "rolling outward," and implies increasing complexity, whereas "entropy" means "turning inward," and implies decreasing complexity.

In the context of our text, the unconcern of the Corinthian Christians that some in their number were "agnostic," or ignorant, about the very existence and nature of God, their Creator, was a measure of their state of "entropy," or "in-turning"—that is, their self-centeredness—and this was a *shameful* state!

There is no excuse for a Christian to be an "entropic" Christian—a self-centered, self-sufficient, self-righteous hindrance to the cause of Christ, indifferent to the unbelief and compromise all around him, concerned only with his own personal affairs and comfort. The urgent command to such a one is "Wake up!"

OCTOBER 10

Adam and Mrs. Adam

Male and female created He them; and blessed them, and called their name Adam, in the day when they were created (Genesis 5:2).

In these days of sensitivity concerning sexism, it is important to focus on God's own evaluation of the two sexes, and their respective roles in the divine plan. As Creator of both, He alone can speak authoritatively about this matter.

Both man and woman were created in God's image (Genesis 1:27), and thus, in the categories of salvation, rewards and eternal fellowship with their Creator, both are surely equal. "For ye are all the children of God by faith in Christ Jesus. . . . There is neither male nor female: for ye are all one in Christ Jesus" (Galatians 3:26, 28).

At the same time, when God created them, He named them *both* "Adam," as our text notes. This is actually the same word as "man," as in Genesis 2:7 ("the LORD God formed man"), etc. Thus it is Biblical to use the word "man" generically, when referring to the human race in general. When the woman was formed out of Adam's side, Adam said, "She shall be called Woman, because she was taken out of Man" (Genesis 2:23). Here a different Hebrew word is used for "man" (*ish*), and "woman" is *isha*.

Adam also gave his new bride a personal name. "Adam called his wife's name Eve ['life-giver']; because she was the mother of all living" (Genesis 3:20).

There is, therefore, nothing demeaning in using "man" as a generic term for both men and women, for this usage is sanctioned by God, Himself. Nevertheless, each individual has his or her own distinctive personal name, and God deals with each of us, individually, on that basis. Our obedience and faithfulness to the divinely ordained role each of us is called by Him to fill, is God's criterion, by which He measures us for eternity.

Created, Formed, Made

Even every one that is called by my name: for I have created him for my glory, I have formed him; yea, I have made him (Isaiah 43:7).

There are three main verbs used to describe God's work of creation in Genesis. These are "create" (Hebrew *bara*), "make" (*asah*), and "form" (*yatsar*). The three words are similar in meaning, but each with a slightly different emphasis. None of them, of course, can mean anything at all like "evolve," or "change," on their own accord.

All three are used in Genesis with reference to man. "And God said, Let us make man in our image. . . . So God created man in His own image. . . . And the LORD God formed man of the dust of the ground" (Genesis 1:26, 27; 2:7).

Although the subject of creation is commonly associated with Genesis, it is mentioned even more frequently by the great prophet Isaiah. The words *bara* and *yatsar* are used twice as often in Isaiah as in any other Old Testament book, and are applied uniquely to works of God. All three verbs are used together in Isaiah 45:18 in order to describe, adequately, God's purposeful work in preparing the earth for man: "For thus saith the LORD that created the heavens; God Himself that formed the earth and made it; He hath established it, He created it not in vain, He formed it to be inhabited: I am the LORD; and there is none else."

God created, formed, made, and established the earth, that it might be the home of men and women. But what was God's purpose for the people who would inhabit it? Our text answers this most fundamental of questions, and, once again, all three key verbs are used: "I have created him . . . I have formed him, . . . I have made him . . . for my glory."

This Biblical perspective alone provides the greatest of all possible incentives to live a godly and useful life. The reason we were created is to glorify God!

OCTOBER 12

The Earliest Pioneers

Therefore is the name of it called Babel; because the LORD did there confound the language of all the earth: and from thence did the LORD scatter them abroad upon the face of all the earth (Genesis 11:9).

The Genesis record makes it abundantly plain that the Noahic deluge was a worldwide cataclysm which destroyed the entire antediluvian human population except those on Noah's Ark. From these, the Bible says, "was the whole earth overspread" (Genesis 9:19). At first, the entire post-Flood human population wanted to remain in Babel, rejecting God's command to fill the earth (Genesis 9:1). Therefore, God forced them to scatter abroad by confusing their languages, thus requiring each family to fend for itself, wherever its members could find (and defend) a suitable homeland.

These emigrants thus went out into a truly "new world," exploring its continents and sailing its oceans—some settling in productive regions where they could develop great civilizations (e.g., Egypt, China), others continuing to wander until they finally reached the remotest regions of earth.

Today archaeologists are beginning to understand the tremendous abilities and contributions of these primeval explorers and builders. In South Africa and Siberia, Peru and the Pacific Islands, the Americas and the Arctic, ancient sites are being excavated and are yielding amazing artifacts of complex cultures.

Evolutionary prejudices have kept these facts unrecognized for evolutionists like to imagine that ancient men were ape-like savages living in gross ignorance. Some of their degenerate progeny may have come to fit such a description, but the earliest people, immediate descendants of the great patriarch Noah, were great explorers, navigators, agriculturalists, husbandmen, and builders, and the modern world is greatly indebted to them for much of its comforts.

Signs of the Times

When it is evening, ye say, It will be fair weather: for the sky is red. And in the morning, It will be foul weather today: for the sky is red and lowring. O ye hypocrites, ye can discern the face of the sky; but can ye not discern the signs of the times? (Matthew 16:2, 3).

This sharp rebuke by the Lord Jesus was well deserved, for His critics were challenging Him to prove His right to be heard by performing a miracle. But they had already been confronted with a tremendous body of evidence, both in their Scriptures and in the very life and teachings of Jesus, as well as in the miracles already wrought by Him, that He was their Messiah. They paid great attention to weather forecasting and other mundane matters, while ignoring or rejecting the evidence that God Himself, in Christ, was in their midst.

Today we are more occupied with daily weather even than they were, with all sorts of forecasting devices in operation. There is also a growing army of doomsday forecasters, loudly concerned about a predicted nuclear winter, over-population, pollution, alien invasions from outer space, and a host of other foreboding secular "signs of the times."

Yet they ignore the overwhelming evidences, both in science and Scripture, that our great Creator/Savior, the Lord Jesus Christ, is still in control and is coming again soon to fulfill His great purposes in creation and redemption. A mere listing of the many real signs of God's times would take many pages. One such sign, of course, is this very proliferation of science and technology. At "the time of the end: many shall run to and fro, and knowledge shall be increased" (Daniel 12:4). Another is the great following achieved by these false teachers, as multitudes "turn away their ears from the truth, and shall be turned unto fables" (II Timothy 4:4). "Hypocrites," Jesus said, are concerned with secular trends, but spiritual discerners can recognize the true signs.

OCTOBER 14

That Ye Might Believe

And many other signs truly did Jesus in the presence of His disciples, which are not written in this book: But these are written, that ye might believe that Jesus is the Christ, the Son of God; and that believing ye might have life through His name (John 20:30, 31).

The Gospel of John is the one book of the Bible specifically written with the purpose of leading men to Jesus Christ and salvation. It is structured around seven specially selected miracles of creation, or "signs" (John 2:11; 4:53, 54; 5:9; 6:13, 14; 6:19–21; 9:6, 7; 11:43–45), each requiring supernatural power as well as knowledge. The book also contains many affirmations of His deity (there are seven great "I am" statements) and many exhortations to believe on Him (e.g., John 3:16), interspersed around the seven signs. Finally, there is the detailed description of the last supper, the crucifixion, and the resurrection, climaxed by the glorious affirmation of faith by doubting Thomas, and then our text stating the purpose of the entire book, as found in our text.

If we are to be effective witnesses for Christ, we can do no better than to follow this same procedure. It is most significant that this begins with a strong emphasis on the special creation of all things, with an exposition showing that Christ Himself is the Creator (John 1:1–14). The judicious use of Christian evidences (e.g., the miracles) demonstrating the truth of His many claims of deity, climaxed by the overwhelming proofs of His own bodily resurrection (John 20:1–29), all interwoven with an uncompromising emphasis on the inerrant authority of Scripture (e.g., John 5:39–47; 10:34–36) and a clear exposition of His substitutionary death and the necessity of personal faith in Him for salvation (especially John 3:1–18) all combine to make the most effective way of bringing men to an intelligent, well-grounded decision to receive Christ as Savior and Lord.

Defending the Gospel

But the other of love, knowing that I am set for the defense of the gospel (Philippians 1:17).

Many Christians today decry the use of apologetics or evidences in Christian witnessing, feeling it is somehow dishonoring to the Lord or to the Scriptures to try to defend them.

But as our text indicates, the Apostle Paul did not agree with this. The gospel does need defending, and he was set for its defense against the attacks of its adversaries. He also told his disciples that "in the defense and confirmation of the gospel, ye all are partakers of my grace" (Philippians 1:7).

The Greek word translated "defense" is *apologia,* from which we derive our English word "apologetics." It is a legal term, meaning the case made by a defense attorney on behalf of a defendant under attack by a prosecutor. Thus, the apostle is saying: "I am set to give an apologetic for the gospel—a logical, systematic (scientific if necessary) defense of the gospel against all the attacks of its adversaries."

Since we are "partakers" with him in this defense, we also need to be set for its defense. We must "be ready always to give an answer [same word, *apologia*] to every man that asketh [us] a reason of the hope that is in [us]" (I Peter 3:15). Any Christian who shares his faith with the unsaved has encountered many who cannot believe the simple plan of salvation until his questions are answered. We must be familiar with the "many infallible proofs" (Acts 1:3) of the deity of Christ and His power to save, both as omnipotent Creator and sin-bearing Savior. We must "search the Scriptures daily" and also study the "witness" He has given in the creation (Acts 17:11; 14:17) if we are to do this effectively, bringing forth fruit that will "remain" (John 15:16) instead of fruit that has withered away, "because it had no root" (Mark 4:6). The gospel is under vicious attack today, so may God help us to be among its victorious defenders.

OCTOBER 16

The Old Paths and the Good Way

Thus saith the Lord, Stand ye in the ways, and see, and ask for the old paths, where is the good way, and walk therein, and ye shall find rest for your souls. But they said, We will not walk therein (Jeremiah 6:16).

Ever since the rise of modern science, and especially since the resurgence of ancient paganism in the guise of modern evolutionary "science," there has developed a sort of social compulsion to follow after whatever seems to be new. There are new philosophies and new religions and "modernized" versions of traditional doctrines—always some new idea. But the eternal God does not change with the times. With Him, there "is no variableness, neither shadow of turning" (James 1:17). "Jesus Christ the same yesterday, and today, and forever" (Hebrews 13:8).

No one questions the value of true advances in science and technology. In fact, this is implicit in the primeval dominion mandate to "subdue" the earth (Genesis 1:28). All these "new" trends in morality and religion, however, are really only ancient immoralities and ancient evolutionism refurbished in modern terminology.

It is such as these that the prophet deplored. The "old paths" constitute the "good way," and God's people will never find true soul-rest until they "walk therein." "Remove not the ancient landmark, which thy fathers have set" (Proverbs 22:28). The New Testament similarly rebukes all those idle "philosophers" who "spent their time in nothing else, but either to tell, or to hear some new thing" (Acts 17:18, 21). When the true gospel comes, however, it is genuine "good news" to all who are not merely curious to hear "this new doctrine" (Acts 17:19), but who will appropriate it for themselves by faith. This new doctrine, in fact, is not new at all, but is that "hope of eternal life, which God, that cannot lie, promised before the world began" (Titus 1:2).

The Light of the Word

Thy Word is a lamp unto my feet, and a light unto my path (Psalm 119:105).

As the sun provides physical light for the world, so Jesus Christ is spiritually "the light of the world" (John 8:12). However, we clearly can see His light only through the light holder, the lamp, as it were, of His written Word. The Word, therefore, is a lamp and, since it contains and reveals the light, is also a light in its own right. Without the Holy Scriptures, this world would lie in the deepest darkness, but "the entrance of Thy Words giveth light" (Psalm 119:130).

The Lord Jesus Christ is the living Word, and "without Him was not anything made that was made. In Him was life; and the life was the light of men. And the light shineth in darkness; and the darkness comprehended it not" (John 1:3–5). Although He "was the true Light, which lighteth every man that cometh into the world" (John 1:9), when He, Himself, came into the world, those who were made by Him refused to receive Him. "Men loved darkness rather than light, because their deeds were evil" (John 3:19).

Just so, although the written Word has come into the world, the world does not receive it, either. The lamp and the light of the written Word have been in the world, in complete and final form, for 1,900 years, but men still reject and ridicule it, and the world still lies in darkness. Nevertheless, for those who receive it, there is wonderful light. "Then Jesus said unto them, Yet a little while is the light with you. Walk while ye have the light, lest darkness come upon you: for he that walketh in darkness knoweth not whither he goeth. While ye have light, believe in the light, that ye may be the children of light" (John 12:35, 36).

God's Word always brings light. His first spoken Word was: "Let there be light" (Genesis 1:3), and wherever He speaks, God sees the light, and it is good!

OCTOBER 18

The Scattering Hammer

Is not my Word like as a fire? saith the LORD; and like a hammer that breaketh the rock in pieces? (Jeremiah 23:29).

One of the most picturesque of the figures used to describe the holy Scriptures is that of the hammer striking and shattering a rock. In this text, however, the "rock" is literally a mighty rock mountain.

Furthermore, the effect of the hammer is to "break in pieces." This phrase actually is a single Hebrew word, which normally means "disperse," or "scatter abroad." It is frequently used, for example, in describing the worldwide dispersion of the children of Israel. It was used even earlier, in connection with the first dispersion at Babel: "So the Lord scattered them abroad from thence upon the face of all the earth" (Genesis 11:8). Perhaps most significantly of all, it is used in the prophecy of Zechariah 13:7: "Smite the shepherd, and the sheep shall be scattered."

This verse was quoted by the Lord Jesus just after the last supper, and applied to Himself: "All ye shall be offended because of Me this night: for it is written, I will smite the shepherd, and the sheep of the flock shall be scattered abroad" (Matthew 26:31). Combining all these themes, our text really seems to be saying: "Is not My Word like a mighty hammer from heaven that shatters the great mountain and scatters it abroad?"

Our text is inserted in the midst of a stinging rebuke by Jeremiah of Israel's false prophets, contrasting their lies with the mighty power of God's true Word. Perhaps it is also a parable of the living Word, who is also the great Rock of ages, as well as the loving Shepherd. When the Rock was shattered, the living stones were ejected from the Rock. The sheep that were thus scattered from the Shepherd became the spreading fire of the written Word, and "they that were scattered abroad went every where preaching the Word" (Acts 8:4).

The Great Divider

Suppose ye that I am come to give peace on earth? I tell you, Nay; but rather division (Luke 12:51).

From the very beginning, God has been a great divider. On the first day of creation, "God divided the light from the darkness," and on the second day, He "divided the waters which were under the firmament from the waters which were above the firmament" (Genesis 1:4, 7). When God first created man, they walked together in sweet fellowship, but then sin came in and made a great division between man and God. Nevertheless, "when we were enemies, we were reconciled to God by the death of His Son" (Romans 5:10).

The price has been paid for full reconciliation with our Creator, but "men loved darkness rather than light, because their deeds were evil" (John 3:19), so Christ, Himself, is now the one who divides. "He that believeth on the Son hath everlasting life: and he that believeth not the Son shall not see life; but the wrath of God abideth on him" (John 3:36).

Jesus Christ divides all history and all chronology. Things either happened "Before Christ" (B.C.) or "in the Year of our Lord" (A.D.). Men are either under the Old Covenant or the New Covenant. Most of all, He divides humanity. "There was a division among the people because of Him" (John 7:43; see also John 9:16; 10:19). These divisions, because of Him, can cut very deep. "The father shall be divided against the son, and the son against the father; the mother against the daughter, and the daughter against the mother" (Luke 12:53).

Finally, when He comes to judge all nations, "He shall separate them one from another, as a shepherd divideth his sheep from the goats: . . . and these shall go away into everlasting punishment: but the righteous into life eternal" (Matthew 25:32, 46). The division is life or death, light or darkness, heaven or hell, Christ or anti-Christ—and the choice is ours!

OCTOBER 20

Great and Precious Promises

Whereby are given unto us exceeding great and precious promises: that by these ye might be partakers of the divine nature, having escaped the corruption that is in the world through lust (II Peter 1:4).

Scripture is full of promises, more than 2,800 in the Old Testament and more than 1,000 in the New. The first of these exceeding great and precious promises was the Protevangel ("first gospel") of Genesis 3:15. Immediately after the fall of Adam and Eve, through the temptation of Satan, that old serpent, God promised the coming Seed of the Woman, the Savior: "And I will put enmity between thee and the woman, and between thy seed and her seed; [He] shall bruise thy head, and thou shalt bruise His heel."

The first New Testament promise, significantly, is this same primeval promise, now made far more specific: "And she shall bring forth a son, and thou shalt call His name JESUS: for He shall save His people from their sins" (Matthew 1:21).

The last promise of the Old Testament speaks of a second coming of "Elijah the prophet," who will "turn the heart of the fathers to the children, and the heart of the children to their fathers" (Malachi 4:5, 6). Then, the final promise of the Bible is the wonderful assurance of Christ concerning His second coming: "Surely I come quickly" (Revelation 22:20).

Sandwiched between these great and precious promises are over 3,800 other promises. Some of these are in the form of promised warnings to the sinner, but promises, none the less. Most promises, however, are to the obedient follower of God, and we know that "He is faithful that promised" (Hebrews 10:23). "For all the promises of God in Him are yea, and in Him Amen, unto the glory of God by us" (II Corinthians 1:20).

Silencing Foolish Men

For so is the will of God, that with well doing ye may put to silence the ignorance of foolish men (I Peter 2:15).

The blasphemous diatribes of modern evolutionary humanists against the Word of God and the testimony of His people are really nothing but arrogant foolishness. "Professing themselves to be wise, they became fools" (Romans 1:22) and "the LORD shall have them in derision" (Psalm 2:4). The Biblical way to "silence the ignorance of foolish men," as our text says, is simply by "well doing." This word (also translated "do well") is used almost exclusively by Peter, but he makes the point quite effectively.

Note the following, for example: "If, when ye do well, and suffer for it, ye take it patiently, this is acceptable with God" (I Peter 2:20). "For it is better, if the will of God be so, that ye suffer for well doing, than for evil doing" (I Peter 3:17). "Wherefore let them that suffer according to the will of God commit the keeping of their souls to Him in well doing, as unto a faithful Creator" (I Peter 4:19).

Our example in this, of course, is none other than Christ Himself, "Who, when He was reviled, reviled not again; when He suffered, He threatened not; but committed Himself to Him that judgeth righteously" (I Peter 2:23). Unbelievers, if they want to badly enough, can reject every argument with some other objection or counter claim, but they have no way to gainsay a godly, righteous, law-abiding, loving life. The unbeliever may ridicule such a life for a time, but he must eventually come to see its sure foundation. "Whereas they speak against you as evildoers, they may by your good works, which they shall behold, glorify God in the day of visitation" (I Peter 2:12). The main reason for "well doing," however, is simply that, as our text says, "so is the will of God," and we can safely leave the response and the results to Him.

OCTOBER 22

No Help from the Hills

I will lift up mine eyes unto the hills, from whence cometh my help (Psalm 121:1).

This oft-quoted verse seems to contradict many other verses in Scripture: "Truly in vain is salvation hoped for from the hills, and from the multitude of mountains: truly in the LORD our God is the salvation of Israel" (Jeremiah 3:23).

In fact, a common error of paganism was to seek salvation and the favor of the "gods" by going to "high places" where, ostensibly, they could commune with spirits in the heavens. Such practices, of course, were vigorously rebuked by God.

He commanded the Israelites, as they entered the promised land: "Ye shall utterly destroy all the places, wherein the nations which ye shall possess served their gods, upon the high mountains, and upon the hills, and under every green tree" (Deuteronomy 12:2).

Thus, the last half of our text above should best be regarded as a sort of rhetorical question: "From whence cometh my help?" (In the original language, the context determines when a statement is a question.) The wonderful answer then immediately follows: "My help cometh from the LORD, which made heaven and earth" (Psalm 121:2).

No object or system in the natural world, regardless of how beautiful or magnificent, can provide help in time of spiritual need. But "we may boldly say, The Lord is my helper" (Hebrews 13:6), for "God is our refuge and strength, a very present help in trouble" (Psalm 46:1).

He alone is the Creator of all things in heaven and earth, whereas the hills and mountains of the present world are merely the remnants of the destructive phenomena of the great Flood (Psalm 104:6–9). All such things are powerless to save, and eventually will "vanish away" (Isaiah 51:6). But "our help is in the name of the LORD, who made heaven and earth" (Psalm 124:8).

The Discerner

For the Word of God is quick, and powerful, and sharper than any two-edged sword, piercing even to the dividing asunder of soul and spirit, and of the joints and marrow, and is a discerner of the thoughts and intents of the heart (Hebrews 4:12).

The Word of God (both the written word and the living Word, Jesus Christ) is "living and energizing" and is the double-edged sword of the Spirit, piercing into the deepest recesses of body, soul, and spirit, where it "discerns" even the very thoughts and intents of our hearts.

This discernment, however, is more than just understanding or insight. The Greek word for "discerner" is *kritikos,* and is used only this one time in the Bible. Our word "critic" is derived from it, and this is an important dimension of its meaning. Its discernment is a critical, judging discernment—one which convicts and corrects, as well as one which understands.

It is paradoxical that men today presume to become critics of the Bible, when it should really be the other way around. There are textual critics, who sort through the various ancient manuscripts of the Bible, trying to arrive at the original text; there are the "higher critics," who critique vocabularies and concepts, trying to show that the traditional authors did not actually write the books attributed to them; and then there are many other purely destructive critics, who criticize the Bible's miracles, morals, and everything else, hoping thereby to justify their rebellion against the Word.

But the Bible still stands! It stands in judgment on our lives and our subconscious motives. It will have the final word when "the books [are] opened . . . and the dead [are] judged out of those things which were written in the books" (Revelation 20:12). It is far better to heed the constructive criticism of the Word now, than to hear its condemnation later.

God's Foundation

His foundation is in the holy mountains. The Lord *loveth the gates of Zion more than all the dwellings of Jacob. Glorious things are spoken of thee, O city of God. Selah* (Psalm 87:1–3).

The 87th Psalm was dedicated to the praise of Jerusalem as the chosen city of God, the site of His temple, where He dwelt with His people. It is on this location that He focuses His continual attention. None of the great fathers of the chosen people—Abraham, Jacob, Moses, Joshua—were ever citizens of earthly Jerusalem, but they all "looked for a city which hath foundations, whose builder and maker is God" (Hebrews 11:10).

The Lord Jesus has gone "to prepare a place" (John 14:2) for us, and God "hath prepared for them a city" (Hebrews 11:16). This is "mount Sion . . . the city of the living God, the heavenly Jerusalem" (Hebrews 12:22), the "Jerusalem which is above" (Galatians 4:26).

The day will come when this beautiful city of God will rest on "a great and high mountain . . . descending out of heaven from God, Having the glory of God" (Revelation 21:10, 11). There on the new earth (Revelation 21:1, 2) it may indeed rest on foundations extending to the center of the earth, for it will be 1,400 miles high, wide, and long (Revelation 21:16). Inscribed on its beautiful foundations are the names of the twelve apostles, but the sure foundation must be Christ Himself (Ephesians 2:20; I Corinthians 3:11). "Nevertheless the foundation of God standeth sure, having this seal, The Lord knoweth them that are His" (II Timothy 2:19).

"Great is the Lord, and greatly to be praised in the city of our God, in the mountain of His holiness. Beautiful for situation, the joy of the whole earth, is Mount Zion, on the sides of the north, the city of the great King" (Psalm 48:1, 2).

The Bible Stands!

Thy Word is true from the beginning: and every one of thy righteous judgments endureth for ever (Psalm 119:160).

Very few books survive very long. Only a few survive the first printing, and science books, especially, get out of date in just a few years.

But one book *is* eternal! The Bible stands! Even its most ancient chapters are still accurate and up to date. Furthermore, despite all the vicious attacks of both ancient pagans and modern humanists, it will continue to endure. Jesus said: "Heaven and earth shall pass away, but my Words shall not pass away" (Matthew 24:35; Mark 13:31; Luke 21:33).

Even after everything else dies and all the bombastic tirades of skeptics and secularists are long forgotten, the Word endures. "The grass withereth, the flower fadeth: but the Word of our God shall stand for ever" (Isaiah 40:8).

Note the oft-repeated testimony to this same effect in Psalm 119. In addition to the comprehensive promise of today's text, this great "psalm of the Word" also contains these affirmations: "For ever, O LORD, Thy Word is settled in heaven. . . . Thy testimonies have I taken as an heritage for ever: for they are the rejoicing of my heart. . . . The righteousness of thy testimonies is everlasting: . . . Concerning thy testimonies, I have known of old that thou hast founded them for ever" (Psalm 119:89, 111, 144, 152). Founded forever, inherited forever, settled forever, lasting forever! God is eternal, and His Word was true from the beginning.

Men may, in these last days, arrogantly think they can "take away from the words of the book of this prophecy" (Revelation 22:19), but such presumption will only "take away [their] part out of the book of life," and the Bible will still stand. "The Word of the Lord endureth forever. And this is the Word which by the gospel is preached unto you" (I Peter 1:25).

OCTOBER 26

Adam and the Animals

And out of the ground the LORD God formed every beast of the field, and every fowl of the air; and brought them unto Adam to see what he would call them: and whatsoever Adam called every living creature, that was the name thereof (Genesis 2:19).

This event occurred on the sixth day of creation week, between the formation of Adam's body and that of Eve (note Genesis 1:26–31; 2:7, 22), and there is no reason not to take it literally. Nevertheless, modern theistic evolutionists, including many seminary professors, have found two imaginary problems which they argue prevent taking it literally.

The first quibble finds a "contradiction" with Genesis 1:21–25, which says the animals were all made before Adam—not afterward. This supposed problem vanishes when the text verse is translated as follows: "The LORD God had formed every beast of the field." This is a legitimate—in fact, preferable—translation of the Hebrew original.

The other alleged difficulty is the supposed inability of Adam to name all the animals in one day. The fact is, however, that he only had to give names "to all cattle, and to the fowl of the air, and to every beast of the field" (Genesis 2:20)—that is, those nearby birds, cattle, and other mammals that might be seen as potential candidates to be a "help meet" for Adam. No marine animals, reptiles, insects, or "beasts of the earth" (Genesis 1:24—i.e., living far away from Eden) were brought to him. Furthermore, he did not need to name every species, but only each relevant "kind"—possibly each "family" (i.e., dogs, horses, eagles, etc.).

Finally, his divinely created mental abilities were not yet limited by the disease of sin, so that he could appropriately name each kind much more rapidly than we could do. Thus, no sincere Bible student should be tempted to doubt Genesis by any such "difficulties" as these.

Men from Mars

The heaven, even the heavens, are the L*ORD's: but the earth hath He given to the children of men* (Psalm 115:16).

Science fiction books and movies movies have conditioned people to believe in extra-terrestrial life, and billions of dollars have been wistfully spent by scientists and politicians dedicated to finding evidence of intelligent life in outer space. All of this is futile, for it is merely arrogant rejection of God's testimony that only planet Earth has been given to man; all else belongs to God.

When God created Adam and Eve, He commissioned them to "have dominion . . . over all the earth" (Genesis 1:26). At Babel, rebellious men made their first attempt to intrude into God's heavenly domain, erecting "a tower, whose top [is] unto heaven"—that is, designed for communicating with, and no doubt worshipping the presumed hosts of heaven, and consequently, God proceeded to "scatter them abroad upon the face of all the earth" (Genesis 11:4, 9).

There are, of course, angels in the heavens, but even these (including Lucifer himself, the highest of all) cannot intrude in those realms restricted by God, and a third of the angels were actually cast out of heaven (note Isaiah 14:12–15; Revelation 12:4, 9), when they attempted it.

"No man hath ascended up to heaven," said Christ (John 3:13). "[God] hath made of one blood all nations of men for to dwell on all the face of the earth, and hath determined the times before appointed, and the bounds of their habitation" (Acts 17:26).

There is no hint in the Bible of men on Mars or anywhere else in space, and all real scientific evidence likewise is against such notions. The planet Earth alone is where God became man, where He died for man's salvation, and where He will establish His universal throne in the ages to come.

OCTOBER 28

The Wisdom Mine

Whence then cometh wisdom? and where is the place of understanding? (Job 28:20).

In one of his monologues, the patriarch Job compares his search for spiritual understanding to man's explorations for metals and precious stones. "There is a vein for the silver," he says, "and a place for gold. . . . Iron is taken out of the earth, and brass is molten out of the stone" (Job 28:1, 2).

These all are easier to find than true wisdom. "It cannot be valued with the gold of Ophir, with the precious onyx, or the sapphire. The gold and the crystal cannot equal it: and the exchange of it shall not be for jewels of fine gold. No mention shall be made of coral, or of pearls: for the price of wisdom is above rubies. The topaz of Ethiopia shall not equal it, neither shall it be valued with pure gold" (Job 28:16–19).

Neither have animals discovered it. "The fierce lion passed by it. . . . It is hid from the eyes of all living, and kept close from the fowls of the air" (vv. 8, 21). "The depth saith, It is not in me: and the sea saith, It is not with me" (vv. 14).

"But where shall wisdom be found? And where is the place of understanding?" (v. 12). Job is driven to ask, "where must one go to find and mine the vein of true wisdom?"

It is certainly "not the wisdom of this world, nor of the princes of this world, that come to nought" (I Corinthians 2:6). The mine of evolutionary humanism which dominates modern education and scholarship will yield only the fool's gold of "science falsely so called" (I Timothy 6:20).

Job found true wisdom only through God, and so must we, for only "God understandeth the way thereof, and He knoweth the place thereof. . . . Unto man He said, Behold, the fear of the LORD, that is wisdom; and to depart from evil is understanding" (Job 28:23, 28). The Lord Jesus Christ Himself is the ever-productive mine "in whom are hid all the treasures of wisdom and knowledge" (Colossians 2:3).

Multitudes in Hell

The strong among the mighty shall speak to him out of the midst of hell with them that help him: they are gone down, they lie uncircumcised, slain by the sword (Ezekiel 32:21).

The subject of hell is largely ignored today, even by evangelical teachers and pastors. This is a tragic mistake, because multitudes are there already, and multitudes living today will soon be there. It is good to preach the love of God, but God also commands us: "Others save with fear, pulling them out of the fire" (Jude 23).

The Lord, through Ezekiel, has given us a graphic picture of those in earlier ages who are now in Hades, awaiting the final judgment. The great Pharaoh of Egypt, along with his countrymen, had practiced the Egyptian religion with all its complex concepts and rituals, but religion, in itself, will not keep one from hell. When Pharaoh died and had "gone down" to "hell" (actually, this word in the Old Testament is *sheol,* equivalent to the Greek *Hades,* a great pit deep in the core of the earth), he found many there already, from the centuries before him. Some specifically named (see vv. 22–30) are Asshur, Elam, Meshech, Tubal, and Zidon, each with their multitudes. Esau, Jacob's brother, was also there (same as Edom). These, significantly, come from all three original branches of Noah's family. All had come from a godly ancestor, but that did not save them. "When they knew God, they glorified Him not as God, neither were thankful; but . . . worshipped and served the creature more than the Creator" (Romans 1:21, 25).

All of this verifies the warning of Christ: "Wide is the gate, and broad is the way, that leadeth to destruction, and many there be which go in thereat" (Matthew 7:13). Only those who worship the true Creator, receiving Christ as personal Savior from sin, will be saved.

OCTOBER 30

The Third Firmament

And the likeness of the firmament upon the heads of the living creature was as the color of the terrible crystal, stretched forth over their heads above (Ezekiel 1:22).

The English word "firmament" in the Bible is a translation of the Hebrew *raqia,* meaning "expanse." Its meaning is not "firm boundary" as Biblical critics have alleged, but might be paraphrased as "stretched-out thinness" or, simply, "space."

Its first occurrence in the Bible relates it to heaven: "And God said, Let there be a firmament in the midst of the waters, and let it divide the waters from the waters. . . . And God called the firmament Heaven" (Genesis 1:6, 8). This firmament obviously could not be a solid boundary above the sky, but is essentially the atmosphere, the "first heaven," the "space" where the birds were to "fly above the earth in the open firmament of heaven" (Genesis 1:20).

There is also a second firmament, or second heaven, where God placed the sun, moon, and stars, stretching out into the infinite reaches of space. "And God set them in the firmament of the heaven to give light upon the earth" (Genesis 1:17).

The firmament in our text, however, is beneath the very throne of God, and above the mighty cherubim (Ezekiel 1:23), who seem always in Scripture to indicate the near presence of God. This glorious firmament, brilliantly crystalline in appearance, must be "the third heaven" to which the Apostle Paul was once "caught up" in a special manifestation of God's presence and power, to hear "unspeakable words" from God in "paradise" (II Corinthians 12:2–4).

All three heavens "declare the glory of God" and all three firmaments "show His handiwork" (Psalm 19:1). Therefore, we should "praise God in His sanctuary" and also "praise Him in the firmament of His power" (Psalm 150:1).

Seducing Spirits

Now the Spirit speaketh expressly, that in the latter times some shall depart from the faith, giving heed to seducing spirits, and doctrines of devils (I Timothy 4:1).

This very cogent warning by the Holy Spirit, spoken "expressly" (or "with special clarity") for those living in the latter days, predicts an unusual outbreak of seductive demonism—not just in pagan, idol-worshiping or animistic cultures, but in "Christian" nations, where they can lead many to "depart from the faith" which their fore-fathers once professed. Christians, therefore, should not be taken by surprise at the vast eruption of witchcraft, new-age mysticism, eastern occultism, rock-music demonism, drug-induced fantasies, altered states of consciousness, and even overt Satan-worshipping cults that have suddenly proliferated in our supposedly scientific and naturalistic society. Behind it all are the "seducing spirits" and "the rulers of the darkness of this world" (Ephesians 6:12).

It should be obvious that Christians must completely avoid all such beliefs and practices. "I would not that ye should have fellowship with devils" (I Corinthians 10:20). "Come out from among them, and be ye separate, saith the Lord, and touch not the unclean thing" (II Corinthians 6:17). Even "innocent" fun (Halloween parties, ouija boards, dungeons-and-dragons games, etc.) and well-intentioned (but many times superficial) exorcism of apparent demon-possession by Christian workers have often led to dangerous demonic influences in the lives of Christian people, as well as in Christians who have sought supernatural experiences or revelations. In anything that even touches on occultism or demonic influence, the advice of Peter is relevant. "Be sober, be vigilant; because your adversary the devil, as a roaring lion, walketh about, seeking whom he may devour: Whom resist steadfast in the faith" (I Peter 5:8, 9).

NOVEMBER 1

Leviathan

In that day the LORD with His sore and great and strong sword shall punish leviathan the piercing serpent, even leviathan that crooked serpent; and He shall slay the dragon that is in the sea (Isaiah 27:1).

There is a remarkable animal called a "leviathan," described in the direct words of God in the 41st chapter of Job. It is surprising that most modern expositors call this animal merely a crocodile. Our text plainly calls it a "piercing serpent . . . the dragon that is in the sea." He is also said to "play" in the "great and wide sea" (Psalm 104:25, 26). God's description in Job 41 says "a flame goeth out of his mouth" (v. 21), and "he maketh the deep to boil like a pot" (v. 31). The entire description is awesome! Whatever a leviathan might have been, it was not a crocodile!

In fact, there is no animal living today which fits the description. Therefore, it is an extinct animal, almost certainly a great marine reptile with "terrible teeth" and "scales" (vv. 14, 15) still surviving in the oceans of Job's day, evidently one of the fearsome reptiles that gave rise to the worldwide tales of great sea dragons, before they became extinct.

But that is not all. In ending His discourse, God called leviathan "a king over all the children of pride" (Job 41:34), so the animal is also symbolic of Satan, whose challenge to God instigated Job's strange trials. He is "the great dragon . . . that old serpent, called the Devil, and Satan, which deceiveth the whole world" (Revelation 12:9). Perhaps, therefore, the mysterious and notorious extinction of the dinosaurs is a secular prophecy of the coming Day of Judgment, when God "shall punish leviathan" (Isaiah 27:1), and the "devil that deceived them" will be "cast into the lake of fire . . . and shall be tormented day and night for ever and ever" (Revelation 20:10).

Maker and Owner

I have made the earth, the man and the beast that are upon the ground, by My great power and by my outstretched arm, and have given it unto whom it seemed meet unto me (Jeremiah 27:5).

"The earth, the man and the beast" are the three entities which God is said to have "created" (Hebrew *bara*—note Genesis 1:1, 21, 27) in the Genesis account of creation. However, they are also said in Genesis to have been "made" (Hebrew *asah*—note Genesis 1:25, 26; 2:4), and that is the emphasis in our text above. Of course, both aspects were accomplished in the six days of creation week, after which God "rested from all His work which God created and made" (Genesis 2:3). This statement makes it abundantly plain that the present processes of nature do not "create" (call into existence out of nothing) or "make" (build up into more complex forms) anything, as our modern theistic evolutionists and evangelical uniformitarians allege. God has rested from both of these works, except in occasional miraculous intervention in the present laws and processes of "nature."

Now, because God did create and make all things, He also "owns" all things. "The earth is the LORD's, and the fulness thereof" (Psalm 24:1). "Every beast of the forest is mine, and the cattle upon a thousand hills" (Psalm 50:10). "The LORD hath made all things for Himself" (Proverbs 16:4).

Therefore, all that we possess—as individuals or as nations—has simply been entrusted to us as God's stewards, and "every one of us shall give account of himself to God" (Romans 14:12). Without a doubt this accounting will be of our handling of our goods, our minds, and our opportunities, among others. For "it is required in stewards, that a man be found faithful" (I Corinthians 4:2). Let us be thankful—not covetous; and industrious—not slothful; in everything He has entrusted to us.

NOVEMBER 3

God and the Whirlwind

The Lord *is slow to anger, and great in power, and will not at all acquit the wicked: the* Lord *hath His way in the whirlwind and in the storm, and the clouds are the dust of His feet* (Nahum 1:3).

The short prophecy of Nahum consists almost entirely of pronouncements of impending judgment against the great and wicked nation of Assyria, and Nineveh, its ancient capital, to which Jonah had earlier preached. Many times the Lord sent witnesses to ungodly nations, giving them opportunity to repent—Moses to Egypt, Daniel to Babylon, Mordecai to Persia, Paul to Rome, for example. He is *slow* to anger, but He will *not* acquit the wicked.

Furthermore, He is great in power! He created the sun and all other sources of power in the universe. He "hast prepared the light and the sun" (Psalm 74:16), and He still controls the use of their power. "He maketh His sun to rise on the evil and on the good" (Matthew 5:45). A great part of the efforts of modern physical scientists is devoted to learning *just how* the power sources in nature (all deriving their energy ultimately from the sun) maintain all the processes and systems of the earth and its living creatures.

The most spectacular and awe-inspiring of these processes, of course, are the great storms, generated in earth's atmosphere in some little-understood fashion by the sun. Scientists may study the mechanisms of the great whirlwinds (or "hurricanes"), and storms, and clouds, and Earth's other great "natural" catastrophes, but they will never *fully* understand, for they are truly "acts of God."

God has His way (i.e., "path") in the mighty whirlwind, and we do well to hear Him speak as He passes by, for He is reminding us once again that, although He is long-suffering, He is still as able as in the days of Nineveh, to cut away "the paths of all that forget God" (Job 8:13).

The Faithful Creator

Wherefore let them that suffer according to the will of God commit the keeping of their souls to Him in well doing, as unto a faithful Creator (I Peter 4:19).

This is the only verse in the New Testament describing the Creator as faithful. God had a very specific purpose in creating the universe, and especially man, and He will surely accomplish that great purpose.

The Scriptures repeatedly stress God's faithfulness. With respect to the physical universe, "Forever, O LORD, Thy word is settled in heaven. Thy faithfulness is unto all generations: thou hast established the earth, and it abideth" (Psalm 119:89, 90). As far as His promises to His people are concerned, "Know therefore that the LORD thy God, He is God, the faithful God, which keepeth covenant and mercy with them that love Him and keep His commandments to a thousand generations" (Deuteronomy 7:9).

The faithful Creator is none other than the Lord Jesus Christ, and He rebukes the compromising church of the last days with these majestic words: "These things saith the Amen, the faithful and true witness, the beginning of the creation of God" (Revelation 3:14). Although many professing believers will prove unfaithful to Him, "yet He abideth faithful: He cannot deny Himself" (II Timothy 2:13).

The triumphant book of Revelation comes directly "from Jesus Christ, who is the faithful witness" (Revelation 1:5); and when He finally returns to Earth in power and glory, His very name shall be "called Faithful and True" (Revelation 19:11). He is both Alpha and Omega, and thus all His "words are true and faithful" (Revelation 21:5). Our salvation is sure, therefore, because "God is faithful, by whom ye were called unto the fellowship of His Son Jesus Christ our Lord" (I Corinthians 1:9). "Faithful is He that calleth you, who also will do it" (I Thessalonians 5:24).

NOVEMBER 5

Dangerous Counterfeits

Prove all things; hold fast that which is good (I Thessalonians 5:21).

Human beings are very gullible, and counterfeiting is a profitable occupation for many deceivers. But spiritual counterfeits are the most dangerous of all, and at times the most difficult to detect. There are many false gods, and this is the subject of the very first of the true God's Ten Commandments: "Thou shalt have no other gods before me" (Exodus 20:3). We are warned also to "beware of false prophets" (Matthew 7:15) and "false Christs" (Matthew 24:24). There are those who preach "another Jesus" (II Corinthians 11:4), and many who come preaching "another gospel" (Galatians 1:6) rather than the true saving gospel of Christ.

There are also counterfeit Christians who are "false brethren" (II Corinthians 11:26), as well as "false teachers" (II Peter 2:1, 2) and "false apostles" (II Corinthians 11:13). They preach "peace; when there is no peace" (Jeremiah 6:14), and some will even "shew great signs and wonders, insomuch that, if it were possible, they shall deceive the very elect" (Matthew 24:24). Satan himself is the greatest counterfeiter, for he "deceiveth the whole world" (Revelation 12:9) in his attempt to become a counterfeit God. Thus we are warned to "try the spirits whether they are of God" (I John 4:1) and to "prove all things"—to test them by God's Word.

In this scientific age, it is especially important that we not be deceived by "science falsely so called" (I Timothy 6:20). So-called evolutionary "science" is not supported by any real scientific evidence, and is contrary both to common sense and the Bible. Many professing Christians have "erred concerning the faith" because of evolution (I Timothy 6:21), which has been made the pseudo-scientific rationale for a multitude of false philosophies propounded by false teachers. May God help us to hold fast only to that which is good!

The Lord Christ

And whatsoever ye do, do it heartily, as to the Lord, and not unto men; Knowing that of the Lord ye shall receive the reward of the inheritance: for ye serve the Lord Christ (Colossians 3:23, 24).

This is the only verse in the Bible where our Savior is called "the Lord Christ." Actually, His three primary names ("Lord," "Jesus," and "Christ") are combined in eight different ways in the New Testament.

"Jesus" was His human name, speaking especially of His mission as suffering Savior. "Christ," equivalent to the Hebrew "Messiah," meaning "anointed," speaks of His office as God's chosen King. As "Lord," He is sovereign Creator and ruler of the universe; victorious over all enemies, even death itself.

"Lord Christ" is the only one of the combination forms of His name which omits the human name. Apparently the reason is that, in this passage, the emphasis is altogether on His exalted position as sovereign Creator and eternal King.

Our service is to be rendered not to men—not even to the man Jesus, in His perfect humanity—but to the Lord and the Christ—the Lord Christ, Creator of all things and King of kings. "Your labour is not in vain in the Lord" (I Corinthians 15:58), for He is "heir of all things" (Hebrews 1:2), and thus can dispense "the reward of the inheritance" to His faithful servants, who are "joint-heirs with Christ" (Romans 8:17). The inheritance is ours because of our position in Christ; the reward is given for service for the Lord.

Because of whom we serve, whatever we do should be done heartily! This is the Greek word *psuches*, usually translated "soul," or "life," as well as "heart." If there is anything we cannot in good conscience do with full heart to the Lord, then it should not be done at all.

Biblical Sarcasm

And Job answered and said, No doubt but ye are the people, and wisdom shall die with you (Job 12:1, 2).

It is remarkable that the Bible, with its great variety of literary forms and numerous personal conversations and discourses, contains very few examples of sarcasm or satire.

Nevertheless, the few examples of Biblical irony are well worth noting, with one of the most notable being Job's response, as above, to the self-righteous platitudes of his three philosophizing "friends." In their intellectual and moral arrogance, and with no real understanding of God's purposes, these critics were far out of line and well deserved Job's cutting sarcasm. Examples of such combined spiritual ignorance and intellectual arrogance are not hard to find today and, occasionally perhaps, a satirical commentary may be effective in changing them or preventing their effect.

One other well-known case of Biblical sarcasm is Elijah's taunting monologue to the prophets of Baal: "Cry aloud: for he is a god; either he is talking, or he is pursuing, or he is in a journey, or peradventure he sleepeth, and must be awaked" (I Kings 18:27). Jeremiah also had a word to say about the ineptitude of false gods and the foolishness of those who put their faith in them, and who were "saying to a stock, Thou art my father; and to a stone, Thou hast brought me forth: . . . But where are thy gods that thou hast made thee? let them arise, if they can save thee in the time of thy trouble" (Jeremiah 2:27, 28).

Much more foolish than those who believe that sticks and stones can generate living beings, however, are those modern-day idolaters who worship "Mother Nature," believing that her "natural processes" can evolve hydrogen atoms, over billions of years, into human beings. The examples of Elijah and Jeremiah, as well as Job, may warrant an occasional touch of sarcasm when discussing such notions!

The Wandering Jew

And the Lord shall scatter thee among all people, from the one end of the earth even unto the other, and there thou shalt serve other gods, which neither thou nor thy fathers have known, even wood and stone (Deuteronomy 28:64).

One of the most convincing evidences of the inspiration of the Bible is found in the numerous prophecies of the dispersion of God's chosen people, Israel, among all the nations of the world.

Our text was written through Moses almost four centuries before the great kingdom of Israel under David and Solomon was even established, and over 700 years before the beginning of the dispersion, but eventually it was fulfilled, literally and meticulously.

No nation was ever scattered so widely as Israel; yet amazingly, they have remained a distinct people, even under great persecution, for over 3500 years. This also was prophesied: "My God will cast them away, because they did not hearken unto Him: and they shall be wanderers among the nations" (Hosea 9:17). "And thou shalt become an astonishment, a proverb, and a byword, among all nations whither the Lord shall lead thee" (Deuteronomy 28:37). "Lo, the people shall dwell alone, and shall not be reckoned among the nations" (Numbers 23:9).

The Scriptures also predicted the long duration of their dispersion, as well as their eventual reestablishment as a nation, and ultimate return to the true God, their Creator and Savior. "For the children of Israel shall abide many days without a king, . . . Afterward shall the children of Israel return, and seek the Lord their God, and David their king; and shall fear the Lord and His goodness in the latter days" (Hosea 3:4, 5).

This is a mere sampling of the Scriptures on this vital subject, all testifying to the prophetic omniscience of the divine author of the Bible.

Mind Control

This I say therefore, and testify in the Lord, that ye henceforth walk not as other Gentiles walk, in the vanity of their mind, Having the understanding darkened, being alienated from the life of God through the ignorance that is in them, because of the blindness of their heart (Ephesians 4:17, 18).

A question that troubles many Christians is why most highly educated leaders in science and other fields—even theologians—seem to find it so difficult to believe the Bible and the gospel of Christ. The answer is in the words of our text: They are "alienated from the life of God" because of self-induced ignorance. It is not that they can't understand, but that they won't understand! They "walk in the vanity of their mind, having the understanding darkened . . . because of the blindness of their heart." They don't want to believe in their hearts, therefore they seek an excuse not to believe in their minds. They are "men of corrupt minds, reprobate concerning the faith" (II Timothy 3:8).

The sad truth is that Satan himself controls their minds. They may be ever so intelligent in secular matters, but the gospel, with all its comprehensive and beautiful simplicity, remains hidden to them. "If our gospel be hid, it is hid to them that are lost: In whom the god of this world hath blinded the minds of them which believe not" (II Corinthians 4:3, 4).

Is there a remedy? Yes. "For the weapons of our warfare are not carnal, but mighty through God to the pulling down of strong holds; Casting down imaginations, and every high thing that exalteth itself against the knowledge of God, and bringing into captivity every thought to the obedience of Christ" (II Corinthians 10:4, 5). In this verse, the word "thought" is the same as "mind." The weapons of truth, of prayer, of love, of the Spirit, can capture even such minds as these!

National Righteousness

Righteousness exalteth a nation: but sin is a reproach to any people (Proverbs 14:34).

Modern Christians place great emphasis on personal salvation, but we must remember that God is also the God of the nations. That being so, our own nation, so greatly blessed of God in the past, may well be in great peril, for "the wicked shall be turned into hell, and all the nations that forget God" (Psalm 9:17).

Our nation was founded by men who had strong faith in God, and its laws were based on the laws of God. The schools all honored the Lord and His Word, taught the truth of special creation, and enforced Biblical morality among the students. Today, God and anything associated with Him are banned from the classroom, His laws are no longer taken seriously in the courts and legislatures, and evolutionary humanism is, in effect, the state-endorsed religion. Divorce and immorality are affecting most of the nation's homes; business and finance are ubiquitously plagued with greed and dishonesty; the sins of homosexuality, drunkenness, and drug use are rampant, and atheistic, New Age globalism is an imminent threat at our gates.

God would even have spared Sodom, though, if there had been ten righteous (Genesis 18:32), and America has evidently been spared thus far because it is still the nerve center of world missions and Christian literature, as well as aid for the sick and needy. The modern revival of true creationism is centered in this nation, and serious Biblical interest is growing in many places, yet worldliness, apostasy, and compromise are eating away at the heart of American Christianity, and there is great need for a revival—not of religious emotionalism, but of genuine commitment to the integrity and authority of God's Word. "Blessed is the nation whose God is the LORD" (Psalm 33:12).

The Peace from God

The LORD lift up His countenance upon thee, and give thee peace (Numbers 6:26).

The beautiful benediction of Numbers 6:24–26 is climaxed by this prayer for God-given peace. The word for "give" is a very strong word, implying a gift which is permanent and secure—that is, the blessing says: "The Lord *establish* peace for you!"

Men have longed for peace all through history, but always there are those who want war. "I am for peace," the psalmist said; "but when I speak, they are for war" (Psalm 120:7). Even today, in our "enlightened" age of science and education, there are perhaps forty local wars raging in the world, and seemingly nothing can be done to stop them.

Those in the "over 60" generation remember how our modern Veterans' Day was once called Armistice Day, established to commemorate the ending of the World War the "war to end all wars," as we were assured. But when World War II came along, then the Korean War and the Viet Nam War, as well as various little wars (Grenada, Somalia, Bosnia, Panama, Iraq, etc., only to mention some of those directly involving our own country), the term "Armistice Day" soon became obsolete.

It is good and right to remember and honor our military veterans, of course, especially those who gave their lives in such wars, but the world seems further away from true world peace than ever. It will always be so, until the Lord Himself lifts up His countenance on His creation and *establishes* peace. Then—but not until then—"of the increase of His government and peace there shall be no end, . . . The zeal of the Lord of hosts will perform this" (Isaiah 9:7), when Christ returns. Nevertheless, the believer can, right now, know true and lasting peace of soul, for the Lord Jesus will "keep him in perfect peace, whose mind is stayed on [Him]: because He trusteth in [Him]" (Isaiah 26:3).

Life in the Blood

For the life of the flesh is in the blood: and I have given it to you upon the altar to make an atonement for your souls: for it is the blood that maketh an atonement for the soul (Leviticus 17:11).

This great verse contains a wealth of scientific and spiritual truth. It was not realized until the discovery of the circulation of the blood by the creationist scientist William Harvey, in about 1620, that biological "life" really is maintained by the blood, which both brings nourishment to all parts of the body and also carries away its wastes.

Its spiritual truth is even more significant. The blood, when shed on the altar, would serve as an "atonement" (literally, "covering") for the soul of the guilty sinner making the offering. In fact, the "life" of the flesh is actually its "soul," for "life" and "soul" both translate the same Hebrew word (*nephesh*) in this text. When the blood was offered, it was thus an offering of life itself, in substitution for the life of the sinner who deserved to die.

Human sacrifices, of course, were prohibited. No man could die for another man, for his blood would inevitably be contaminated by his own sin. Therefore, the blood of a "clean animal" was required. Animals do not possess the "image of God" (Genesis 1:27), including the ability to reason about right and wrong, and therefore cannot sin. Even such clean blood could only serve as a temporary covering, and it could not really "take away" sin. For a permanent solution to the sin problem, nothing less was required than that of the sinless "Lamb of God, which taketh away the sin of the world" (John 1:29). "Neither by the blood of goats and calves, but by His own blood He entered in once into the holy place, having obtained eternal redemption for us" (Hebrews 9:12). Since His life was in His blood, He has "made peace through the blood of His cross" (Colossians 1:20).

NOVEMBER 13

The Eternal Flame

The fire shall ever be burning upon the altar; it shall never go out (Leviticus 6:13).

The so-called "eternal flame" at the tomb of former President John Kennedy will surely eventually be extinguished. The same proved to be true for the continual burnt offering ordained by God in Israel's ancient tabernacle sacrifices. The continual sacrifices for sin were of no more avail, once God's own sacrifice had been slain. "Every priest standeth daily ministering and offering oftentimes the same sacrifices, which can never take away sins: But this man, after He had offered one sacrifice for sins for ever, sat down on the right hand of God; . . . For by one offering He hath perfected for ever them that are sanctified" (Hebrews 10:11, 12, 14).

There is one flame, however, which is truly eternal. Jesus spoke of it several times. For example: "It is better for thee to enter into life maimed, than having two hands to go into hell, into the fire that never shall be quenched" (Mark 9:43). "Depart from me, ye cursed, into everlasting fire, prepared for the devil and his angels" (Matthew 25:41). Then, in the last book of the Bible describing the final judgment, "the devil that deceived them was cast into the lake of fire and brimstone, where the beast and the false prophet are, and shall be tormented day and night for ever and ever. . . . And whosoever was not found written in the book of life was cast into the lake of fire" (Revelation 20:10, 15).

But there is also another symbolic significance to the continual burnt offering: "Did not our heart burn within us, . . . while He opened to us the Scriptures?" (Luke 24:32). "His Word was in mine heart as a burning fire shut up in my bones" (Jeremiah 20:9). "By Him therefore let us offer the sacrifice of praise to God continually" (Hebrews 13:15). Set on fire by the Word of God and the love of Christ, our hearts should burn with His praises continually.

Adam's Rib

And the L*ORD* *God caused a deep sleep to fall upon Adam, and he slept: and He took one of his ribs, and closed up the flesh instead thereof; And the rib, which the* L*ORD* *God had taken from man, made He a woman, and brought her unto the man* (Genesis 2:21, 22).

This amazing record of how the first woman came into being has been the object of much ridicule, but it is completely and literally true. However, the "rib" which God used was most likely not a rib at all. Rather, the Hebrew word in most of its occurrences is translated either "side" or "side chamber." This would probably be a better translation here, as well.

It may be that Eve's body was formed by God from Adam's side, or from something within the "chamber" of his side. Any such "surgery" must at least have involved the shedding of blood. Since "the life of the flesh is in the blood" (Leviticus 17:11), and since the circulating blood in one's body cleanses and renews both flesh and bones, such a primeval blood transfusion from Adam's body would be uniquely appropriate to bring life to Eve's body.

Adam's "deep sleep" thus becomes a prophetic foreshadowing of the deep sleep of death into which one day "the last Adam" (I Corinthians 15:45) would enter, when a spear "pierced His side, and forthwith came there out blood and water" (John 19:34). As Adam's sacrifice gave life to his bride, so did the death of Christ quicken "the church of God, which He hath purchased with His own blood" (Acts 20:28). "Christ also loved the church, and gave Himself for it; . . . That He might present it to Himself a glorious church" (Ephesians 5:25, 27). As Eve thenceforth shared Adam's very life, so do believers today constitute Christ's beloved Bride, and we are "hid with Christ in God," so that Christ Himself is "our life" (Colossians 3:3, 4).

NOVEMBER 15

Made New in Christ

Therefore if any man be in Christ, he is a new creature: old things are passed away; behold, all things are become new (II Corinthians 5:17).

To appreciate this wonderful verse properly, it is helpful to remember two things: In the New Testament, both "creature" and "creation" represent the same Greek word and so can be used interchangeably. Secondly, in both Testaments, only "God" or "the Lord" can be the subject of the verb "create" or "created," because God alone is the Creator. Men can "make" things, or "form" things, but only God can *create!*

As far as the physical creation is concerned, the work of creation was finished long ago (Genesis 2:1–3; Hebrews 4:3, 10), except for the very special case of miracles (e.g., the miracle of the multiplied loaves and fishes).

Nevertheless, He is still the Creator, and the miracle of regeneration is a *spiritual* creation which does occur every time an individual truly receives Christ as Savior and Lord and is, thereby, "born again." Only God can create! No psychologist, or guru, or anyone else can make a "new man" of an "old man." Only God is Creator, and an unregenerate person must be "born of the Spirit"—that is, God the Holy Spirit—to be truly "born again" (John 3:3–8).

But then he does become a new creation, and his life is changed! We "put off . . . the old man," and "put on the new man, which after God is created [note—*created!*] in righteousness and true holiness" (Ephesians 4:22, 24). We "have put off the old man with his deeds; And have put on the new man, which is renewed in knowledge after the image of Him that created him" (Colossians 3:9, 10). This is Christ's work, for "Christ liveth in me: and the life which I now live in the flesh I live by the faith of the Son of God" (Galations 2:20).

A Created People

This shall be written for the generation to come: and the people which shall be created shall praise the L*ORD* (Psalm 102:18).

Only God can create, and whenever this verb (Hebrew *bara*) is used in the Bible, the subject of the verb, either explicitly or implicitly, is *God!* However, certain "progressive creationists" contend that "creation" does not have to be instantaneous, but can be a protracted process—some form of evolution. The verse above is used as a proof text for this position, the idea being that the Jewish "people" are being gradually created ("molded") into a nation that will eventually bring praise to God.

This type of Scriptural distortion illustrates the extremes to which theistic evolutionists and progressive creationists will go, in order to force long evolutionary ages into Scripture. In the context, the psalmist is not speaking of a long process, but a future event. He is speaking of a future time to "have mercy upon Zion," when "the time to favour her, yea, the set time, is come" (v. 13). At that future time, "the LORD . . . shall appear in His glory" (v. 16). Then will come the glorious day "when the people are gathered together, and the kingdoms, to serve the LORD" (v. 22).

It is only then that "the people shall be created" who "shall praise the LORD." When a person receives the Lord Jesus Christ, by faith, as his Creator and Savior, he does, indeed, become "a new [creation]" (II Corinthians 5:17), and the miracle of regeneration is always recognized in Scripture as an instantaneous event accomplished by the Creator in the mind and heart of the believer at the time of conversion. As for the Jews who are alive when the Lord returns, "in that day there shall be a fountain opened to the house of David" (Zechariah 13:1). Multitudes will believe and become, at that time, "new creature(s) in Christ Jesus."

NOVEMBER 17

The Rainbow and the Cloud

And I saw another mighty angel come down from heaven, clothed with a cloud: and a rainbow was upon His head, and His face was as it were the sun, and His feet as pillars of fire (Revelation 10:1).

This is the last reference in Scripture to the beautiful rainbow, and a most majestic picture it is. A mighty cloud descends from heaven enveloping the great Creator/Savior Himself, here called (as is often true in Scripture) an "angel," but with a description applicable only to the glorified Son of Man (note Revelation 1:7, 13–16). The rainbow is above the cloud, crowning the head of the Mighty One, as He stands astride both land and sea, thus claiming possession of all the earth (Revelation 10:2).

There seems here to be a clear correlation with the first reference in Scripture to the rainbow and the cloud, neither of which had existed prior to the great Flood, "for the LORD God had not caused it to rain upon the earth" (Genesis 2:5) until that awful day of judgment. At the conclusion of the Flood, when the vast "waters above the firmament" (Genesis 1:7) had all condensed and poured down on the ground, then God had said: "I do set my bow in the cloud, and it shall be for a token of a covenant between me and the earth" (Genesis 9:13), a sign of God's promise never again to destroy the earth with water, as He had just done. It has, ever since, been a beautiful reminder that God cares for His creation, and that, even in the midst of judgment, He is the God of all grace. It also reminds us that He still rules the world He made.

The time is soon coming, when, once again, there shall be no rain and no cloud and "no more sea" (Revelation 21:1), so there shall be no more need for the reminder of the rainbow. All of God's judgments will be over and gone, and there shall "be glory in the church by Christ Jesus throughout all ages, world without end. Amen" (Ephesians 3:21).

The End of the Lord

Behold, we count them happy which endure. Ye have heard of the patience of Job, and have seen the end of the Lord; that the Lord is very pitiful, and of tender mercy (James 5:11).

The Lord often allows godly men and women to go through severe difficulties, but the Apostle says we should "count them happy which endure." "Blessed are they which are persecuted for righteousness' sake: . . . Rejoice, and be exceeding glad: for great is your reward in heaven" (Matthew 5:10, 12).

The patriarch Job is the classic example. He was a godly and righteous man in the highest degree, according to the testimony of God, Himself, who said that "there is none like him in the earth, a perfect and an upright man, one that feareth God, and escheweth evil" (Job 1:8). Yet God allowed Satan to take away all his possessions, and his health, and even his children. Nevertheless, Job remained faithful, and testified: "For I know that my Redeemer liveth . . . yet in my flesh shall I see God" (Job 19:25, 26).

The chastenings of the Lord may seem grievous, especially when they are not sent as punishment for known sin but rather for development of character in likeness to Christ, but "the end of the Lord" (that is, "the final goal and purpose of the Lord") always manifests His love and tender mercy.

In Job's case, once the testing was finished, "the LORD gave Job twice as much as he had before" (Job 42:10), giving him precisely twice as many head of livestock as those he had lost (compare Job 1:3; 42:12). In addition, "He had also seven sons and three daughters," precisely the number who had died in a great storm at the beginning of his troubles (Job 1:2, 18, 19; 42:13). He knew he would also see his first set of children again, because they, like he, would live again, giving him twice as many children as he had before. The "end of the Lord" is tender mercy, always, to those who love Him.

God's Work of Providence

Thou visitest the earth, and waterest it: Thou greatly enrichest it with the river of God, which is full of water: Thou preparest them corn, when Thou hast so provided for it (Psalm 65:9).

The 65th psalm speaks especially of God's great work of "providence" as supplementing His primeval work of creation. The latter was completed in the six days of Creation Week (Genesis 2:1–3). The work of providence, however, still goes on, perpetually reminding us of God's care for His creatures. "He left not Himself without witness, in that He did good, and gave us rain from heaven, and fruitful seasons, filling our hearts with food and gladness" (Acts 14:17).

God's providential concern, however, extends not only to men and women. "He causeth the grass to grow for the cattle" (Psalm 104:14). "So is this great and wide sea, wherein are things creeping innumerable, both small and great beasts. . . . These wait all upon thee; that thou mayest give them their meat in due season" (vv. 25, 27). "Behold the fowls of the air: . . . your heavenly Father feedeth them" (Matthew 6:26).

Note that He is not *their* Heavenly Father, He is *your* Heavenly Father—yet He feedeth *them!* He is merely their Maker and Provider; yet a single sparrow "shall not fall on the ground without your Father" (Matthew 10:29).

He even provides for the inanimate creation, "upholding all things by the word of His power" (Hebrews 1:3). The omnipotent God of Creation is thus the ever-sustaining and ever-caring God of Providence.

Still, some choose not to believe, even though "that which may be known of God is manifest in them; for God hath shewed it unto them. For the invisible things of Him from the creation of the world are clearly seen . . . so that they are without excuse" (Romans 1:19, 20).

The God of Israel

Know therefore this day, and consider it in thine heart, that the Lord *He is God in heaven above, and upon the earth beneath: there is none else* (Deuteronomy 4:39).

It is the standard cliché among modern intellectuals that Jehovah, the God of Israel, was nothing but a tribal "god," like Dagon of the Philistines or Baal of the Zidonians. Nothing could be further from the truth, of course. As our text proclaims: "Jehovah (or Yahweh) is God in heaven above, and upon the earth beneath: there is none else!"

This statement is found in what has been called the "valedictory address" of Moses. In fact, most of the book of Deuteronomy (meaning "second law") consists of Moses' exhortations and reminders to the children of Israel as they were about to enter the Promised Land. The great burden of his message was that the God of Israel was *not* like other gods, for they were nothing but nature gods, mere personifications of natural forces, energized to some degree by demonic spirits. "Jehovah, *He* is God!" He is the Creator of heaven and earth, and the various forces of nature, even of the spirits the heathen were worshiping.

"Behold, the heaven and the heaven of heavens is the Lord's thy God, the earth also, with all that therein is" (Deuteronomy 10:14), Moses reminded them. Then, in even stronger language, he said: "For the Lord your God is God of gods, and Lord of lords, a great God, a mighty, and a terrible, which regardeth not persons, nor taketh reward" (Deuteronomy 10:17). One cannot gain God's favor either by position or by purchase, but only by obedient faith.

This God of Israel is Maker of heaven and earth! Therefore, said Moses, "ascribe ye greatness unto our God. He is the Rock, His work is perfect: for all His ways are judgment; a God of truth and without iniquity, just and right is He" (Deuteronomy 32:3, 4).

NOVEMBER 21

God Our Habitation

Lord, thou hast been our dwelling place in all generations (Psalm 90:1).

These are the tremendous opening words of the oldest psalm in the book of Psalms, called, in its superscript, the "prayer of Moses the man of God." Moses must have written it shortly before his death, as he looked out over the promised land and realized that he, himself, would never live there (Deuteronomy 34:4, 5). It did not really matter, though, for he had lived in many places, and none of them were really his home. As a baby, he had lived for a brief while in a basket on the river, then in a queen's palace, then forty years in Midian, and forty more years wandering in the wilderness.

Furthermore, he had been meditating on the men of God of previous generations (after all, he had compiled all their ancient records in the book of Genesis) and had found that they, too, like the Apostle Paul 1500 years later, had "no certain dwellingplace" (I Corinthians 4:11). Adam had been expelled from his Garden; Noah lived for a year in an Ark on a worldwide sea, then the rest of his life in a devastated earth; Abraham, Isaac, and Jacob lived in tents in Canaan, and their descendants lived as slaves in Egypt.

Yet wherever they were, the Lord was with them. *He* had been their dwelling place, and this was Moses' first thought as he composed his great prayer. He also had written down "the blessing, wherewith Moses the man of God blessed the children of Israel before his death" (Deuteronomy 33:1). Its climax was this great assurance: "The eternal God is thy refuge, and underneath are the everlasting arms" (v. 27). The "refuge" of this promise is the same Hebrew word as "dwelling place" in our text.

We, like they, are "strangers and pilgrims on the earth" (Hebrews 11:13), but "underneath are the everlasting arms." Where the Lord is—there home is!

Where Is Wisdom?

But where shall wisdom be found? and where is the place of understanding? (Job 28:12).

Men have been searching for this most valuable of all treasures since time began. Eve first fell into sin as she was led by Satan to believe that the forbidden fruit would make her wise. Even before Abram left Ur of the Chaldees, the patriarch Job was asking this ancient question of his three critical friends, but they could not answer.

In this chapter, Job notes that while valuable metals can be dug from the rocks of the earth (Job 28:1, 2), wisdom cannot be mined by hard searching and labor. Neither can it be purchased like some commodity (vv. 13–19). In terms of modern categories, wisdom is not acquired through college degrees or philosophical meditation, or any variety of human experience or study.

It can only be found in God, Himself, for "God understandeth the way thereof, and He knoweth the place thereof" (Job 28:23). "The fear of the Lord, that is wisdom; and to depart from evil is understanding" (Job 28:28).

True wisdom is to be found in the Lord Jesus, "who of God is made unto us wisdom" (I Corinthians 1:30). In Him alone "are hid all the treasures of wisdom and knowledge" (Colossians 2:3).

Then, of course, since the Holy Scriptures constitute His written Word, we find wisdom there. "Let the word of Christ dwell in you richly in all wisdom" (Colossians 3:16).

If one desires wisdom—*real* wisdom—he must find it in the fear of the Lord, a departure from all evil, receiving Jesus Christ as Savior and sovereign Lord, and in diligence to learn and obey His Word. "For the Lord giveth wisdom: out of His mouth cometh knowledge and understanding. He layeth up sound wisdom for the righteous: He is a buckler to them that walk uprightly" (Proverbs 2:6, 7).

NOVEMBER 23

The Designed Creation

Understand, ye brutish among the people: and ye fools, when will ye be wise? He that planted the ear, shall He not hear? He that formed the eye, shall He not see? (Psalm 94:8, 9).

The concept of evolution, according to this verse, is nothing but brute-like foolishness. If an automobile presupposes an automaker, and a clock implies a clockmaker, surely the infinitely more intricate and complex eyes and ears of living creatures require an ear-maker and an eye-maker! "The hearing ear, and the seeing eye, the LORD hath made even both of them" (Proverbs 20:12).

The most basic of all scientific laws—the law of cause and effect (no effect greater than its cause)—becomes utmost nonsense if the cosmos is the product of chaos and the universe evolved by chance. "The fool hath said in his heart, There is no God" (Psalm 14:1).

Every creature, from the single-celled amoeba to the amazing human body, bears the impress of intricate planning and construction. The notion that such complex structures could evolve by random mutations and natural selection is simply a measure of the audacity of human rebellion and the absurdity of humanistic reasoning. Such things never happen in the real world, and there is no real scientific evidence whatever for "vertical" evolution from one kind to a higher kind.

The *only* genuine evidence for evolution is the fact that the leaders of intellectualism believe it, and the only reason *they* believe it is their frantic desire to escape God. "Professing themselves to be wise, they became fools" (Romans 1:22).

The ear did not "evolve"; it was planted. The eye did not "happen by chance"; it was formed. Every *wise* man and woman will say with the psalmist, "I will praise thee; for I am fearfully and wonderfully made: marvelous are thy works; and that my soul knoweth right well" (Psalm 139:14).

When Jesus Gave Thanks

And He took the seven loaves and the fishes, and gave thanks, and brake them, and gave to His disciples, and the disciples to the multitude (Matthew 15:36).

This is the first reference in the New Testament to the grace of thankfulness, and it is appropriate that it should refer to a prayer of thanksgiving coming from the lips of Christ, Himself, as He fed the multitude with a few fragments of bread and meat.

There are ten references to Christ giving thanks: four of them (Matthew 15:36; Mark 8:6; John 6:11, 23) are in the accounts of His feeding the two multitudes. Five of them tell of His giving thanks at the last supper (Matthew 26:27; Mark 14:23; Luke 22:17, 19; I Corinthians 11:24). On the other occasion, as He prepared to raise Lazarus from the grave, Christ thanked His Father for hearing His prayer (John 11:41).

Since He left "us an example," that we "should follow His steps" (I Peter 2:21), it is pleasing to God when we give thanks. Not only should we thank God for all His material blessings, as Christ did when He fed the multitude, but also when He answers our prayers, as Christ did at Lazarus' tomb.

We also ought to thank Him for the privilege of suffering for Him, as He did for us (Philippians 1:29, I Peter 2:19–24). When He gave thanks for the bread and "the fruit of the vine" at the last supper, He reminded His disciples that the elements represented His broken body and His shed blood, which were "given for you" and "shed for you" (Luke 22:19, 20).

Thus, if we would be like Jesus in the spirit of thanksgiving, we will thank God for everything—even for suffering. In fact, this is exactly what God has told us to do! "In every thing give thanks: for this is the will of God in Christ Jesus concerning you" (I Thessalonians 5:18). "In every thing . . . with thanksgiving let your requests be made known unto God" (Philippians 4:6).

NOVEMBER 25

Thanksgiving in Heaven

And the four and twenty elders, which sat before God on their seats [thrones], fell upon their faces, and worshipped God, Saying, We give thee thanks, O Lord God Almighty, which art, and wast, and art to come; because thou hast taken to thee thy great power, and hast reigned (Revelation 11:16, 17).

This is the final reference in the Bible to the giving of thanks. It records a scene in heaven where the 24 elders, representing all redeemed believers, are thanking God that His primeval promise of restoration and victory is about to be fulfilled. The petition, "thy kingdom come" (Matthew 6:10), is now ready to be answered.

Similarly, the final reference to the offering of praise is also set in heaven. "And a voice came out of the throne, saying, Praise our God, all ye His servants, and ye that fear Him, both small and great. And I heard as it were the voice of a great multitude, and as the voice of many waters, and as the voice of mighty thunderings, saying, Alleluia: for the Lord God omnipotent reigneth" (Revelation 19:5, 6).

The word "alleluia" is the same as the Hebrew word "hallelujah," meaning, "Praise ye the Lord!" Thus, the joyful notes of praise for who He is and thankfulness for what He has done will resound through heaven when Christ returns. Then, forevermore, the very lives of all His saints will be perpetual testimonies of thanksgiving and praise.

This is our destiny, if we have received Christ by faith as Savior and Lord. It is important that our lives even now begin to reflect such a character, that we may be the better prepared as the day approaches. "In every thing give thanks: for this is the will of God in Christ Jesus concerning you" (I Thessalonians 5:18). "By Him therefore let us offer the sacrifice of praise to God continually, that is, the fruit of our lips giving thanks to His name" (Hebrews 13:15).

God Will Provide

And Abraham said, My son, God will provide Himself a lamb for a burnt offering: so they went both of them together (Genesis 22:8).

When Abraham was tested in the matter of offering his beloved son as a sacrifice, God finally provided a ram which could be used for the sacrifice in place of his son. As a result, Abraham named that place *Jehovah-jireh,* meaning "the Lord will provide" (Genesis 22:13, 14). It was in that very place that God's Lamb would be provided for the sin of the world.

Abraham learned a great lesson in this experience, having faith in God's providing grace under the worst of circumstances. The God who created all things can surely provide anything to His children when they ask. This is the testimony of both the Old and New Testament.

He will provide the right person needed for any of His ministries. For example, when his people desired a king, God told Samuel: "I have provided me a king," and directed him to David (I Samuel 16:1). God also provides the necessities of life, even for the least of His creatures. "Who provideth for the raven his food?" was the rhetorical question God asked of Job. He surely, therefore, will supply the physical needs of His own people. "I will abundantly bless her [Zion's] provision: I will satisfy her poor with bread" (Psalm 132:15).

More importantly, He satisfies our spiritual needs, especially for us in this present age of grace, "God having provided some better thing for us" (Hebrews 11:40). He provides us, for example, with "the supply of the Spirit of Jesus Christ" (Philippians 1:19). Finally, we have the glorious promise of Philippians 4:19: "But my God shall supply all your need according to His riches in glory by Christ Jesus." Like Abraham and Isaac, we can go together to do God's will, knowing by faith that God will always provide.

NOVEMBER 27

The Pilgrims

Peter, an apostle of Jesus Christ, to the strangers scattered throughout Pontus, Galatia, Cappadocia, Asia, and Bithynia (I Peter 1:1).

These "strangers" to whom Peter wrote his two epistles were actually "pilgrims." He used the same Greek word (*parepidemos*) in I Peter 2:11: "Dearly beloved, I beseech you as strangers and *pilgrims,* abstain from fleshly lusts." The word means a resident foreigner, and its only other New Testament usage is in Hebrews 11:13, speaking of the ancient patriarchs, who "confessed that they were strangers and *pilgrims* on the earth."

We give honor today to the American "pilgrims," as they called themselves (thinking of these very verses), who left their homelands in order better to serve God in a foreign land. The "pilgrims" to whom Peter was writing likewise had been "scattered abroad" for their faith (note Acts 8:4).

For that matter, every born-again believer in the Lord Jesus Christ is really just a pilgrim here on Earth, ambassadors for Christ in a foreign land. "For our conversation is in heaven" (Philippians 3:20). That is, we are citizens of heaven (the Greek word translated "conversation" in this verse is *politeuma,* meaning "a community" or "citizenship"), and are here only for a time to serve our Lord until He calls us home.

And while we are here, we may endure many trials and sorrows—just as did those Massachusetts pilgrims—but He nevertheless supplies our needs—just as He did for them—and we ought to abound in thanksgiving, as they did.

Of all people in the history of the world, none have more cause for thanksgiving than American Christians. Therefore, since we are "enriched in every thing," through our Savior, this "causeth through us thanksgiving to God" (II Corinthians 9:11), and we should be "abounding therein with thanksgiving" (Colossians 2:7).

Praise and Thanksgiving

Praise ye the Lord. O give thanks unto the L*ORD; for He is good: for His mercy endureth for ever* (Psalm 106:1).

In this verse there are two commandments: "Praise ye the Lord," and "give thanks unto the Lord." Although the meaning of each exhortation is similar to the other, there is one important difference.

When we thank the Lord, our prayer deals with what He has done for us and those with whom we are directly concerned. When we praise the Lord, on the other hand, our praise is for what He is and what He does intrinsically, with no necessary reference to how these truths may affect us personally.

It may be significant that there are approximately twice as many references to "praise" in the Bible as there are to "thanks." On the other hand, our personal prayers usually spend far more time in thanksgiving for personal blessings than in simple praise to God, Himself. For that matter, our prayers are usually far more occupied with requests, than with praise and thanksgiving put together.

Every type of prayer is good, of course, if offered in accord with Biblical criteria. Every Christian needs to spend much time before the Lord, both in petition and thanksgiving. But an even greater need is to increase the element of praise in our lives.

The distinctive meaning of "praise" is first suggested in its first occurrence in the Bible. In Genesis 12:15, it is said that the princes of Pharaoh "commended" Sarai to their king. In this verse, the Hebrew *hallal* ("to praise") is translated "commended," though later it is almost always rendered "praise." Thus "praise" is essentially a commendation.

In a very real sense, our ministry of creationism—that is, of exalting God as Creator and showing that all the wonderful works of "nature" are in reality the products of His loving, creative power and purpose—is a ministry of praise.

NOVEMBER 29

The Foolishness of Human Wisdom

Professing themselves to be wise, they became fools (Romans 1:22).

The Lord Jesus, in Matthew 5:22, warned His disciples against calling anyone, "Thou fool," since we can only judge by outward acts. Yet the Scriptures, in general, and Christ, in particular (who *could* discern the inward character), do not hesitate to describe certain types of people as fools.

For example: "The fool hath said in his heart, There is no God" (Psalm 14:1). Anyone who tries to explain away all the innumerable evidences of God is a fool, the Bible says. So is anyone who rejects the teachings of Christ: "And every one that heareth these sayings of mine, and doeth them not, shall be likened unto a foolish man, which built his house upon the sand" (Matthew 7:26). In particular, one who lays up riches for himself is in this category. "But God said unto him, Thou fool, this night thy soul shall be required of thee: then whose shall those things be" (Luke 12:20). Christ rebuked the Pharisees as "fools and blind" (Matthew 23:17, 19) because of their hypocrisy.

But perhaps the most foolish of all are those who proclaim themselves to be wise and then seek to rationalize their rejection of the Word of God. The Apostle Paul gravely warns against all such man-centered wisdom: "For the wisdom of this world is foolishness with God" (I Corinthians 3:19).

Such "wisdom" led to ancient paganism, and is now centered in evolutionary humanism. They "became vain in their imaginations, and their foolish heart was darkened. Professing themselves to be wise, they became fools, And . . . worshipped and served the creature more than the Creator" (Romans 1:21, 22, 25, as in the context of Romans 1:18–32). Such humanistic philosophy commonly masquerades as "science," but God has warned: "I will destroy the wisdom of the wise" (I Corinthians 1:19).

The Offense of the Cross

And I, brethren, if I yet preach circumcision, why do I yet suffer persecution? then is the offense of the cross ceased (Galatians 5:11).

The cross is profoundly offensive to the natural man, for it brands him as a hell-deserving sinner. It makes his only hope of salvation a humbling acknowledgment of Christ, the rejected Creator, as his personal Savior, who died for his sins.

It is especially sad when Christians seek to escape this offense of the cross by accommodating their preaching of the cross to the opinions of those who reject it. In the case of the Galatians, legalistic Christians were insisting that Christian converts from paganism be circumcized, in order to avoid offending the Jews. When Paul, instead, preached salvation by grace alone, he was persecuted for it.

This particular compromise has long been forgotten, but a multitude of others have arisen during the ensuing centuries to take its place. Whenever some new philosophy or practice becomes popular in the world, a Christian party will soon be found advocating its adoption in the church, ostensibly to promote easier acceptance of the gospel, but in reality seeking to mitigate the offense of the cross.

Whenever the pagan world follows after a new dress trend or a new music form, a new philosophy or a new life style, many Christians are sure to follow. Witness the widespread compromise with pantheistic evolution and its so-called geologic "ages" by Christian accommodationists, for example. Or, consider the current acceptance of Eastern or Freudian thinking by Biblical counsellors, or the common sanction of divorce for trivial reasons.

Instead of fleeing from the offense of the cross, we need to say with Paul, "God forbid that I should glory, save in the cross of our Lord Jesus Christ, by whom the world is crucified unto me, and I unto the world" (Galatians 6:14).

DECEMBER 1

Lessons for Angels

Unto whom it was revealed, that not unto themselves, but unto us they did minister the things, which are now reported unto you by them that have preached the gospel unto you with the Holy Ghost sent down from heaven; which things the angels desire to look into (I Peter 1:12).

This is an amazing revelation. Many Christians speak of what they call the "simple gospel," and yet its scope is so great that angels, whose wisdom and power are far greater than those of human beings, are continually learning about its riches as they watch from heaven.

Angels, like humans, are created beings. They are not omniscient, and they evidently are learning more and more about Him as they observe the outworkings of His great plan of creation and redemption through the lives of redeemed men and women on Earth.

In fact, "the principalities and powers in heavenly places" are somehow being instructed "by the church the manifold wisdom of God, According to the eternal purpose which He purposed in Christ Jesus our Lord" (Ephesians 3:10, 11).

Satan and the angels who are following Him in his long war against God are also learning. They learned long ago that they could not destroy Job's faith in God, nor Peter's testimony for Christ, though they surely tried! And they will soon start learning, in the "everlasting fire, prepared for the devil and his angels" (Matthew 25:41), that God alone is Creator and eternal King.

Now if angels are still learning about God and His ways, though they have already been in God's presence for thousands of years, we can also learn from them, that our future translation to heaven will not immediately enable us to understand all things. We, like they, shall continue learning forever, "the depth of the riches both of the wisdom and knowledge of God!" (Romans 11:33).

Formed to Be Inhabited

For thus saith the LORD that created the heavens; God Himself that formed the earth and made it; He hath established it, He created it not in vain, He formed it to be inhabited: I am the LORD; and there is none else (Isaiah 45:18).

This verse is the key proof-text for the "gap theory," which attempts to accommodate the evolutionary "ages" of geology by placing them in a hypothetical gap between the first two verses of Genesis. Genesis 1:2 states: "The earth was without form" (Hebrew *tohu*), but Isaiah says, "He created it not in vain" (same word, *tohu*). Thus it is argued that the earth *became* "tohu" long after the primeval creation, as a result of Satan's rebellion in heaven supposedly allowing the geological ages to be inserted between these two events.

Actually, the meaning of *tohu* is very flexible; it occurs 20 times and is translated 10 different ways, depending on context. In our text above, Isaiah was not writing about the initial state of the creation, but the *purpose* of the creation—to provide a beautiful and appropriate home for mankind.

The translation "in vain" was required by Isaiah's context, just as "without form" best fits the context in Genesis 1:2. There is no conflict, since the two passages are dealing with two different subjects, and Isaiah's message simply extols God's ultimate and certain goal for His creation.

When God first created the space/time universe, only the basic elements of the earth (Genesis 1:1) were created, with neither structure nor inhabitants, but that was not its full purpose. God had merely "created" the heavens according to this verse. But then, with great care, He *formed* the earth, *made* the earth, and *established* the earth, and all this was done to make it ready to be inhabited by men and women who would share His image and know His love.

DECEMBER 3

From the Beginning of the Creation

But from the beginning of the creation God made them male and female (Mark 10:6).

These words of the Lord Jesus Christ ought to settle once and for all, for those who take His words seriously, the controversial question of the age of the earth. The earth was created essentially at the same time, He said, as the creation of Adam and Eve. Christ was quoting from Genesis 1:27: " . . . male and female created He them." This greatest of God's creative works was "from the *beginning* of the creation," not 18 billion years *after* the beginning of the creation, as modern old-earth advocates allege.

One can understand why atheists believe in evolution and an almost infinitely old universe, for they really have no other alternative. One who believes in a personal God, on the other hand, only dishonors God if he believes such humanistic speculations rather than God's Word. God is omniscient and omnipotent, as well as loving and merciful, and He would never do anything like this. The great ages assumed by evolutionary geologists supposedly involved billions of years of suffering and dying by billions of animals before man ever evolved. Surely this would have been the most inefficient, wasteful, and cruel method that ever could have been devised for "creating" human beings. Since man's creation was God's main purpose, there is no conceivable reason why He would waste billions of years in such a meaningless charade as this before getting to the point. In fact, the only reason He took six days was to serve as a pattern for man's work week (Exodus 20:8–11).

In fact, the Lord Jesus Christ was not only a creationist, but was, Himself, the Creator of all things (John 1:3; Colossians 1:16; etc.). Therefore, He is the best possible witness as to *when* He created man and woman, and *He* said it was "from the beginning of the creation!"

The Poetry of God

For we are His workmanship, created in Christ Jesus unto good works, which God hath before ordained that we should walk in them (Ephesians 2:10).

The word "poem" is derived from the Greek *poiema.* Used only twice in the New Testament, it refers to great works of God Himself. Thus, God is the divine poet who has created two great masterpieces—artistic creations of marvelous intricacy and surpassing beauty.

The first is the entire physical universe: "For the invisible things of Him from the creation of the world are clearly seen, being understood by the things that are made, even His eternal power and Godhead; so that they are without excuse" (Romans 1:20). In this key verse, *poiema* is translated "things that are made." Everything in the universe, animate and inanimate, constitutes a marvelous product of God's creative forethought and inventive skill. If a beautiful poem requires a poet to create it, so much the more does the complex cosmic Poem of the universe demand a great Poet of consummate wisdom and infinite power. The rejection of the Poet and the message of the Poem not only leaves one "without excuse" (v. 20), but facing "the wrath of God" (v. 18).

Yet an even more amazing poem is the work of transforming redemption accomplished in a lost soul saved "by grace through faith" (Ephesians 2:8). For then it is we, ourselves, who become His poem! This also is a great creative masterpiece, for "we are His workmanship [same word, Greek *poiema*], created in Christ Jesus unto good works." A life once dead in sin, now born again and walking in good works—*this* is God's greatest poetic masterpiece of all!

Both the mighty universe and the soul made new in Christ are special creations of God, and both manifest His greatness and His love. "Thanks be unto God for His unspeakable gift" (II Corinthians 9:15) of grace.

The Deep Sleep

And the LORD God caused a deep sleep to fall upon Adam, and he slept: and He took one of his ribs, and closed up the flesh instead thereof (Genesis 2:21).

This is the first of seven occurrences of the unusual term "deep sleep" (Hebrew *tardema*) in the Old Testament. In each case, it seems to refer to a special state induced by the Lord Himself, in order to convey an important revelation to, or through, the person experiencing it.

In Adam's case, God made a bride for him during his deep sleep, from whose seed would be born all the nations of the earth. "And the rib, which the LORD God had taken from man, made He a woman, and brought her unto the man" (v. 22). The covenant God made with Adam and Eve delegated dominion over the earth to their descendants.

The second deep sleep was that which "fell upon Abram" (Genesis 15:12), when God passed between the sacrificial animals and established His great covenant with him, promising that from his seed would be born the chosen nation. "And I will make of thee a great nation" (12:2). The Abrahamic covenant also delegated the central land of the earth to Isaac's descendants (15:18–21) and promised that "in thee shall all families of the earth be blessed" (12:3).

But Adam was a type of Christ and Abraham was a type of Christ, and their deep sleeps pre-figured His own deep sleep of death on the cross. There He became the last Adam and the promised Seed, dying to give life to His great Bride and living again to establish a holy nation of the redeemed, fulfilling all of God's ancient covenants, and instituting the eternal New Covenant in His own blood.

When Adam fell into a deep sleep, a bride was born; when Abraham fell into his deep sleep, a nation was born. But when Christ slept deeply in death, on the cross and in the tomb, death and hell were judged, and a new world was born.

The Stars Also

And God made two great lights; the greater light to rule the day, and the lesser light to rule the night: He made the stars also (Genesis 1:16).

On the fourth day of Creation Week, God made the two lights for day and night, and then—almost like an afterthought—"He made the stars also." Nothing, of course, is an afterthought with God, but this emphasizes the relative importance of these parts of His creation. Whether or not the earth is the *geographical* center of the universe, Earth is the center of God's *interest* in the universe. This is where He created man and woman in His own image, and where He will reign over His creation in the ages to come.

The primary purpose of the stars, as well as the sun and moon, was "to divide the day from the night; And . . . to be for signs, and for seasons, and for days, and years: and . . . to give light upon the earth" (Genesis 1:14, 15). They could not fulfill these functions, of course, if their light could not be seen on the earth, so we can be sure that these heavenly bodies and their light rays were created—like Adam and Eve—"full-grown," in a state of functioning maturity.

All that can be known scientifically about the stars must be determined from their light intensity and spectra. (Their distances can be measured geometrically only to about 300 light-years.) Any other information—any greater distances, size, temperature, etc.—must be derived by inference, based on some theory of stellar evolution.

Although the stars all look alike (even through a telescope, they all appear as mere points of light), these calculations have shown that each one is unique, as revealed long ago in Scripture: "One star differeth from another star in glory" (I Corinthians 15:41). Those who believe can learn more about them in the ages to come, for "they that be wise shall shine . . . as the stars for ever and ever" (Daniel 12:3).

Given by Inspiration

All scripture is given by inspiration of God, and is profitable for doctrine, for reproof, for correction, for instruction in righteousness: That the man of God may be perfect, throughly furnished unto all good works (II Timothy 3:16, 17).

This passage is the most definitive of all passages on the inspiration of the Bible. It explicitly repudiates all the false concepts which men have developed to try to escape this vital doctrine.

For example, it repudiates the *humanistic theory of inspiration,* which says that the writers were "inspired" with the same quality of exalted feelings that inspired other great writers. But this verse attributes it not to human inspiration, but to the "inspiration *of* God."

Then, there is the *partial theory of inspiration,* which says that part of the Bible is inspired (the "religious" parts), but that part of it is not (the scientific and historical parts). But our verse says that *all* Scripture is inspired! The *dynamic theory* says the thoughts are inspired, but not the words. However, it is the *Scriptures* that are inspired, not the thoughts of the men who wrote them. The "Scriptures" mean the "writings"—the actual words written.

The *encounter theory* says the Scriptures are not inspired in themselves, but only become inspired when a reader "encounters" God through reading them. This, also, is false. The Scriptures are inspired regardless of how they affect the reader. Actually, the phrase "given by inspiration of God" is one word in the Greek, meaning "God-breathed."

Thus, plenary verbal inspiration and complete divine origin and authority of all the Holy Scriptures is the true Biblical doctrine. When one does accept the God-breathed authority of Scripture, however, he has an infinite resource, serving as an inerrant framework for all true wisdom and knowledge, and leading him into full maturity in the Christian life.

My Glory

O God, my heart is fixed: I will sing and give praise, even with my glory (Psalm 108:1).

This seems a somewhat strange expression. A similar statement is found in Psalm 30:12. "To the end that my glory may sing praise to thee, and not be silent." Also, note Psalm 57:8: "Awake up, my glory; awake, psaltery and harp."

The Hebrew word is the normal word for "glory," as in Psalm 19:1, for example: "The heavens declare the glory of God." But what, then, is meant by "*my* glory"? The explanation is found in the way the New Testament quotes Psalm 16:9: "Therefore my heart is glad, and my glory rejoiceth." In Acts 2:26, this verse is applied to Christ, and translated: "Therefore did my heart rejoice, and my tongue was glad."

It becomes clear, then, that in such passages "my glory" simply means "my tongue." In fact, the word was translated "tongue" in these and other similar passages in the Greek Septuagint translation of the Old Testament.

But why, then, did the inspired Hebrew text here use the words "my glory" instead of the usual Hebrew word for tongue? The answer probably is that, when our tongues are used to praise the Lord, they do, indeed, become our glory!

It is this very ability, in fact, that primarily distinguishes man from the animals. Animals can bark, roar, grunt, and send out sonar signals, but they cannot speak in intelligible, symbolic, abstract speech. This is an unbridgeable evolutionary gulf that cannot be crossed, because only men and women were created in the image of God.

Mankind alone has the ability to speak, for the simple reason that God desires to communicate with us so that we can respond in praise to Him. This is our glory! "I will sing of the mercies of the LORD for ever: with my mouth will I make known thy faithfulness to all generations" (Psalm 89:1).

Inherit the Wind

He that troubleth his own house shall inherit the wind: and the fool shall be servant to the wise of heart (Proverbs 11:29).

This verse was selected to provide the title for one of the most widely distributed movies ever produced in Hollywood. *Inherit the Wind* was a black-and-white movie produced in 1960, starring Spencer Tracy as the famous atheist lawyer, Clarence Darrow. The theme of the picture was the Scopes evolution trial held in Tennessee in 1925. The picture glorified Darrow and evolutionism, portraying creationists and Bible-believing Christians as fanatical buffoons.

Although the movie grossly distorted history, it has continued all these years to be shown over and over. The Scopes trial itself—in the absence of any real scientific evidence for evolution—is repeatedly rehashed in print by evolutionists in their zeal to destroy creationism. This is typical of the "profane and vain babblings, and oppositions of science falsely so called" (I Timothy 6:20), to which evolutionists resort in lieu of evidence.

As far as the Scripture verse itself is concerned, it should serve rather as a sober warning to those evolutionary humanists who are still troubling our nation's homes and schools and churches with this false and deadly doctrine of evolution. *They* are the ones who will inherit the wind. "The ungodly . . . are like the chaff which the wind driveth away" (Psalm 1:4). They are the ones who, "professing themselves to be wise" have become fools (Romans 1:22), "who changed the truth of God into a lie, and worshipped and served the creature more than the Creator" (Romans 1:25).

It is the one who proclaims "no God," who is "the fool" (Psalm 53:1) of our text. Evolutionists, humanists, atheists, and other anti-Biblicists will inherit nothing but wind, but "the wise shall inherit glory" (Proverbs 3:35).

Questions about Creation

Where wast thou when I laid the foundations of the earth? declare, if thou hast understanding (Job 38:4).

Chapters 38–41 of Job records a remarkable series of 77 questions about the creation—questions which God asked Job and his philosophizing friends, and which they were utterly unable to answer. At the end of the searching examination, Job could only confess: "Therefore have I uttered that I understood not; things too wonderful for me, which I knew not" (Job 42:3). Modern evolutionists, despite all their arrogant pretentions, still are not able to answer them either, over 35 centuries later.

But there is One who can answer them, and His answers echo back from another ancient document, the marvelous 8th chapter of Proverbs. To God's first question, "Where wast thou when I laid the foundations of the earth?" comes His answer: "When He appointed the foundations of the earth: Then I was by Him" (Proverbs 8:29, 30). The speaker here is the divine Wisdom. He is the Word of God, the pre-incarnate Son of God, soon to become the Son of man. In this amazing chapter, He echoes an answer to the most searching of God's inscrutable questions to Job and his friends:

"Who shut up the sea with doors, when it brake forth?" (Job 38:8). "He set a compass [literally 'sphericity'] upon the face of the depth: . . . When He gave to the sea His decree, that the waters should not pass His commandment" (Proverbs 8:27, 29). "Hast thou commanded the morning . . . and caused the dayspring to know his place?" (Job 38:12). "When He prepared the heavens, I was there" (Proverbs 8:27).

Our Savior was there! "For by Him were all things created" (Colossians 1:16). One more question: "Have the gates of death been opened unto thee?" (Job 38:17). Yes, and they have not prevailed! "For whoso findeth me findeth life, . . . all they that hate me love death" (Proverbs 8:35, 36).

Ascending Vapors

He causeth the vapors to ascend from the ends of the earth; He maketh lightnings for the rain; He bringeth the wind out of His treasuries (Psalm 135:7).

This striking verse is practically identical with Jeremiah 10:13 and Jeremiah 51:16, suggesting the possibility that the prophet Jeremiah may have written the otherwise anonymous Psalm 135. The two Jeremiah passages do preface this statement with the note that there is "a multitude of waters in the heavens" in connection with the processes described in the verse.

In any case, this thrice-mentioned mechanism beautifully summarized what we now call the hydrologic cycle, and it did so over 2,000 years before the cycle began to be understood by modern scientists. In order to provide rain to water the earth, there must be vapors ascending all over the earth (that is, evaporation from the world's great oceans), winds then blowing from God's unseen treasury (actually the global atmospheric circulation), and, finally, lightnings for (or "with") the rain (electrical discharges associated with the condensation and coalescence of the particles of water vapor in the atmosphere). All of this repeatedly transports purified waters from the ocean back over the lands to fall as rain and snow, there finally to run off back to the oceans after performing their life-sustaining ministries on the lands. "Unto the place from whence the rivers come, thither they return again" (Ecclesiastes 1:7).

Not only does this hydrologic cycle sustain physical life on Earth, but it also is a type of the spreading of God's Word, giving spiritual life. "For as the rain cometh down, and the snow from heaven, and returneth not thither, but watereth the earth, . . . So shall my Word be that goeth forth out of my mouth: it shall not return unto me void, but it shall accomplish that which I please" (Isaiah 55:10, 11).

As Far As East from West

For as the heaven is high above the earth, so great is His mercy toward them that fear Him. As far as the east is from the west, so far hath He removed our transgressions from us (Psalm 103:11, 12).

Critics of the Bible often claim that it pictures a four-cornered, flat earth, with a solid "firmament" high above, on which the stars traverse regular pathways, along with the sun and moon. But nothing could be further from the truth, as evident from our text.

The heavens extend as high above the earth as the infinite mercy of God, which provides free salvation for lost sinners. This surely fits the modern scientific belief in an infinite universe. "Behold the height of the stars, how high they are!" (Job 22:12). The same concept is implied in Isaiah 55:9: "For as the heavens are higher than the earth, so are my ways higher than your ways, and my thoughts than your thoughts."

Consider also the implication of the second verse in our text. Our transgressions have been removed from us as far as the east is from the west. And how far is that? One can start traveling east and continue forever without coming to the end of "east." The same is true if he tries to find the end of "west." The only way this could be true is for the earth to be round. The Bible no more teaches a flat earth than a finite universe. "It is [God] that sitteth upon the circle [or 'roundness'] of the earth" (Isaiah 40:22).

But such great scientific truths, revealed in Scripture long before their confirmation in modern science, are given primarily to illustrate the character of our loving Creator and Savior. His mercy is as infinite as the universe, and His forgiveness never ends. We can never judge His infinite thoughts or analyze His inscrutable ways with our finite understanding. But we can always rejoice in His mercy and praise Him for our great and eternal salvation.

DECEMBER 13

The Powerful Hand of God

Mine hand also hath laid the foundation of the earth, and my right hand hath spanned the heavens: when I call unto them, they stand up together (Isaiah 48:13).

The human hand is an anatomical marvel; nothing remotely comparable exists among the primates or any other animals. It is a marvel of design. But surely the "hand of God"—of which man's hand is only a very dim shadow—is infinitely more powerful and skillful.

Note the testimony of Isaiah 45:12: "I have made the earth, and created man upon it: I, even my hands, have stretched out the heavens, and all their host have I commanded." God did not have to use intermediate processes or pre-existing materials. Everything was "commanded" into existence and "I, even my hands," made all of it, including man. Creation was direct—a *direct* product of God's mighty hands.

Not only was it direct, it was also *immediate,* as our text above makes emphatically plain. His hand laid the earth's foundation and spanned the heavens. Then, "When I call unto them," He says, "they stand up together!" Not one by one—first the universe, then the sun, then the earth, and so on. No, "*they stand up together*." "He spake, and it was done" (Psalm 33:9). It did not take 16 billion years; it took six days—and the only reason it took that long was so that God's work week could serve as a pattern for man (Exodus 20:8–11).

God's hand is omnipotent, and "He's got the whole world in His hand." It is wonderful to know His hand is gentle and loving as well as powerful. His hands will bear eternal scars, where they were spiked to the cross, because He loved us, and died for us. "My sheep hear my voice," He says, "and I give unto them eternal life; and they shall never perish, neither shall any man pluck them out of my hand" (John 10:27, 28). The hand that spanned the heavens can hold on to those who trust Him.

Parable of the Star

I shall see Him, but not now: I shall behold Him, but not nigh: there shall come a Star out of Jacob, and a Sceptre shall rise out of Israel, and shall smite the corners of Moab, and destroy all the children of Sheth (Numbers 24:17).

A parable is not an illustrative story, as most people think, but a "dark saying" (note Psalm 78:2) designed to reveal some hidden truth only to those who are prepared to understand (note Jesus' assertion in Matthew 13:10–17).

The first reference in the Bible to parables is in connection with the seven parables of the false prophet Balaam (Numbers 23:7, 18; 24:3, 15, 20, 21, 23). The central parable of these seven verses is the one in our text speaking of a mysterious Star out of Jacob and a Sceptre out of Israel, both the Star and the Sceptre representing a great person coming in the far future, destined both to guide and to rule all nations.

The wise men of the East somehow recognized His star rising, and came seeking the King. The star they saw, appearing perhaps in one of the constellations long associated by ancient peoples with the primeval promise of a coming redeemer/king—was but a type of the true "bright and morning star" (Revelation 22:16) and the "day star" that one day shall "arise in your hearts" (II Peter 1:19), that "light of the world" (John 8:12) who would be "the light of life" for all people who follow Him in faith.

He is also the Sceptre, the King of all kings, that "rod of iron" by which all nations must one day be ruled (Revelation 19:15) in righteousness. The babe in Bethlehem became the suffering servant on the cross, then rose from the grave like a bright and morning star out of the darkness and will also very soon be acknowledged as "the blessed and only Potentate, the King of kings, and Lord of lords" (I Timothy 6:15).

The Center of the Earth

Thus saith the Lord God; This is Jerusalem: I have set it in the midst of the nations and countries that are round about her (Ezekiel 5:5).

It is doubtful that enough was known about geography in Ezekiel's day for him to be able to know that Jerusalem was "in the midst of the nations and countries" of the world. In fact, he also said that the people of Israel in the last days "dwell in the midst of the land" (Ezekiel 38:12). The last phrase could better be rendered "the center of the earth."

In any case, Ezekiel was right! It would have been essentially impossible to determine the center of the earth's land masses before the advent of modern computers, but this has now been done. A computer study sponsored by the Institute for Creation Research over 20 years ago determined that the sum of the distances from a point in the "Bible lands" to all other increments of land areas on Earth would be smaller than from any other point on the earth's surface.

Not only is this region (and probably Jerusalem itself, if we had precise information on the exact shape of the continents and their continental shelves) the geographic center of the earth, but it is also the spiritual center. It was there where Christ died and rose again and it is also there where He will come again and reign over the earth (Zechariah 14:4, 9).

For that matter, the New Jerusalem will, in the ages to come, be the center of the entire universe. We do not know where the center of the universe is now, for one cannot even define the center of infinite space. The best we can do is to assume that the universe is centered around the throne of its Creator, from where it was "stretched out" in the beginning (Psalm 104:2). And, of course, when the New Jerusalem comes down to the new earth, "the throne of God and of the Lamb shall be in it" (Revelation 21:2; 22:3), and all who know Him now will live there too.

When God Became Man

Thou madest Him a little lower than the angels; thou crownedst Him with glory and honor, and didst set Him over the works of thy hands (Hebrews 2:7).

We cannot comprehend what it meant for the infinite Creator God to become finite man, even coming "in the likeness of sinful flesh" (Romans 8:3). Nevertheless, we can, and must, believe it, for "every spirit that confesseth not that Jesus Christ is come in the flesh is not of God" (I John 4:3).

The Scriptures have given us a glimpse of the "emptying" that His incarnation required—the setting aside of certain outward aspects of His deity. He had been "so much better than the angels" (Hebrews 1:4), but He had to be "made a little lower than the angels for the suffering of death" (Hebrews 2:9—"put to death in the flesh") (I Peter 3:18).

The eternal Word "was God" (John 1:1), but it was necessary that "the Word was made flesh" (John 1:14). "The world was made by Him" (John 1:10), but "the princes of this world . . . crucified the Lord of glory" (I Corinthians 2:8).

He, "being in the form of God, thought it not robbery to be equal with God" (Philippians 2:6). That is, He was not fearful of losing His deity and, therefore, did not have to cling to His divine nature and attributes as He became man. Thus, He "made Himself of no reputation" (emptying Himself of the outward form of God), "and took upon Him the form of a servant" (Philippians 2:7).

Yet that was only the beginning. "For He hath made Him to be sin for us, who knew no sin; that we might be made the righteousness of God in Him" (II Corinthians 5:21). He suffered hell for us, that we might enjoy heaven with Him.

Because He was willing to be so humiliated, He will one day be crowned with glory and honor. "God also hath highly exalted Him, . . . that every tongue should confess that Jesus Christ is Lord" (Philippians 2:9, 11).

DECEMBER 17

A Special Son

The book of the generation of Jesus Christ, the son of David, the son of Abraham (Matthew 1:1).

These opening words of the New Testament identify this "book of the generation [literally 'genesis'] of Jesus Christ" as telling of the wonderful fulfillment of the promise to both Abraham and David of a very special Son.

To Abraham, God had promised: "Because thou hast done this thing, and hast not withheld thy son, thine only son; . . . in thy seed shall all the nations of the earth be blessed; because thou hast obeyed my voice" (Genesis 22:16, 18). This prophecy was directed immediately through Isaac, but focused finally on Jesus Christ, Abraham's greater Son. "Now to Abraham and his seed were the promises made. He saith not, And to seeds, as of many; but as of one, And to thy seed, which is Christ" (Galatians 3:16).

Similarly, a unique promise was made to David concerning his own special Son. "I will set up thy seed after thee, . . . I will be His Father, and He shall be My Son. . . . And thine house and thy kingdom shall be established for ever before thee" (II Samuel 7:12, 14, 16). Once again, this promise applied precursively to Solomon, but ultimately to the greater Son of David, "made of the seed of David according to the flesh; And declared to be the Son of God with power, . . . by the resurrection from the dead" (Romans 1:3, 4). He was greater than Abraham, greater than David, and even "better than the angels. . . . For unto which of the angels said He at any time, . . . I will be to Him a Father, and He shall be to me a Son?" (Hebrews 1:4, 5).

In the fullest sense, this Son was the fulfillment of the primeval promise of the coming seed of the woman (Genesis 3:15). He is the virgin's Son (Isaiah 7:14), the Son given (Isaiah 9:6), "the last Adam . . . the Lord from heaven" (I Corinthians 15:45, 47).

When the Angels Worshipped Christ

And again, when He bringeth in the firstbegotten into the world, He saith, And let all the angels of God worship Him (Hebrews 1:6).

Jesus Christ is "the only begotten Son, which is in the bosom of the Father" (John 1:18), but the day finally came when He had to proceed all the way to Earth, and the eternal Word "was made flesh, and dwelt among us, (and we beheld His glory, the glory as of the only begotten of the Father) full of grace and truth" (John 1:14). A little later, He would be "declared to be the Son of God . . . by the resurrection from the dead" (Romans 1:4). By eternal generation, by the incarnation, by the virgin birth, and by the resurrection, He is in every sense God's "first begotten"—His only begotten—Son.

Our text says that when He first entered the world, born of the virgin, His heavenly Father called on all the innumerable angels in the heavenly host to bow down and worship Him. It is not clear whether this command is a quotation from the Old Testament, although it is cited in a passage which also quotes several other Messianic prophecies as applied to Jesus Christ. Psalm 97:7 and Deuteronomy 32:43 have been suggested as possible source verses, but neither of these seems to fit very well in context.

Thus it may be that our text refers directly, and solely, to a specific decree of God, proclaimed throughout the universe at the time of the human birth of His Son, and recorded here alone. All the angels of the infinite cosmos bowed in solemn worship, but a special contingent was commissioned to watch directly over the birth, and proclaim the good news to those nearby. "And suddenly there was with the angel a multitude of the heavenly host praising God, and saying, Glory to God in the highest, and on earth peace, good will toward men" (Luke 2:13, 14). The angels saw and worshipped; the shepherds heard and told. And "all they that heard it wondered" (Luke 2:18).

DECEMBER 19

The Eternally Begotten Son

When there were no depths, I was brought forth; when there were no fountains abounding with water. Before the mountains were settled, before the hills, was I brought forth (Proverbs 8:24, 25).

It is unfortunate that many modern Bible translations (RSV, NIV, NEB, and others) dilute such key verses as John 3:16 by changing "only begotten Son" to merely "only son." This makes the Bible contradict itself, for Jesus was *not* the *only* son of God. Adam is called "the son of God" (Luke 3:38), angels are called "sons of God" (Job 1:6), and, in fact, all believing Christians are called "sons of God" (John 1:12).

But Jesus was the only *begotten* Son of God! The Greek word is *monogenes,* clearly meaning "only generated" or "only begotten." The word is used only six times in the New Testament (John 1:14, 18; 3:16, 18; Hebrews 11:17; I John 4:9). Five of these refer to Jesus. One refers to Isaac as Abraham's only begotten son (Hebrews 11:17), indicating him as a type of Christ. The first (John 1:14) is a favorite Christmas verse, telling us that the eternal "Word was made flesh, and dwelt among us . . . the glory as of the only begotten of the Father." The last (I John 4:9), is also a beloved Christmas verse, reminding us that "God sent His only begotten Son into the world." *This* verse tells us also that He was God's only begotten Son *before* He came into the world.

But just *when* was He begotten of the Father?

Our text for the day, speaking of the divine Wisdom, tells us that He was "brought forth" before there were any hills or mountains or depths or fountains. In fact, He says, "The LORD possessed me in the beginning of His way. . . . I was set up from everlasting" (Proverbs 8:22, 23).

No wonder the old theologians spoke of Him as the *eternally* begotten Son. And it was *this* Son that the Father gave, that we might have everlasting life!

The Word Made Flesh

And the Word was made flesh, and dwelt among us, (and we beheld His glory, the glory as of the only begotten of the Father,) full of grace and truth (John 1:14).

This is the definitive verse on the divine Incarnation, when "God was in Christ, reconciling the world unto Himself" (II Corinthians 5:19), and the wealth of truth implied therein is beyond human comprehension. We can never understand how the infinite God could become finite man, but where the intellect fails, faith prevails.

It was the Word who "was God" and by whom "all things were made" (John 1:1, 3), yet He made His own human body, in the womb of Mary, and therein "dwelt among us" for thirty-three years. The Greek word here for "dwelt" is unusual, literally meaning "tabernacled."

How could this be? "Without controversy great is the mystery of godliness: God was manifest in the flesh, justified in the Spirit, seen of angels, preached unto the Gentiles, believed on in the world, received up into glory" (I Timothy 3:16). This is, indeed, a great mystery, "but with God all things are possible" (Matthew 19:26). God made a body for Adam; surely He could also make a perfect body in which He Himself could "tabernacle." He was made "in the likeness of sinful flesh" (Romans 8:3), and "was in all points tempted, [i.e., 'tested'] like as we are, yet without sin" (Hebrews 4:15). Since "God cannot be tempted with evil," (James 1:13) and since the Word, who was God, was merely tabernacling in the likeness of sinful flesh, this testing was to demonstrate to man (not to Himself) that He was without sin and therefore able to save sinners. Therefore, John could testify: "We *beheld* His glory!"

Jesus Christ is, indeed, true man—in fact, He is man as God intended man to be. Neither in the womb of Mary, nor on the cross, did He ever cease to be God.

DECEMBER 21

That Holy Thing

And the angel answered and said unto her, The Holy Ghost shall come upon thee, and the power of the Highest shall overshadow thee: therefore also that holy thing which shall be born of thee shall be called the Son of God (Luke 1:35).

This revelation of the Angel Gabriel to Mary refers, of course, to the miraculous conception of the incarnate God in the virgin's womb. It is noteworthy that the developing babe was called "that holy thing." The birth of Jesus had to be a perfectly normal human birth with His infant form being carried in the womb through full term from conception to birth, for "in all things it behooved Him to be made like unto His brethren" (Hebrews 2:17).

This suggests that every other growing embryo could also be called a "holy thing" (actually, the Greek simply says "holy"). John the Baptist, in fact, was said to be "filled with the Holy Ghost, even from his mother's womb" (Luke 1:15).

In any case, there can be no doubt that the growing body of Jesus in Mary's womb was (apart from innate sin) truly human from the moment of conception, and this must therefore be true of every human embryo. The modern abortionist's idea that the fetus only becomes "human" after the first trimester, or even later, is based on the infamous "recapitulation theory" of 19th century evolutionists who taught that the embryo "recapitulated" the evolutionary history of an animal ancestry. This bizarre and long-discredited notion is still offered as a "proof" of evolution and as the pseudo-scientific rationale for abortion—its advocates claiming that the fetus progresses through invertebrate, fish, reptile, and monkey stages before evolving into a human being. No knowledgeable embryologist teaches such a thing today, of course. Abortionism is not only contrary to Scripture and the purposes of God, but unscientific, as well.

Mary and the Grace of God

And the angel said unto her, Fear not, Mary: for thou hast found favor with God (Luke 1:30).

This announcement by the angel Gabriel to the virgin Mary, that she had been chosen as the mother of the coming Savior, contains the first mention in the New Testament of the Greek word for "grace" (*charis*). Mary was chosen, not for anything she had done, but because she had "found grace."

In a remarkable parallel, certainly implying divine inspiration, the first mention of "grace" in the Old Testament is also associated with the coming of a new dispensation in God's dealings with men. "But Noah found grace in the eyes of the LORD" (Genesis 6:8).

Just as Mary found grace, so Noah had found grace. Grace is not something one earns or purchases; grace is a treasure that is *found!* When a person—whether Noah or Mary or someone today—finally realizes that salvation is only by the grace of God, received through faith in the saving work of Christ, he or she has made the greatest discovery that could ever be made, for it brings eternal life.

But there is an even greater dimension to the grace of God. When we do "find" grace, it is actually because God in His infinitely precious grace has found us, and revealed to us the Savior of our souls. Just as God found Moses in the desert, and found Paul on the road to Damascus, then saved and called them to His service, so He finds us, and then we also find His saving grace.

Mary's discovery of God's grace in salvation, through the coming of the "seed of the woman" into the world, is revealed in her *Magnificat*. "My soul doth magnify the Lord, And my spirit hath rejoiced in God my Savior" (Luke 1:46, 47). This could well have also been the testimony of Noah long ago, and it surely should be the testimony of each of us who has found grace today.

The Second Man

The first man is of the earth, earthy: The second man is the Lord from heaven (I Corinthians 15:47).

Paleoanthropologists, seeking to trace man's supposed evolutionary ancestry, have widely different opinions as to the when and how of it. As one evolutionist has recently lamented: "Paleoanthropologists seem to make up for a lack of fossils with an excess of fury, and this must now be the only science in which it is still possible to become famous just by having an opinion."

There is no need to speculate. The Bible solves the problem when it speaks of "the first man Adam" (I Corinthians 15:45) and says that Eve "was the mother of all living" (Genesis 3:20). There were no "pre-Adamite men" (as even some Christians have alleged, hoping thereby to accommodate evolutionary speculations).

Adam, alone, was "the first man," and he had been formed directly by God "of the dust of the ground" (Genesis 2:7)—that is, out of the same basic elements as those in the earth (carbon, oxygen, hydrogen, etc.). He was "earthy," like the materials of Earth. But, then, how can Jesus Christ, who is "the Lord from heaven" be "the second man?" Adam had millions of male descendants before Jesus was born.

The answer can only be that He was "the second man" in the same way that Adam was "the first man." That is, His human body, like that of Adam, was directly made by God, from Earth's elements—not produced by reproduction, like all other men. He was "made flesh" (John 1:14), but only made "in the *likeness* of *sinful* flesh," for He must not inherit the sinful flesh of His human parents, if He is to "condemn sin in the flesh" (Romans 8:3). "A body hast Thou prepared Me," He said (Hebrews 10:5), and as the angel told Mary: "That holy thing which shall be born of thee shall be called the Son of God" (Luke 1:35).

The Babe in Bethlehem

But thou, Bethlehem Ephratah, though thou be little among the thousands of Judah, yet out of thee shall He come forth unto Me that is to be ruler in Israel; whose goings forth have been from of old, from everlasting (Micah 5:2).

This is a very remarkable prophecy, explicitly predicting that the future king of Israel would be born in the little village of Bethlehem, some 700 years before He finally came. Then, to assure its fulfillment, the great Emperor Augustus had to decree a comprehensive census, compelling Joseph to take Mary with him to Bethlehem for her child to be born.

That the prophecy involves an actual birth is clear, not only from the phrase "come forth," but also from the succeeding verse, which warns that God will "give them up, until the time that she which travaileth hath brought forth" (v. 3). The preceding verse had also predicted that "they shall smite [this coming ruler] the judge of Israel with a rod upon the cheek" (v. 1), speaking of His initial rejection and execution.

But that is not all. The prophecy not only foresees His birth in Bethlehem, His repudiation by His own people, and His eventual installation as King over all Israel (not merely Judah), but also that this same remarkable person was none other than God Himself! His "goings forth" had been "from everlasting." That is, He is eternally proceeding forth from His Father. He did not become God's Son when He was born in Bethlehem; He has been coming forth eternally.

There is still another truth implied in the remarkable Hebrew word for "goings-forth." It is also used for such things as the flowing of water from a fountain or the radiations from the sun. Thus, the never-ending flowing forth of power from God, through the Son, is nothing less than the sustaining energy for the whole creation, as He is "upholding all things by the Word of His power" (Hebrews 1:3). And this was the Babe in Bethlehem!

God Gave Himself

For God so loved the world, that He gave His only begotten Son, that whosoever believeth in Him should not perish, but have everlasting life (John 3:16).

It is singularly appropriate that we look at this greatest of all verses on Christmas Day, for it records the greatest of all gifts. The theme of giving is very prominent in the Bible, with such words as "give," "gift," "gave," etc., occurring more than 2,100 times. The first is Genesis 1:17, when God created the sun, moon, and stars "to give light upon the earth," and the last is Revelation 22:12, when Christ will return with His rewards, to "give every man according as his work shall be." "He . . . gave us rain from heaven, and fruitful seasons," as well as "life, and breath, and all things" (Acts 14:17; 17:25).

But the greatest gift, clearly, was when God gave Himself for a lost and undeserving world. It was the greatest gift because it met the greatest need, revealed the greatest love, and had the greatest scope and greatest purpose of any gift that could ever be conceived in the heart of an omniscient Creator.

That was not the end of His giving, of course. "He that spared not His own Son, but delivered Him up for us all, how shall He not with Him also freely give us all things?" (Romans 8:32). "Trust . . . in the living God, who giveth us richly all things to enjoy" (I Timothy 6:17).

This great gift of God is abundantly sufficient to provide salvation and everlasting life for the whole world. But a gift only becomes a gift when it is accepted, and the greatest of all tragedies is that this greatest of all gifts has been spurned and even ridiculed, or—worst of all—simply ignored, by multitudes who need it so greatly. When they brazenly refuse God's free gift of everlasting life, they can only perish in everlasting death. God did all He could do when He gave His Son; for when He gave His Son, He gave Himself.

The Rain and the Word

For as the rain cometh down, and the snow from heaven, and returneth not thither, but watereth the earth, and maketh it bring forth and bud, that it may give seed to the sower, and bread to the eater: So shall my word be that goeth forth out of my mouth: it shall not return unto me void, but it shall accomplish that which I please, and it shall prosper in the thing whereto I sent it (Isaiah 55:10, 11).

In these familiar verses, there is a beautiful anticipation and spiritual application of the so-called "hydrologic cycle" of the science of hydrogeology. The rain and snow fall from the heavens and eventually return there (via the marvelous process of river and ground water run-off to the oceans). This water then later evaporates by solar radiation and is translated inland high in the sky by the world's great wind circuits, finally to fall again as rain and snow on the thirsty land.

But they do *not* return until they first have accomplished their work of watering the earth, providing and renewing the world's water and food supplies to maintain its life.

Analogously, God's Word goes forth from heaven via His revealed Scriptures and their distribution and proclamation by His disciples. It does not return void, for it accomplishes God's spiritual work on Earth. But it *does return,* for it is "for ever . . . settled in heaven" (Psalm 119:89).

The fruitful spreading of God's Word is presented in many other Scriptures. For example: "Cast thy bread upon the waters: for thou shalt find it after many days. . . . In the morning sow thy seed, and in the evening withhold not thine hand: for thou knowest not whether shall prosper, either this or that, or whether they both shall be alike good" (Ecclesiastes 11:1, 6).

Thus, as we sow and water the seed, which is the Word of God, we have God's divine promise that it will accomplish that which He pleases.

Fighting the Creator

Fear ye not Me? saith the L*ORD: Will ye not tremble at My presence, which have placed the sand for the bound of the sea by a perpetual decree, that it cannot pass it: And though the waves thereof toss themselves, yet can they not prevail; though they roar, yet can they not pass over it?* (Jeremiah 5:22).

Jeremiah, warning his Jewish countrymen of their imminent exile into a pagan land, reminded them how futile it had been for them to rebel against their Creator (v. 19). He did this by noting one of God's mighty works of providence.

The earth is dominated by water, which covers over 70 percent of its surface. If the earth were completely smoothed out, the waters would be almost two miles deep all around the globe. In the primeval creation, water was present everywhere, and the earth was "without form" (Genesis 1:2). But then God had energized the universe's gravitational forces, and the waters soon had a "surface," with this "sea level" controlled ever since by gravity and the configuration of land surfaces established on the third day of creation week. Let the waves of the sea become ever so violent; all they do is abrade more sand from the rocky shores and still further stabilize the seashore with the beaches so produced.

At the time of the Flood, great masses of water were added to the earth's surface through the fountains of the great deep and the windows of heaven (Genesis 7:11), and the permanent sea level was increased. But this again was stabilized after the Flood, and God promised that the waters would never again prevail over the earth (Genesis 9:15; Psalm 104:9).

Ever since, the tossing waves may produce more sand, but they cannot transgress God's "bound." They even provide a striking picture of the futility of fighting the Creator. Evolutionary humanists, like the pagans of old, may toss and roar, but like the sea, they can never prevail.

The Bible's Central Verse

It is better to trust in the LORD than to put confidence in man (Psalm 118:8).

In the present chapter-and-verse divisions of the Bible, it is striking that this verse, Psalm 118:8, turns out to be the middle verse of the Bible. Although these verse divisions were not part of the original inspired text, this particular verse is very appropriate as a key verse for the Word of God.

It presents the great truth of theism versus humanism; belief and trust in God as the ultimate measure of reality and meaning rather than in man. The Bible begins by setting forth God as Creator (Genesis 1:1) and ends by invoking the grace of the Lord Jesus Christ (Revelation 22:21), but mankind's greatest and most basic sin has always been that of seeking to replace God with man. "Ye shall be as gods," was the Satanic lie which induced man's initial rebellion (Genesis 3:5).

All the ancient pagan religions were based on the arrogant evolutionary prescription that "changed the truth of God into a lie, and worshipped and served the creature more than the Creator, who is blessed for ever" (Romans 1:25). This false religion, in modern garb as secular evolutionary humanism, dominates the intellectual establishment in every nation of the world today, as well. The infamous Humanist Manifesto of 1973 declared: "No deity will save us; we will save ourselves." But humanism is utter folly. Only God can save, since only God is the true Creator of life.

There are really only two basic religions or philosophies among men, one of which is man-centered; one God-centered. One is based on evolutionism; one on creationism. One is humanism; the other is theism. And the only truly creationist, theistic religion is Biblical Christianity, for it alone acknowledges that the eternal God is both Creator and Savior, the Lord Jesus Christ. It is infinitely, eternally better to trust in the Lord, than to put one's confidence in man.

The Heavens Are the Lord's

Thus saith the LORD; If heaven above can be measured, and the foundations of the earth searched out beneath, I will also cast off all the seed of Israel for all that they have done, saith the LORD (Jeremiah 31:37).

There are some things God has reserved for Himself, at least in this present age. One of these is the domain of the stars. Cosmogonic speculations and wistful searches for extra-terrestrial life are basically nothing but expressions of man's rebellion against his Creator, seeking to explain the origin and meaning of the universe without God.

God placed man in dominion over this earth (Genesis 1:26–29), telling him to "subdue it." so science and technology are well within the divine mandate when applied to systems on the earth, or related to it, including the use of stars for chronology and navigation (Genesis 1:14–19).

But we have no jurisdiction over the heavens. "The heaven, even the heavens, are the LORD's: but the earth hath He given to the children of men" (Psalm 115:16). "When I consider Thy heavens, the work of Thy fingers, the moon and the stars, which Thou hast ordained; What is man, that thou art mindful of him?" (Psalm 8:3, 4). "God that made the world and all things therein, seeing that He is Lord of heaven and earth; . . . hath made of one blood all nations of men for to dwell on all the face of the earth, and hath determined the times before appointed, and the bounds of their habitation" (Acts 17:24, 26).

The study of astronomy is appropriate, of course, if dedicated to revealing the majesty of God's creative handiwork, for "The heavens declare the glory of God" (Psalm 19:1). But any hope of travel to distant stars, or of finding extraterrestrial life, or of devising a naturalistic evolutionary cosmogony, is blasphemously arrogant, as well as utterly foolish.

God of the Cosmos

Thou, even Thou, art Lord alone; thou hast made heaven, the heaven of heavens, with all their host, the earth, and all things that are therein, the seas, and all that is therein, and Thou preservest them all; and the host of heaven worshippeth Thee (Nehemiah 9:6).

These are the opening affirmations of the prayer of the Levites after the return of the Jews from captivity in Babylon and the completion of the walls of Jerusalem under Nehemiah's leadership. This prayer followed immediately after a great revival of Bible reading led by Ezra, the priestly scribe (Nehemiah 8:1–18; 9:1–3).

The natural outcome of such a return to the Word of God by all the nation was this great national affirmation that Jehovah was the true Creator of all the universe. He had created all things in heaven and in earth—even the stars!

Such an acknowledgment was especially significant for a people who had just emerged from more than 150 years of captivity in Babylon—the very center and archetype of the polytheistic evolutionism of the ancient world. Furthermore, the Jews had been sent into captivity in the first place, because they had fallen into the same sin as the Babylonians—that of blasphemously worshipping the "host of heaven."

But now God's people had recognized and acknowledged once again that this very host of heaven had been created by God, and that the faithful host of heaven (the unfallen angels) still worshipped this same Creator God who had now brought His people back to their promised land. If mighty angels worship their Creator, how can we do less?

Herein is an important lesson for our own nation today. A true national revival must begin with a great renewal of sincere Bible study, with a foundational emphasis on the basic fact of special creation, recognizing that control of all things must be by the true God of the universe.

Count Your Many Blessings

Thou crownest the year with Thy goodness; and Thy paths drop fatness (Psalm 65:11).

At year's end, a Christian should stop to count his blessings. If he does this honestly and fully, no matter what his problems may have been during the year, he will have to confess that God, as always, has crowned the year with goodness.

The coronation figure is frequently used in Scripture to speak of God's blessings in the Christian life. For example: "Who redeemeth thy life from destruction; who crowneth thee with lovingkindness and tender mercies" (Psalm 103:4). Even our testings and trials are always in the context of God's grace and love. Christ Himself wore a crown of thorns so that we may be crowned with mercy and salvation.

Consider also Psalm 5:12: "For Thou, LORD, will bless the righteous; with favor wilt Thou compass him as with a shield." The word "compass" is the same Hebrew word as "crown," the basic meaning being "encircle." Other jewels in the year-end crown for the believer are God's grace and glory. "[Wisdom] shall give to thine head an ornament of grace: A crown of glory shall she deliver to thee" (Proverbs 4:9).

Then there is the wonderful testimony that "Thou hast made Him a little lower than the angels, and hast crowned Him with glory and honor" (Psalm 8:5). Finally, the believer's crown is none other than the Lord Himself: "In that day shall the LORD of hosts be for a crown of glory, and for a diadem of beauty, unto the residue of His people" (Isaiah 28:5).

Most Christians also have an abundance of material blessings to count at the end of the year, for which to thank the LORD. Even if they have none of these, however, God has crowned the year with goodness and favor, with loving kindness and tender mercies, with grace and glory and honor and, best of all, with His own presence. "Bless the LORD, O my soul, and forget not all His benefits" (Psalm 103:2).

Subject Index

SUBJECT INDEX

Principal Scripture Index

PRINCIPAL SCRIPTURE INDEX